PRAISE FOR TRA

McConnaughey's book builds on the research of psychologists, neuroscientists, and theologians in the study of trauma and its impact on human persons. She addresses how trauma, which is often undetected, inhibits a person's ability to grow spiritually. She also addresses some of the deep wounds of guilt, shame, and failure of some Christian communities—communities intended to be safe places for healing—that have become places of spiritual trauma. *Trauma in the Pews* provides practical guidance to pastors and church leaders on how to break the cycle of perpetuating spiritual trauma and how to experience God and the church as a place of healing.

—Mark A. Maddix, PhD, Dean,
School of Theology & Christian Ministry:
Point Loma Nazarene University

Dr. McConnaughey takes us on an eloquent journey through a land of difficult, painful, and even taboo topics related to trauma. Everyone experiences and is affected by trauma differently—mentally, physically, spiritually, and emotionally. Sharing her own personal trauma narrative and those of other survivors, McConnaughey gives us glimpses of her expertise in everything from spiritual disciplines to medical science. In a society where the outward world and conscious cognitive sciences trump any and all things internal and subconscious, this book is a welcomed and cathartic treat. McConnaughey gives great insight into faith and spirituality as experienced by trauma survivors. But this book is not just for those who have suffered or even simply for ministry staff and laity. *Trauma in the Pews* will benefit anyone who works with survivors of trauma; pastors, teachers, foster parents, social workers, etc. This book is one of the first commentaries I have read regarding what it truly means for a church to be trauma responsive. In a sense, Dr. McConnaughey is gently inviting us into a more sensitive and informed worldview—as if she is saying,

"Welcome. Come on in. View the world through a trauma lens. And do so safely—with no judgment or shame."

—David Stevens, EdD, Director: M.Ed.
in Neuroscience and Trauma, Tabor College

In this important book, Janyne has given us three things that are needed more than ever in the moment in which we find ourselves: The willingness to do the hard work of healing, the capacity to acknowledge the complexity and precarity of the human experience, and the hope and imagination necessary to cultivate and sustain lives and communities that are nurturing, sustainable, and attainable. *Trauma in the Pews* is not an exercise in theory or a mere abstraction, but is, instead, a deeply grounded enactment of vulnerability, truth-telling, and possibility.

—Michael Hanegan, Senior Fellow,
The Dietrich Bonhoeffer Institute

Dr. Janyne McConnaughey wraps empathy around those who've experienced trauma, no matter on what side of the pulpit they stand. *Trauma in the Pews: The Impact on Faith and Spiritual Practices* is filled with meaningful conversations written with love and acceptance—a type of opening up of the soul that honors the trauma survivor and strengthens the spirit of the reader.

—Shana Lynn Schmidt, LPC, IMHS, Early Childhood
Mental Health Specialist and award-winning author:
Over Our Hearts: A Mother's Journey Learning to Listen In

Trauma in the Pews broadens the definition of trauma from our standard diagnostic manual, which is valuable for many people who may not meet those specific criteria of life-threatening events. It also acknowledges the impact of trauma on our emotional, physical, and spiritual well-being. Janyne describes her personal trauma history and how she navigated her own emotional and spiritual healing journey. She "gets it."

The book focuses on a Christian perspective, but the principles apply to all Judeo-Christian traditions and encompasses the impact of trauma in any context. Recent research in trauma has identified the importance of Trauma Informed Healers—that Healers are not only mental health professionals, but the spiritual leaders that people trust and turn toward for guidance. Since most aspects of survivor's lives are colored by their experience, including their physical and spiritual well-being, increasing trauma-informed, trauma-sensitive, and trauma-responsive clergy is a necessary step.

—Nancy Stella, PhD, PsyD, Award Winning Author, *Fear Traps: Escape the Triggers that Keep You Stuck*

Given the current upsurge of interest in spiritual abuse and religious trauma, this is an essential and timely book for anyone in ministerial leadership as well as those whose own traumatic experiences have resulted in a belief that they are spiritual failures. The author's vulnerability in sharing her own story makes the text highly accessible as she convincingly argues for the importance of spiritual practices being viewed through a trauma-informed, -sensitive, and -responsive lens. My hope and prayer is that this book will prevent further trauma from occurring while enabling deep healing to happen as spiritual communities such as churches become safe(r) places. After all, as the author quotes, "People need healing. The church needs healing. Nations need healing. We all need healing." (page 217).

—Gillian Harvey, D.Psych, Therapeutic Counsellor/Psychotherapist, Supervisor, Researcher & Trainer

As a therapist working with individuals in private practice, I have found an overwhelming number of people who are living with some form of significant trauma. Many who experience childhood traumatic events enter adulthood with hope that having a faith community will bring them relief and comfort. They very often find that their pain is minimized through rote spiritual practices, and often the view is that if those spiritual practices don't work, it's because the person is living without faith. This creates a compounding effect on an already intolerable pain. What Janyne has accomplished in her marvelous work of *Trauma in the Pews* is a real compassionate response to both the faith community and to those who are continuing to be wounded by communities that don>t know how to respond. Janyne has given a gift to the faith community. Let those who have ears hear its timely message.

—Kiersten (Adkins) Moore, MA, LPC,
Executive Director: Pathway to Hope

Many are becoming aware of the power trauma has in our lives and in the lives of those we love. But we're still learning how to deal with trauma in realistic and life-affirming ways. Janyne McConnaughey offers us wisdom and resources as both a professional and as one who has worked the through trauma in her own experience. This book is just what we as individuals, leaders, and churches need as we seek healing!

—Thomas Jay Oord, Director: Doctoral Program at
Northwind Theological Seminary/Center for Open
and Relational Theology, author of *God Can't:
How to Believe in God and Love after Tragedy,
Abuse, and Other Evils*

Janyne McConnaughey takes readers on a journey into the world of trauma, all while embracing various spiritual practices that will help readers lean into God for healing and strengthening of their faith. This book is full of important information for spiritual leaders, spiritual communities, and all those who long to better understand trauma and its impact on individuals and how to embrace the art of spiritual formation to gently walk alongside them. Janyne McConnaughey has written a must-read for anyone who desires to meet others right where they are in their healing journey and for those who have experienced their own trauma in the Church and are seeking a way to connect with God. As an LGBTQ+ Jesus-follower, and someone who works with LGBTQ+ young adults of faith who are being traumatized by the Church, I look forward to using the spiritual practices discussed in this book, and I pray this book will help the demographic God has invited me to encourage to hold on tightly to their faith.

—Jen Eckles, Spiritual Director and Founder/Owner
of Saguaro Roots Spiritual Direction

To be honest with you, there is nothing more important in today's world than getting a grasp on what trauma has done and is doing to millions of people. There are many places that should provide a safe environment for our children—for instance, home, school, and church. But, as we all know, these places often become the location where the trauma raises its ugly head and no longer feel safe to the traumatized. Our society needs to open their eyes to what is happening in our places of worship and fix this issue. What is the best way to get an understanding of this huge issue today? Education. Janyne's latest book, *"Trauma in the Pews: The Impact on Faith and Spiritual Practices,"* is a great place to start. I have read this book multiple times already and she presents a perfect foundation of understanding while exposing the evil and addressing the problem head on. I highly recommend this book to each person in the hope that it begins a conversation that ultimately helps expose, educate, and heal those who have been hurt and help turn these victims into victors.

—Dr. Gregory Williams, Best-Selling Author,
Counselor, Speaker/Trainer, Radio Talk Show Host,
Ordained Minister

This book is a bold and generous invitation to everyone in the pews and those preaching from the stage or the altar to understand trauma and its consequences. McConnaughey seamlessly weaves spiritual wisdom, neuroscientific acumen, and personal reflections that leave the reader hungry to participate in the trauma-informed transformation of the Body of Christ and the individual bodies of Christ.

—Ryan Kujah, Trauma therapist, spiritual director and author of *From the
Inside Out: Reimagining the Mission, Recreating the World*

Trauma in the Pews: The Impact on Faith and Spiritual Practices is a necessary read for the churches of today. Janyne McConnaughey, PhD, wisely and compassionately explains how faith supports the entire healing journey by utilizing techniques and exercises specific to those impacted by trauma. This book is a detailed manual for both clergy and faith community members on how to be sensitive to the needs of many who've lived to tell their story. An expert in the field of psychology, and a trauma survivor herself, Janyne recognizes the reality of suffering and identifies the importance of trauma-informed healing practices, demonstrating how well it all fits together to strengthen the church body and provide a safe sanctuary for survivors to develop emotionally and spiritually.

—Susan Frybort, Author of *Look To The Clearing,*
Open Passages and Hope is a Traveler

In the last few years, we have seen waves of people boldly sharing their stories of spiritual abuse, church hurt, and religious trauma. But these stories are often met with ridicule, mockery, and shaming. Instead of listening with compassion and investigating culpability, Christian leadership most commonly deflects blame by accusing or ignoring the wounded and bypassing root issues.

The intersection of faith and science has historically been fraught with conflict and disagreement resulting in vast division across faith communities. Religious trauma is one of the aftereffects of binary, dogmatic thinking. When a faith leader bristles to the idea of becoming trauma informed, they risk being the conduit of compound harm directed at those they claim to serve. But that need not be the case, as Dr. McConaughey so clearly helps readers acknowledge.

McConaughey guides those who are willing to witness the marriage of faith and science into an expansive understanding of how becoming a trauma informed faith leader or individual can result in revolutionary healing. Readers will learn how to evolve from a reticent position on trauma in their lives and work toward becoming informed with vocabulary, sensitivity, and a deeper understanding of the inner workings of the human soul.

—Rebekah Drumsta, MA, CPLC, Spiritual Abuse
Advocate & Consultant, Author of *When Family Hurts:*
30 Days to Finding Healing and Clarity

Wow! I feel on some soul level that this book is going to go viral—it's brilliant, insightful, inspired by the Holy Spirit, trauma-informed, and hope-filled. As a trauma-survivor turned trauma-warrior, and daughter of a theologian who spent eight years in the seminary, I send you heartfelt gratitude and applause. Thank you for offering us this guide, a trauma bible, really, and being a BRAVE soul, yet again, in sharing needed truth!

—Teri Wellbrock, Trauma-Warrior, Author,
Speaker, Podcaster: The Healing Place

Every ministry leader needs this book. As a trauma survivor, my heart wept with hope for those suffering feelings of spiritual failure for reasons beyond their control. McConnaughey delivers a paradigm shift for real and honest change.

—Danielle Bernock, Founder 4F Media and Victorious Souls Podcast,
Author of *Emerging With Wings* and *Because You Matter*

Finally! *Trauma in the Pews* is a book that helps faithful and spiritual leaders and church communities understand the impact of trauma on development and spirituality. Becoming trauma informed, then trauma sensitive, and finally trauma responsive should not be optional for any organization in this day and age. Janyne's explanation of the impact of trauma on our development as children and on our functioning as adults is clear and compassionate. It has been said that one of the most effective treatments for childhood trauma is connection with others. Where better to find connection with God and with our community members then in our houses of worship? Thank you, Janyne, for providing a roadmap to becoming trauma responsive for faith communities and faith leaders all over the world.

—Melissa Sadin, EDD, Author of *Teachers Guide to Trauma: 20 Things Kids with Trauma Wish Their Teachers Knew*

Fostering and adopting play significant roles in the lives of many people of faith, so they have a genuine need to know about the critical issues facing the children they bring into their families through these processes. Trauma is unambiguously among the most critical of those issues, which is why this book is so important. It meets foster and adoptive parents—as well as their communities—"where they are," providing the knowledge and resources they need to help every child heal and thrive.
—Adam Pertman, President of the National Center on Adoption and Permanency (NCAP) and Author of *Adoption Nation*

I first heard about trauma-informed care in 2014 while working for the police department to reduce drug related and violent crime. This subject impacted me in a powerful way, not because I was working in the justice system, but because of my own life of faith. I saw it was a message that paralleled the Gospel. It is a message, for those who listen, to extend empathy and grace toward others. As I began training a wide sector of professionals, one thing I did not foresee in this journey was the number of stories I would hear from people who experienced trauma within their houses of faith. *Trauma in the Pews: The Impact on Faith and Spiritual Practices* is an invaluable resource that has been missing in the trauma-informed conversation. Sadly, for many who turn to the religious system for help, they are met with an environment of judgement, messaging of missing the mark and not measuring up. In transparent fashion, Janyne eloquently shares how this system was a source of trauma in her own life. As you read, you will find she is sharing her heart and wisdom. This must-read for those in the faith community will provide you essential tools for transforming a retraumatizing environment into one of healing.
—Becky Haas, International Trauma-Informed Care Author/Speaker/Trainer

In *Trauma in the Pews*, Dr. McConnaughey not only makes the case for why churches and their leaders should be trauma informed but shows how leaders can truly be trauma responsive. And she does this through an attachment-focused lens. We must recognize that reaching and healing a traumatized world requires us to truly see each person the way God does and put relationships first.

—Julie Beem, MBA, Executive Director:
Attachment & Trauma Network, Inc.

I highly respect Dr. Janyne McConnaughey, my dear colleague in the trauma-informed care movement, who wrote this resourceful book with her vulnerable but courageous sharing of her own personal stories and well-informed knowledge of traumatology. I highly recommend this book to those who seek to understand how trauma interplays with individual and communal faith tradition practices which will tremendously support building healthy trauma-informed faith communities and practices.

—Rev. Dr. Sanghoon Yoo, Founder of The Faithful City
and Arizona Trauma Informed Faith Coalition

Trauma in the Pews is the book that I needed when I was in seminary. My ministry training did not adequately prepare me to care for people who had experienced trauma. Most of my ability to listen, empathize, and walk slowly with people who had experienced profound suffering came on the fly. I wish that hadn't been the case. Janyne's book is a gift to a new generation of ministers who are primed and ready to be more equipped than I was. At the same time, to those of us who have been in ministry for a while, it provides a much-needed course correction. The only way God's church will relate to and serve vulnerable people in the coming decades is if we grow corporately in our understanding of trauma, how it affects people, and how to respond to it in compassionate, gentle, Jesus-like ways. Janyne's book will help you and your church do that.

—James Pruch, Director of Programs at
Christian Heritage, Former Pastor

In this compassionately prophetic, spiritually therapeutic, and vulnerably powerful text, trauma survivor and lifelong educator Janyne McConnaughey both brilliantly and beautifully lays the groundwork for helping ministries become more trauma informed, trauma sensitive, and trauma responsive. We arguably cannot adequately understand or address the human condition without such awareness, sensitivity, and responsiveness. This is the book my clients' churches have needed for years.

—Shane Moe, MA, MDiv, LMFT, Psychotherapist,
Certified EMDR Clinician and Consultant

Little do we know the depths of trauma experienced by those in our pews. Too often that trauma has been caused by those that held sacred trust, who have abused their power, influence, and control as church leaders and clergy. Too often, the trauma has been compounded as we ineptly respond to those that have been harmed. Janyne's newest book echoes what my own doctoral research found among victim-survivors of child sexual abuse. We have a God that heals! God uses His people who live incarnationally and who practice spiritual disciplines to nurture that healing. However, to do this, we must be trauma informed and sensitive to the Spirit's leading. Janyne has provided an excellent resource to guide readers on how to view the pain of others through a trauma lens. Through this lens, we will witness the transformation process from trauma to triumph. I applaud Janyne for this much-needed book. I strongly encourage this book to be on the top of your reading list.

—Melodie Bissell, MDiv, DMin, Victim Advocate

It was as if my current life reconnected to my childhood as I gripped every word in *Trauma in the Pews*. Having been raised in a church that filled my mind and heart with fear and shame, I continue to struggle with unpacking what I know about trauma and how it relates to the impact of my evangelical upbringing. McConnaughey took me through a facts-based science-focused journey of how to navigate the impact of my religious trauma throughout this book! *Trauma in the Pews* will serve as a healing catalyst for those of us who did experience trauma in the pews while supporting faith-based leaders on how to transform truth into practice moving into the future.

—Mathew Portell, M.Ed, Founder of Trauma Informed
Educators Network, Director of Communities
at PACEs Connection

OTHER BOOKS BY THE AUTHOR

BRAVE
A Personal Story of Healing Childhood Trauma

JEANNIE'S BRAVE CHILDHOOD
Behavior and Healing Through the
Lens of Attachment and Trauma

A BRAVE LIFE
Survival, Resilience, Faith and Hope
After Childhood Trauma

TRAUMA
IN THE PEWS

The Impact on Faith and Spiritual Practices

JANYNE MCCONNAUGHEY, PHD

BERRY POWELL PRESS

PageMill Press

Trauma in the Pews: The Impact on Faith and Spiritual Practices

COPYRIGHT @ 2022 Janyne McConnaughey. All Rights Reserved. No part of this book may be reproduced or re-transmitted in any form or by any means without the written permission of the publisher.

Cover Design: Kay McConnaughey
Interior Design: Formatted Books
Copyediting: Valeri Mills Barnes

Co-published by:

Berry Powell Press
Glendora, California
www.berrypowellpress.com

PageMill Press
Transpersonal Books for Spiritual Renewal
Alameda, California
www.pagemillpressbooks.com

ISBN: 978-1-957321-06-6 (paperback)
ISBN: 978-1-957321-07-3 (ebook)
LCCN: 2022914249

The content, suggestions, and resources contained in this book have been drawn from the personal experiences of the author and are neither prescriptive nor intended as a substitute for seeking assistance from a professional trauma-based therapist. The inclusion of resources is intended to further the reader's understanding of trauma, but inclusion does not indicate full endorsement of all material. Updated or additional resources can be found on the author's website.

DEDICATION

To my husband, Scott, who has faithfully and lovingly walked
with and served beside me for over forty years. This book
is ours, with both the heartache and the hope that spiritual
leaders and faith communities can more compassionately
respond to those who have experienced trauma.

CONTENTS

SECTION ONE
RECOGNIZING THE IMPACT OF TRAUMA IN THOSE WE SERVE

SECTION TWO
ACKNOWLEDGING THE IMPACT OF TRAUMA ON SPIRITUAL PRACTICES

SECTION THREE
EFFECTIVELY MINISTERING TO THOSE IMPACTED BY TRAUMA

FOREWORD

To be a minister today must be one of the hardest jobs in the world. Helping congregants and those they minister to navigate death, a pandemic, mass shootings, racism, wars, political rifts, dissolution of marriages, abuse, crises of faith, church hurts, and a host of other traumas, requires the utmost knowledge, skill, wisdom, and spiritual and emotional maturity. Additionally, simultaneously managing their own family relationships and kaleidoscopic spiritual and emotional lives is quite challenging, especially while remaining balanced and healthy.

Speaking of trauma, the word comes from a Greek word meaning "wound" or "injury." Traumatic events can cause various degrees of injury affecting our physiology, spirituality, and relationality. For most people, trauma disrupts their emotional GPS causing overpowering emotions, disruptive thoughts, and even painful physical sensations. Though everyone experiences stressful events throughout their life, not everyone perceives them as traumatic. Each individual has a unique tolerance level to traumatic events determined by their upbringing, temperament, their feeling of support and safety at home, their network of safe and supportive friends, and current life stressors. Unlike a badly bruised arm that people can physically see, trauma is insidious. It hides in the deepest recesses of our hearts and bodies, often to the detriment of those affected by it and those they love.

Since trauma is ubiquitous in today's world, ministers need someone qualified and trustworthy to guide them through the rocky terrain of trauma and its effects on those they serve. Why? Because the effects of trauma prevent people from knowing God more fully. Trauma ensnares people in repetitive cycles and destructive patterns causing fractures and divisions in the body of Christ. It mires people in cycles of shame and addictions that lure them from their paths of becoming more like Christ.

Jesus, in his first-ever sermon preached in the synagogue, stated that his primary mission and the very reason that the Spirit was upon him, was to preach good news to those affected by the dragon of trauma. He came to heal and set free the traumatized who felt like they were poor, prisoners, blind, oppressed, and those desperately needing to hear about God's favor (Luke 4:18-19). How can people be informed about trauma and its effects without a teacher? Thankfully, this is where Janyne comes in.

I have known Janyne for many years. I have borne witness to the countless transformational workshops and seminars she has given on trauma-related topics. I have watched her from a distance and have been inspired by how she compassionately encourages people on their journey. I have been awed by reading her books and how eloquently she describes God's healing journey into the deepest recesses of her being. As a licensed therapist and ordained pastor, I have deeply appreciated her fascinating and brilliant integration of psychology and theology, helping all of us become *trauma informed*, *trauma sensitive*, and *trauma responsive* with the goal of healing and spiritual and emotional formation.

Janyne's book, *Trauma in the Pews*, is prophetic, wise, educational, compassionate, autobiographical, and beautifully challenging. Ministers, lay people, spiritual directors, counselors working with spiritual concerns, and Christians affected by trauma will highly benefit from reading this book. Take it slow. Sip it like a healthy tea. And, let this literary delight inform and change you from the inside out, for the sake of yourselves and those you walk alongside on their sacred journeys.

—**Mark Gregory Karris**,
PsyD, MDiv, LMFT, Ordained Pastor,
Best-Selling Author

INTRODUCTION

Growing older creates a longing to go back to the beginning with the wisdom that I now have—back to when I was just starting to serve in churches and church-related ministries. Back to my teaching days with children and adults. Back to my parenting days. Back to the days when I longed to grow in faith while following the spiritual instruction of the churches I attended.

As did many in the church, I viewed life through a "spiritual" lens. I believed that my struggles could ultimately be traced back to a lack of discipline on my part in following the traditional spiritual practices. I was taught that engaging in spiritual practices would bring me closer to God. These practices included daily scripture reading, a more consistent prayer life, serving within the church, exhibiting self-control by following the prescribed rules, participating in worship, and regular church attendance.

I did my best to pursue all of these avenues, finding most to be challenging for reasons I could not understand. It was discouraging to come away feeling more like a spiritual failure than an effective believer. After publishing my first book, many others began to share similar feelings of spiritual failure while talking with me about their childhood trauma. It was then that I began to wonder if the impact of trauma and feelings of spiritual failure were connected.

Once I understood the prevalence and impact of trauma—in my life and in those around me—my paradigm was completely altered. I suddenly viewed myself and others through a different lens, a broader lens, that had more nuance and compassion. Revisiting conversations I'd had with friends, students, family, and ministry leaders, I realized that many of their stories included elements of suffering from the impact of trauma.

Without understanding the effects of trauma, I am certain that I had blind spots to the pain and suffering of some of the people who came across my path. Once I saw the effects of trauma, I couldn't unsee the impact it made. I realized that many of the issues were not spiritual but the result of traumatic events so many have suffered.

This new awareness of the impact of trauma doesn't cause me to regret the ways I interacted with those who suffered. I did the best I could. I cannot hold myself responsible for something that wasn't understood. During forty years as an educator, thirty-three as a teacher educator, I never mentioned trauma; no one did. It simply was not on anyone's radar. The lens we shared focused on behavior and couldn't bring trauma into focus.

But that has changed. As a society, our understanding of the effects of trauma has advanced exponentially in the past ten years. The increasing availability of resources since I began my healing journey in the fall of 2014 is astounding—and growing so fast that keeping up is difficult, if not impossible.

> During forty years as an educator, thirty-three as a teacher educator, I never mentioned trauma; no one did. It simply was not on anyone's radar. The lens we shared focused on behavior and couldn't bring trauma into focus.

My current work with educators as a Distinguished Visiting Professor for Tabor College's Master of Education in neuroscience and trauma, as well as my work as President of the Board for the Attachment & Trauma Network, is redefining how I view and respond to others. This is true for all those who have become a part of the movement to bring the understanding of the impact of trauma to all sectors of society.

While the network is expanding and the conversations among disciplines are increasing, what we understand about trauma is not adequately informing the church's faith practices. I am one of many who are making this connection. But we need to engage more intentionally. Bringing together these two perspectives opens up a new potential for fulfilling the mission of the church. With an understanding of trauma, laypeople and ordained ministers can be catalysts for tremendous healing. Without it, the church risks becoming irrelevant to a world that is searching for answers.

There are three questions I seek to answer in this book. How can ministry leadership and laypeople recognize and better understand the impact of widespread trauma that is present among its members? How can leadership develop resources and instruction that acknowledge the impact of trauma and facilitate healing within the framework of spiritual practices? And how must the past behavior-based paradigm be revised to provide clearer vision and more effectively serve the needs of so many impacted by trauma?

We couldn't know what we didn't know in the past. But the information is available to us now. Today, we can do better by becoming 1) trauma informed – acquiring knowledge and understanding about trauma, 2) trauma sensitive – recognizing how trauma impacts our lives and faith, and 3) trauma responsive – ministering to people who have experienced trauma in effective and compassionate ways. There are still many in our churches whose suffering has been overlooked, and perhaps they aren't fully aware themselves how they've been affected. But with a different lens, our faith communities will become safer places for everyone; those who have experienced trauma and those who walk beside them in families, faith communities, schools, and businesses alike.

HOW TO GET THE MOST OUT OF THIS BOOK

Section One will answer the question, "How can becoming trauma informed provide better knowledge and understanding of the effects of trauma in the lives of those who sit in the pews?" This will include information about how trauma affects the brain and the prevalence of trauma in the lives of church members, both collective and individual.

Section Two answers the question, "How can we view the struggles of those who suffer from the effects of trauma more compassionately?" Becoming trauma sensitive—recognizing the many ways trauma impacts our lives—can help us better understand how trauma affects an individual's efforts to access spiritual practices.

Many of the spiritual practices of the church find their origins in Jewish tradition. But over the past two-thousand-plus years, believers from various Christian traditions have modified and added practices that were viewed as helpful, if not essential, to living out our faith. Rather than attempt an overview of these varied practices, I have chosen to utilize the Spiritual Disciplines proposed by Richard Foster in his book *Celebration of Discipline*, published in 1978.

Foster's presentation of spiritual practices initiated a spiritual formation movement that has impacted generations of Christians. Entire programs, degrees, many a sermon, and an untold number of personal spiritual plans have been based on his Spiritual Discipline framework (throughout this book, when capitalized, Spiritual or Discipline will indicate that the term refers to Foster's work). The stories of those who have been positively impacted by this book leave no question as to its validity and value. The importance of spiritual practices over the centuries is an undisputed fact—something well documented in *Celebration of Discipline*.

Organizing my thoughts around Foster's framework enabled me to utilize a common language to describe how so many struggle with implementing traditional spiritual practices—both because the impact of trauma decreases our ability to access these practices but also because it has been incorrectly assumed that these practices are sufficient to bring about a full healing from trauma. The positive impact that Richard Foster's work has had on faith practices cannot be overstated. But many individuals were negatively impacted by how some misapplied these spiritual practices as rules to live by and then over-promised the possible benefits.

Seeing my difficulty with certain spiritual practices allowed me to hear the same concerns in the emails and conversations I had with others who had been impacted by trauma. The stories included in Section Two are created from elements of personal stories shared with me—always written to protect confidences. A trauma-sensitive reflection on the stories can help us understand why so many struggle with spiritual practices.

Section Three answers the question, "How can we better serve those who suffer from the effects of trauma?" This is the question that being trauma responsive—responding in informed and compassionate ways—answers. Faith communities in general, and Christians in particular, have the potential to help those impacted by trauma turn their struggles into joy. Without understanding trauma and its effects, our efforts are often misguided and have the opposite effect.

We are at the beginning of a significant and necessary change in our perceptions of those who suffer silently in the pews. We still have far to go, but with an understanding of the impact of trauma guiding our efforts, we can more effectively minister to those who are impacted. It is possible for our compassionate efforts to reap much greater dividends in the lives of those who sincerely desire a closer walk with God.

Section One

RECOGNIZING THE IMPACT OF TRAUMA IN THOSE WE SERVE

Nathan and I sat talking over our cups of coffee. His life had been both a harrowing story of trauma and an example of human determination. He had lived a good life and was known as a kind, generous, and caring man. What most did not know was how much he loathed his younger self.

"You understand now that it wasn't your fault, right?"

His response was the most beautiful healing words I had ever heard him say. "Yes, I do understand that now. It wasn't my fault. And I think I like myself now."

What caused this remarkable transformation?

Because I spent my career helping prepare men and women for ministry, I wanted the reason for Nathan's transformation to be his involvement in the church. He had served as both a volunteer and a staff member in various ministries. But this was not the case. The change came about when he began to view his life experiences in terms of his childhood trauma and the effects those experiences had on his mind and body. The help he needed to experience this new perspective was found outside of the church, rather than within.

Nathan hadn't understood anything about trauma, and ministry leaders didn't either. While some early forms of trauma-based professional help might have existed at the time, Nathan was not directed to any form of therapy because ministry leaders did not know enough about trauma to recognize its effects on people. Their lack of understanding caused them to misinterpret his struggles and offer nothing that was genuinely helpful. Instead, their efforts unwittingly added layers of additional pain on top of his traumatic childhood experiences.

And to be fair, these ministry leaders could not know what they did not know. For the most part, ministry leaders, including myself, have done the best with what we knew. But as Maya Angelou once said, "Do the best you can until you know better. Then when you know better, do better."

Thankfully, it is now possible to know better *if we are willing to learn*. To help Nathan and all of those seeking support through faith communities, both ministry leaders and laypeople can become trauma informed, trauma sensitive, and trauma responsive. For those who suffer, we can do better. Much better. Because now we know.

UNDERSTANDING TRAUMA[1]

Trauma is often more about how an event is processed than the event itself. *The Diagnostic and Statistical Manual of Mental Disorders* (DSM-V) defines trauma as requiring a sense of "actual or threatened death, serious injury, or sexual violence."[2] This definition fails to encompass all aspects of trauma. It also fails to address the effects of chronic stress and physical or emotional neglect that most do not recognize as having many of the same debilitating effects as traumatic events. In cases of domestic violence, verbal abuse is equally as damaging as physical abuse. Emotional and physical pain "light up" the same part of the brain. The body cannot distinguish the difference—studies show that ibuprofen works to soothe both physical and emotional pain.[3]

When considering the effects of trauma, it is helpful to think of a traumatic event as anything that causes an individual to feel threatened emotionally or physically, feel powerless, and/or affect their capacity to cope while overwhelmed. The age of an individual at the time of the trauma is also an important factor in their ability to cope.

In experience, traumatic events can vary greatly and can include things like car accidents, natural disasters, and physical or verbal abuse. Anytime trauma occurs within relationships, the long-term effects involve damage to one's ability to trust and create negative internalized messages—such as being unlovable. Trauma includes physical and emotional pain as well as neglect. Traumatic experiences in childhood increase the likelihood of registering events later in life as a trauma—the internalization of the experience.

Section One: Leadership Reflection Questions

- Section One begins with Nathan's revelation that he now understands that the abuse that occurred in his childhood was not his fault. Have you had similar conversations with survivors who blamed themselves? How did you respond?
- What struggles were you aware of that they faced in their lives? Did you understand those struggles and whether they helped or hindered their spiritual journeys?
- In what ways did you provide guidance or assistance for the individual? Did this seem helpful for them?

What Don't We Understand About Trauma?

My father and I were having our regular afternoon chat when he said, "I think I would do a lot of things differently if I could go back and do it again." I was surprised because he had led an exemplary life as a pastor and loved his family well. Now at the age of ninety-seven, it seemed sad for him to have regrets. I was curious.

"What would you have done differently?" I asked.

He sighed. "I would have handled things differently as a pastor."

Since I had seen him navigate some very difficult church situations with wisdom much like Solomon's, I was even more curious.

"Like what?" I probed.

He mumbled about a few things. It really didn't seem like he could have done anything differently in those situations.

And then he said, "I wish I had understood people better."

I do not know a single person in ministry that wouldn't make that statement during these difficult times! Life in ministry has never been an easy life, but it does seem so much harder now. Yet, I do not believe the questions we would ask are much different than those that have been asked for generations.

- Why do people struggle with choices after salvation?
- Why do people have difficulties with relationships?
- Why does salvation transform some and not others?
- Why is there so much discord among church members?
- Why do people who sincerely desire to grow spiritually have difficulty following through with the practices that promise to help?

The questions I asked as an educator in ministry-preparation colleges were not much different. In fact, the problems people face in education, work, communities, and relationships are consistent inside and outside of the church. However, inside the church we often view problems as being primarily spiritual in nature. But I pose an important question: What if some of the problems we face as Christians are not spiritual at all?

What if we are trying to solve a problem with the wrong answer? Or what if our answer is only partially correct? Does salvation matter? Yes. Is it transforming? Often yes, but not always. What if it isn't because people aren't trying? What if they're trying but sidetracked by the wrong solution?

During my years as a professor in Bible colleges, I eagerly watched as new groups of freshmen arrived on campus. So much potential! In most cases, they were eager to prepare to serve God and others. Yet, I knew the attrition rate would be dismally high. Not all would be successful students. I spent the majority of my adult life encouraging students to succeed while secretly questioning whether the answers I offered accurately matched their needs.

When I talk with my friends who currently serve in ministry, they often express the same doubts that I had. Not understanding how to meet the needs of those they minister to often exhausts their will to serve. And this sense of falling short isn't reserved for those in leadership. Many who sit in the pews share this same tension. We work hard, doing what we believe at the time to be the best actions, and yet wonder if we're missing the mark. What is it, exactly, that we sense is lacking but can't quite articulate or define?

WHAT IF OUR PROBLEMS AREN'T SPIRITUAL AT ALL?

My pursuit to find the answer to these questions was personal. I was raised in a faith tradition that believed salvation could be "lost," and so I probably prayed to be re-saved more often than most Christians. Then I changed to a faith tradition that believed salvation could never be lost. At that point, I no longer needed to be saved again and again. Did either path help me to lessen the inner turmoil that I erroneously believed was conviction? No, my internal turmoil never lessened from year to year, no matter how much I desired to follow God.

Neither of these traditions solved the problem of the deep inner turmoil and darkness that I could not explain. Since my entire life was lived within the church, albeit in differing doctrinal traditions, the message was the same. I simply needed to control myself better, be more disciplined, and try harder to use spiritual practices. So, I did just that, year in and year out, in spite of the fact that nothing improved. Not once—and I am amazed to admit this—did I question the basic assumption that the only things that mattered were spiritual in nature, and that being the case, believed all my problems had a spiritual solution.

Then, at the age of sixty-one, my inner turmoil overwhelmed me, and God prompted me to begin therapy, specifically, trauma-based therapy. Before I experienced this approach, I didn't even know such a thing existed—or that the vague dark shadow flitting on the edge of my awareness was trauma trying to get my attention. For the next five years, my story of childhood trauma, which I had consciously and unconsciously repressed and denied, poured out in a million tears during a countless number of therapy sessions.

When I came out on the other side of this intense process of healing, I fully understood that my problems had never been spiritual. Unbeknownst to me, I could have found descriptions of these symptoms in information about Post Traumatic Stress Disorder (PTSD). The information I needed could never be found in biblical studies or doctrinal teachings. All the ways I struggled had been mislabeled and misunderstood. The struggles I endured were misjudged by me, my family, my employers, and church leaders. And sadly, that blocked me from fully experiencing the joy that is possible in a faith experience by those who have not been affected by trauma.

POST-TRAUMATIC STRESS DISORDER (PTSD)[4]

Post-Traumatic Stress Disorder is a psychiatric disorder that may develop when an individual experiences or witnesses a traumatic, often life-threatening event. This severe mental illness was brought to the public's attention through the military and their experiences in the wars of Vietnam, Afghanistan, and Iraq. We now understand that those who experience *any* form of severe trauma, such as rape, can develop PTSD. It is estimated that twenty-four million people—eight percent of the population—suffer from this disorder. Women are twice as likely to develop the disorder as men.

Individuals with PTSD often have lasting and frightening thoughts and memories of the event and tend to be emotionally numb. They experience high levels of anxiety, emotional and physical arousal, and avoidance of interpersonal contacts or situations that can remind them of the trauma they experienced.

Some people develop PTSD after a trauma and others do not. Theories suggest that both learning and biological factors may contribute to the cause of PTSD. The number and types of traumatic events a person experiences are also a factor. The effects of repeated traumas may have a cumulative effect and result in more severe symptoms. Though not included in the DSM 5, this is often referred to as Complex PTSD (C-PTSD).

PTSD may develop anytime in an individual's life after experiencing a traumatic event. For most people, the symptoms of PTSD gradually disappear over weeks or months, but for other people, the symptoms may get worse over time. With treatment, a person may fully recover from PTSD, although some may continue to experience symptoms after treatment. PTSD is diagnosed with a clinical interview in which the interviewer identifies the symptoms and determines whether the individual has experienced specific symptoms for more than a month.

HOW DOES TRAUMA AFFECT SPIRITUALITY?

Eventually, we will explore how trauma is caused, but for now, it is reasonable to ask if all inner turmoil is caused by trauma. No, but my study of trauma and its effects helps me understand that it is the root cause of most mental health problems. I will make the case for it also being the cause for most of the spiritual struggles that result in many Christians feeling like spiritual failures as they confuse the inner dys-regulation created by trauma with what the church calls "conviction."

My thoughts on this perspective began to take form when I submitted a proposal to speak at an eConference on religious trauma. Though many of my experiences within the context of faith communities were traumatic, I felt the problem went much deeper than the results of humans behaving badly. It struck me that my sense of worthlessness and spiritual failure—with hell hovering close by—were both a result of trauma and a form of trauma itself.

The messages offered in faith communities provided ineffectual solutions for the effects of my traumatic experiences, unwittingly undermined any sense of being worthy of God's love and increased my feelings of worthlessness and spiritual failure. Instead of compassion for the challenges the traumatized face, there is often judgment and admonitions to try harder. I believe that an understanding of trauma, both the historical significance and effects, can shift this paradigm from judgment to compassion. We can do better!

My long and complicated history within faith communities gave me many reasons to stay and an equal, if not greater, number of reasons to leave. Leaving is exactly what I did; for several years. Ironically, becoming

> I believe that church communities can help the hurting heal. This will require embracing the historical contexts of the times when the church has not gotten it right because they did not understand the effects of trauma.

trauma informed is what brought me back to the church. My hope is to share what I now know with those who also long to understand why salvation does not solve the problem of inner turmoil. I believe that church communities can help the hurting heal. This will require embracing the historical contexts of the times when the church has not gotten it right because they did not understand the effects of trauma. We cannot leave the past behind us if we ever hope to change ourselves, the church, or the future.

FINAL THOUGHTS

Becoming trauma informed is the first step in transforming how we engage with ourselves and the world around us. This is true for all believers who comprise faith communities but especially for its leaders. It's essential to understand the effects of trauma on our brains and bodies. The term "mental health" is a misnomer because it limits healing to "thinking differently." Thinking differently can never reach the trauma that continues to live in in every cell of our bodies.

In addition, our trauma did not occur only to us as individuals. In fact, trauma permeates our communities, our country, and around the globe. It's rooted in our history, our cultures, the stories we tell about our ancestors, our societies, and the cultural context of who we are—collectively. But this global and national problem must first heal at the individual level. Then, and only then, can the church become a powerful force for healing in trauma-informed, sensitive, and responsive ways.

Chapter 1: Leadership Reflection Questions

- At the beginning of the chapter, a series of questions were posed that ministry leaders often ask. Have you asked any of those questions? With what answers?

- Do you ever wonder about unpredictable or repeated unhealthy behaviors in those who attend your church? What are examples of that? What do you wish you understood better?

- Have you ever connected the dots between a parishioner's childhood trauma and their adult behaviors? Did you feel confident in how to approach the situation? What did you want to understand better?

- Do you have a list of counselors for referral? Are you aware if they have expertise in addressing trauma?

- As you read about what some may call "struggles of faith" not being spiritual, what were your thoughts?

- Have you had members of your congregation diagnosed with PTSD? If so, how did the effects of this diagnosis appear to affect their spiritual life and participation in the church?

Why is it Important to Understand Trauma?

One of the most challenging aspects of ministry is to continue to have compassion for someone who seems determined to keep making the same mistakes. John Wesley faced this problem. His revolutionary methods of spiritual guidance through class meetings have become, in various forms, a foundational part of spiritual discipleship. The challenge was that some people just didn't seem to benefit. Wesley created what he called *penitent bands* for those with severe social and moral problems. The solution, he believed, was a "more stringent and forceful treatment." [5]

Controlling behavior has been the gold standard for parenting, classroom management, the judicial system, and the spiritual lives of believers. It is thought that if someone's behavior was not in line with spiritual and societal standards, it was because they were choosing to not control themselves. This was assumed to be true for those Wesley placed in the bands. What if what Wesley saw was not willful turning from God but, instead, the effects of trauma?

Dr. Bessel van der Kolk, in the book *The Body Keeps the Score*, stated:

> We now know that trauma compromises the brain area that communicates the physical, embodied feeling of being alive. These changes explain why traumatized individuals become hypervigilant to threat at the expense of spontaneously engaging in their day-to-day lives. They also help us understand why traumatized people so often keep repeating the same problems and have such trouble learning from experience. We now know that *their behaviors are not the result of moral failings or signs of lack of willpower or bad character—they are caused by actual changes in the brain.*[6] (Emphasis added.)

The last sentence in van der Kolk's quote brings up so many questions! What qualifies as trauma? How does trauma change the brain? Isn't destructive behavior, regardless of cause, still considered a sin? Isn't it possible to control behaviors? Do we not hold people accountable for behavior? I am aware of these questions and many more. For now, I will address the first two as an introduction to what will be discussed more extensively later.

WHAT QUALIFIES AS TRAUMA?

Unlike in the past, the word "trauma" is now commonly heard in our society. While this is a significant change, the word often loses its meaning as more and more people talk about many daily events as traumatizing—though they may very well be.

It is essential to understand the difference between traumatic events that everyone experiences—that most can leave in the past—and trauma that leaves long-lasting, debilitating effects.

Understanding this difference involves knowing how the body responds, what people believe about themselves because of the event or events, and how they process, or cannot process, what happened.

In other words, does a memory fade into the past without harmful impact, or does it continue to control the individual, consciously or unconsciously? Disliking certain places or objects can be related to childhood events but isn't life altering. However, sometimes these experiences do become life altering when unconscious or conscious avoidance keeps people from living fully.

> It is essential to understand the difference between traumatic events that everyone experiences—that most can leave in the past—and trauma that leaves long-lasting, debilitating effects. Understanding this difference involves knowing how the body responds, what people believe about themselves because of the event or events, and how they process, or cannot process, what happened.

No human can escape this life without experiencing some form of trauma. With appropriate support after a traumatic event, most can recover without debilitating effects. This process builds resilience. But trauma without appropriate help leads to unimaginable suffering for many. The path to healing is more complicated for those who have experienced early developmental trauma or lived under constant threat—emotionally or physically—that leads to Complex Post Traumatic Stress Syndrome (C-PTSD).

COMPLEX PTSD (C-PTSD)

While not included in the DSM-5, Complex PTSD is clinically recognized by practitioners who work with individuals who have a history of trauma. It occurs as a result of long-term exposure to traumatic stress or repeated traumatic events that have typically occurred in childhood. (This differs from

Chronic PTSD which indicates symptoms lasting six months or longer.)

Many people with a history of complex PTSD often feel misunderstood and are misdiagnosed and inappropriately medicated. This failure to diagnose is due to several factors, including similarity of symptoms to other disorders, co-occurring disorders, and unfamiliarity of practitioners with trauma and its impact. C-PTSD is commonly mistaken and can co-occur with personality disorders, bipolar disorder, ADHD, anxiety disorders, somatic disorders, and substance use disorders. How this disorder develops is multifaceted and includes several contributing factors in addition to experiencing childhood trauma. The following is a list of contributing variables:

Intensity, Duration, and Timing – The more intense or longer the abuse or traumatic event lasts, the more likely C-PTSD will develop. Individuals are most at risk during the first three years of life when the nervous system develops and also during adolescence as personal identity begins to take shape.

Genetics – Some research suggests that there is a biological factor in how a person experiences trauma. This is a fascinating area of study called epigenetics.

Environment – Whether or not a child feels safe contributes to their ability to recover. A parent's presence, their ability to provide adequately for all the child's physical and emotional needs, unexpected disruption in a child's life, and other environmental factors can have significant impact.

In-Utero Influences – While still being studied, infants who were born to mothers who were pregnant during a traumatic event that could have resulted in the mother experiencing PTSD had physical attributes such as lower birth rates and decreased cortisol levels.

They are often reported to be harder to soothe, more prone to colic and at increased risk for PTSD.

Family Dynamics – Factors such as birth order, a family's interactions, and whether a child is planned or wanted are all possible contributors.

Modeling – Children learn from what they experience and when parents don't have health promoting behaviors, children are at risk for developing similar practices.

Presence of a Learning Disability or ADHD – The extra need for compassion and understanding for this child can be easily missed, and a child's brain experiences chronic stress with things other children can easily accomplish, compounded by a lack of patience and/or understanding.

Lack of Resilience Factors – Protective resources like secure attachment, positive peer relationships, activities outside of the home, and an understanding community help a child see that they can be human, recovering from mistakes and growing through challenges.[7]

HOW DOES THE BRAIN REACT TO TRAUMATIC EVENTS?

Our bodies and brains were created for survival. When a car is speeding toward us, considering our options is too time consuming—we need to react and react quickly. In the center of our brain, in the limbic brain, the amygdala is always on guard for danger. We have all felt the rush of adrenaline when we perceive danger. The amygdala signals "Danger!" to a part of our brain in the more primal area located in the brain stem, and we will autonomically respond with a fight, flight, or freeze response. "Fawn response" is also being recognized by some as a behavior that enables us to try to "make friends" with the danger.

When this reaction occurs, the amygdala also shuts down the prefrontal cortex—the thinking part of the brain. This is especially important to understand when children or adults react to a perceived threat. Asking them what they were thinking is useless. They weren't thinking; they were reacting. We see this every day on the news or in our schools. Why would people resist arrest? What were they thinking? They weren't. Why do children run out of the school building and into the street? What were they thinking? They weren't.

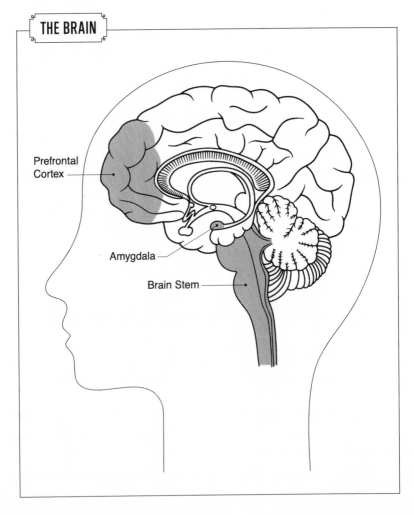

THE BRAIN

Prefrontal Cortex

Amygdala

Brain Stem

How often have you heard, "That triggered me"? It is probably the most-used and least-understood trauma-related term, and it has become part of our common cultural vocabulary. In essence, a trigger is a physical reaction to a stimulus. Pavlov's dogs were, essentially, triggered to react to the bell. That experiment wasn't a harmful thing—maybe manipulative, but not harmful.

Being trauma informed requires more than an understanding that people get triggered by things that remind them of a traumatic event. It requires us to accept that we are humans—created, evolved, or both—with bodies designed to survive. That means that smells can direct us to sources of food and can also take us back to terrifying events. These reminders of the event alert the amygdala to prepare to fight, flee, or when those options aren't available, freeze.

When trauma is triggered, the body floods with stress hormones that take the prefrontal cortex offline, and the individual feels as if the trauma is happening now. This is far different than remembering something that was upsetting. When the trigger leads to "the bell rang, and I am hungry," as in the case of Pavlov's dogs, it is a benign thing. In my personal story, the smell of Old Spice cologne had to be avoided at all costs, and it was not benign. It was a trauma trigger that eventually became a clue that helped me unravel my story. I am also triggered in a benign way by the smell of pine needles, which transport me back to my days at camp as a child and teenager. Both are physical reactions and completely normal. The difference is that a trauma trigger is terrifying and releases a completely different set of hormones in my body.

It is important to understand that the effects of trauma are *felt* in the body. The emphasis on transforming the mind asks the traumatized person to *think* their way out of physical reactions. To do this, they must unconsciously learn to ignore the sensations in their body. When a trigger overrides this, the bodily sensations are overwhelming.

Dr. Stephen Porges's polyvagal theory is helping us better understand how the body responds to threat and why behavior is a symptom of an overwhelmed autonomic nervous system (ANS).[8] Viewing outward responses (fight or flight) or shutting down (freeze response) as being a result of an overwhelmed nervous system is helpful. With this understanding, it is possible to assist ourselves and others in developing the skill to pause and breathe before reacting to a threat that doesn't currently pose a danger.

These internal sensations are often misinterpreted by those who cannot see the internal state of the individual. Many examples of this will be shared as we discuss the impact of trauma more deeply, but one example involves the pressure to participate in worship. When we minister to people who feel physically or emotionally unsafe, it can be detrimental to pressure them to participate, especially if it involves being vulnerable. What may appear on the surface as shyness or reluctance may have a much deeper significance to those dealing with past tragedies or relational trauma. Unwittingly, we can try to include someone in an effort to be friendly, when in fact, the person is in a fragile or overwhelmed state.

FINAL THOUGHTS

Becoming trauma informed is essential to every ministerial leader. In education, medicine, and judicial systems, those who understand trauma are beginning to realize that many of the methods and strategies they use are only making matters worse. Faith communities are no different.

The only path to fully healing trauma, especially relational trauma, is through relationships that provide unconditional love or regard. Peter Levine states, "Trauma is not what happens to us, but what we hold inside in the absence of an empathetic witness." Healing comes not because we offer answers, but because we listen and compassionately believe the stories traumatized people tell us. Current neuroscience findings and my own personal experience supports this. Why was therapy so healing in my life? There are many reasons, but the primary one was the nonjudgmental and empathetic listening of my therapist. Felt safety is a cornerstone of healing. It must also become the central theme in our churches if we are to compassionately minister to those who suffer.

TRAUMA-INFORMED THERAPY[9]

The current understanding of the mind/body reactions during a traumatic event is helping researchers and mental health professionals to expand the available options for trauma-informed/focused treatments. In addition, meeting the attachment needs of the child as a precursor for developing self-regulation has demonstrated the importance of a therapeutic relationship to heal trauma.

To understand the concept of trauma-informed care, the Substance Abuse and Mental Health Services Association (SAMSHA) has outlined six key principles. At the top of the list is safety—something not felt in any type of trauma. The second is trustworthiness and transparency, two factors specifically impacted when trauma is caused by those the child should be able to trust. These three components are at the foundation of basic human needs and require building or rebuilding in the process of healing from trauma or stressor-related disorders. The remaining principles are collaboration, empowerment, voice/choice and cultural, historical and gender issues.

A trauma-informed clinician will demonstrate empathy, non-judgment, positive regard and collaboration in the treatment process with their client. Key ingredients of trauma-informed clinical practices include involving patients in the treatment process, screening for trauma, training staff in trauma-specific treatment approaches, engaging referral sources, and partnering organizations in trauma-informed care.

Chapter 2: Leadership Reflection Questions

- Were you familiar with the difference between PTSD and C-PTSD? How would you explain this in a trauma-informed way to your congregation?

- Bessel van der Kolk, when referring to behavior, stated, "Their behaviors are not the result of moral failings or signs of lack of willpower or bad character—they are caused by actual changes in the brain." What are your thoughts concerning this quote?

- Have you counselled or worked with an individual who was unable to leave a tragic event in the past? How can understanding trauma explain why that might be happening?

- Have you ever said, "What were they thinking?" about someone's actions? How does understanding trauma help you to comprehend this in a more compassionate way?

- Why is it impossible to avoid those things that might trigger people? How can you help those who find many aspects of church life and expected behaviors triggering?

How Prevalent is Trauma in the Pews?

O n any typical Sunday, how many who sit in our church pews are experiencing the effects of trauma? Statistically, at least a quarter of any congregation has experienced sexual abuse. This type of abuse is only a small portion of the types of traumas that people experience. In fact, the Adverse Childhood Experiences (ACE) research found that 65 percent of adults had experienced at least one type of ACE documented in the study.[10]

Trauma is prevalent in the lives of many of those who are part of our faith communities. If a specific congregation is representative of the general population, 65 percent of the congregation will have suffered trauma. Since many who suffer seek help from spiritual communities, the percent is likely higher.

> If a specific congregation is representative of the general population, 65 percent of the congregation will have suffered trauma. Since many who suffer seek help from spiritual communities, the percent is likely higher.

Is the prevalence of trauma a new phenomenon? Or do we just talk about it now? To consider the answers to these questions, it is necessary to reflect on the means by which the cumulative effects of trauma have been building in our homes, communities, churches, and nation. In truth, trauma has lived as an undercurrent in our churches for many generations.

THE ADVERSE CHILDHOOD EXPERIENCES STUDY (ACES)[11]

In the 1990's, Kaiser Permanente and the Center for Disease Control (CDC) conducted a study on adverse childhood experiences. The ACE Study, as it is called, formed the foundation for our understanding of trauma experienced during childhood. The study asked participants, all employees of Kaiser Permanente, to answer ten questions to indicate if they had experienced any adverse events during their childhoods. The questions focused on three major categories: abuse, neglect, or household dysfunction.

The researchers compared the results from the questionnaires to the employee's medical records and discovered a correlation: the higher the number of ACEs a person experienced, the more likely the person was to have a variety of medical conditions and mental health concerns. The study also confirmed that "Toxic stress from ACEs can change brain development and affect how the body responds to stress." ACEs are linked to chronic health problems like heart disease, stroke, cancer and diabetes, in addition to mental illness and substance misuse in adulthood."

The most promising aspect of this study is the understanding of trauma as a significant underlying cause of many physical and psychological conditions. With this knowledge, healthcare professionals can recognize the symptoms caused by ACEs and provide more effective treatments that will reduce their long-term effect on a person's physical and mental health.

THE GROWTH OF THE POST-WAR CHURCH

During the era that followed World War II, our nation was embracing the "American Dream." The war was over, and the country was prospering. It's easy to look back on those years as achieving the spiritual and societal example we should regain. In truth, they were the years in which the effects of trauma were beginning to rumble in both society and faith communities, and everyone was ill-prepared to help. It didn't mean that there weren't good intentions and many who sincerely worked to help the hurting—mostly succeeding.

My father was the pastor of a growing church that was organized the year of my birth. We stayed at this new-start church from 1953 to 1963, a decade of devoted ministry by my parents. It was part of the greatest period of church growth in our nation's history. Carol Tucker wrote in an article in the USC News, "On a typical Sunday morning in the period from 1955–58, almost half of all Americans were attending church—the highest percentage in U.S. history. During the 1950s, nationwide church membership grew at a faster rate than the population, from 57 percent of the U.S. population in 1950 to 63.3 percent in 1960."[12]

During these years was when I came to understand the divided character of the church. It was also when I learned to hide the truth of the darkness that existed alongside spirituality. Yes, faith communities were growing but they were also unknowingly building spiritual practices on quicksand by not recognizing the reality of the mental health needs of those who hid their pain while sitting in the pews of churches. Few understood the effects of the trauma that had visited our nation since its inception.

Still, the stories of how faith communities and their leaders got it right are everywhere. I would never want to diminish the good that followers of Jesus have brought to our world. I am not a throw-the-baby-out-with-the-bathwater church hater. Not at all. I do not believe that I could have survived the trauma in my life without the pastors, youth workers, and lay members who cared about me. Despite this, I suffered deeply from the trauma I experienced and erroneously believed its effects were a spiritual problem.

THE TRAUMA OF WAR

I was a freshman in college when they began to post the draft numbers on the wall of the cafeteria. The Vietnam War seemed to be an ever-present shadow across my childhood after I completed a report about the country in fifth grade and learned about the political and social issues that would eventually consume our national conversations during my teen years. Sadly, those conversations did nothing to honor those of my generation who served.

One of the most important mental health advances resulted from the study of Vietnam veterans who returned from the war with what we now understand as PTSD. The efforts to help veterans heal from the effects of combat-related trauma gave us answers about what had been called "shell shock" in previous wars. There was never a question that some soldiers seemed to fare well while others returned from combat with overwhelming mental health problems. Bessel van der Kolk, in the book *The Body Keeps the Score*, thoroughly discussed the history of care for these veterans—the failures and successes. We now know it wasn't just soldiers who experienced PTSD; anyone facing a real or perceived life-threatening experience—trauma—can develop symptoms.

The prevalence of PTSD in combat soldiers is important because the history of our nation began with war and has seldom not been warring in some form. During our country's history, there have been around a hundred wars or rebellions in which our military has been involved. Though PTSD was not recognized as a diagnosis until 1980, the symptoms have been evident throughout recorded history and called by a variety of names such as nostalgia, soldier's heart, or shell shock.[13]

Without a doubt, every conflict sent traumatized men and women home to their families. Many of them also returned to places of worship. While growing up and then serving in the church, I always honored those who served our country. However, I seldom heard their stories. For the most part, they did not talk about the horrors of war. There was one exception, a man who attended my church for many years. I am not sure why this remarkable man decided to talk. He shared how his unit was one of the first to enter a concentration camp at the end of World War II. As he walked through the horrific scene, he noticed his boots were covered with ash and he had the blinding realization that he was covered with the ashes of human beings.

Not every veteran has a story like this man's experience, but those who do rarely share. We now know that repeated sharing of stories does not always promote healing and without trauma-based therapy, can make matters worse. On the other hand, never telling anyone is a sure way to suffer. For this reason, my complete lack of knowledge about the stories of veterans who served in wars and sat beside me in church pews is rather unsettling.

We are a warring nation and for many who were traumatized, the war within them never ended. Many children of World War II and Vietnam veterans share about their parents' unpredictable tempers, mood swings, and alcohol abuse. All of these are common effects of unresolved trauma. The generations traumatized by the world wars—not to mention the Dust Bowl and Great Depression—were flocking to churches in the 1950s with the belief that spirituality was the answer. Many suffered from PTSD, depression, and anxiety. The only answer ministry leaders had for them was salvation and the forgiveness of sin.

Unresolved trauma lives on in the shadow of our unconscious minds and guides our behaviors and actions. Often incorrectly called "inner demons" or "original sin," the unconscious mind lives out unresolved trauma in ways people do not understand without deep healing. When their actions do not match who they believe themselves to be (or who they want to be), they say, either as a joke or with conviction, "The devil made me do it." It is impossible to understand adult behaviors without understanding the past. Repeated trips to the altar never solve the problem because it is not a spiritual problem.

Ministry leaders and laypeople misidentified the effects of various types of trauma—combat related, physical or sexual abuse, or neglect—as sin and told people that accepting Jesus would heal the turmoil. By following the admonition to leave the past behind, these traumatized individuals tried to distance themselves from the pain but could not achieve this goal. Still in pain and confused by their lack of success, this generation unknowingly passed the effects of trauma on to the next generation.

While hiding their pain, church members often lived out a joyless faith. Subsequent generations began to leave churches in droves because they determined that faith communities in that present form did not have the answers for which they were searching. The findings of "The State of Religion & Young People 2020: Relational Authority" documented this trend. "Nearly 40% of young people ages 13–25 indicate they are unaffiliated, whether agnostic, atheist, or 'nothing in particular.' Young people do not necessarily feel that they are bound by the limits of a religion's traditional edges. They take what they perceive to be true, just, and good, and integrate it into a wider worldview."[14]

> It is impossible to understand adult behaviors without understanding the past. Repeated trips to the altar never solve the problem because it is not a spiritual problem.

RACIAL TRAUMA

Recently, I received a document that detailed my mother's ancestry. I was excited to add this information to my father's family history. Both documents are filled with religious information about salvation, baptisms, and church membership. The obituaries contained comments about the strong faith of my ancestors. On my father's side, my lineage information dates back to the Revolutionary War and contains documentation about the property value of slaves.

Family lore says that my great-great-grandfather, who lived in Virginia, released his slaves at the beginning of the Civil War and went to fight for the Union Army. I hope that story is true, but it doesn't change the fact that my "God-fearing" family may have owned the ancestors of those who now carry the generational trauma of slavery. It is a historical fact that many slave owners who attended church also abused their slaves. It is a neuroscientific fact that trauma carries on from one generation to another through the epigenetic process. The trauma of slavery is still living within the descendants of slaves.

Every new generation inherits their parents' unresolved trauma, and until we accept this truth and take active steps to address the past, the church will soon become irrelevant. There are faith communities that are leading the way in taking these steps. One example is the decision by the leadership of First United Methodist Church of Boise, Cathedral of the Rockies, to remove a stained-glass window with an image that includes George Washington, Abraham Lincoln, and Robert E. Lee. Chair of the church council, Susie Pouliot, stated, "We cannot have a banner above our door that says, 'All means all – you are welcome here' and continue to have a symbol of white supremacy in the form of Gen. Lee's visage just a few feet away. It's wrong. It doesn't represent who we are as a church and as individuals."[15]

> Every new generation inherits their parents' unresolved trauma, and until we accept this truth and take active steps to address the past, the church will soon become irrelevant.

I would also be remiss to not mention that many members of various faith communities were integral in the abolitionist movement. Black churches were also powerful forces in the survival of freed slaves. In the same way, I passionately believe that the church has the power to make healing choices that acknowledge the painful parts of our nation's history.

As a child, except for a visiting Black evangelist, I never saw a Black person in my church. I heard many explanations about why that was true. None of those explanations included discrimination and racial prejudice. The demographics in most churches have not changed much. What has changed is my recognition that the American church cannot deny the trauma of an entire segment of our population and continue to proclaim that we have the answers. We have not been honest about our past and slavery is only one aspect of that.

Racial trauma affects all minority groups. I live in the Pacific Northwest, and the names of many of our cities, towns, and roads remind me that the land on which our houses, businesses, and places of worship sit was not ours to own. Our attempts to honor the tribes seem feeble in light of the decimation of entire cultures. Recent revelations about the abuse and death of children in religious-run schools are also part of our history that requires us to take an honest look at our personal and collective histories.

EPIGENETICS

According to the Center for Disease Control (CDC), "Epigenetics is the study of how your behaviors and environment can cause changes that affect the way your genes work. Unlike genetic changes, epigenetic changes are reversible and do not change your DNA sequence, but they can change how your body reads a DNA sequence."[16]

Epigenetic changes can result from life choices such as diet and exercise, as well as environmental factors including trauma. The impact of trauma on gene expression is being researched for how epigenetic changes may help to explain many physical and mental long-term effects.

RELIGIOUS TRAUMA

Somewhere along the line, faith communities began to promote the image of the "perfect Christian" and based on many cultural constructs, created rules to help sinners be that person. This was true during the adult years when I served, worked in schools, and attended churches that leaned heavily toward legalism. It was intriguing to notice that the rules were similar to the accepted 1950s culture of my childhood. We went to church, we followed the dress code, we didn't partake of "sinful substances," we were to be morally pure, and we did not dance or listen to rock 'n' roll. It was as if faith was frozen in time, and we were desperately trying to return to the glory days that never actually existed. It was a place where people could look spiritual by following rules. It was a perfect scenario for the abuse by those who appeared to be upstanding church members to go unrecognized—especially in a culture that did not believe those who tried to speak about the abuse.

I wish there was DNA testing for faith communities—the kind of testing that brings hidden stories to light. Genetic test results do not deny the truth. We have no such truth-teller in the church, and therefore the secrets remain in the graveyard of "prove it." Recent revelations of the intentional repression of claims of sexual abuse by church leaders is evidence of a culture that has not only repressed but ignored and further traumatized victims. This has always been true. Now we have "Me Too/Church Too" signs pointing to the stories that were buried. The call to protect the church and its leaders only increased the pain of those who already suffered.

Many who experienced trauma outside of faith communities came into the church and stared at the stained glass assuming it to be a place where they could finally be safe. All they had to do was repent. So, they did, often believing themselves responsible for the sins of others who had hurt them. They also believed that salvation would solve the inner turmoil of their trauma. They were told to leave the past behind and not trust their feelings and emotions. They struggled to fulfill spiritual expectations and were certain they were the only ones to do so. They felt the longing to return to the ways they had survived before salvation and without the help they needed to heal, they slipped back into old patterns. Ministry leaders and laypeople called it "backsliding" and said they should have tried harder. In essence, the traumatized were retraumatized.

What no one understood was that their problems weren't spiritual. We joked about putting on our "church masks" before walking in the door. For some, that meant the arguments in the car stopped at the church door. For others, it required that the family secrets remained hidden. In current-day vocabulary, we would say that our faith communities lacked authenticity. Those outside faith communities—or those who left—began hurling accusations of hypocrisy. They were told to keep their eyes on Jesus. No one understood the problem was not spiritual.

Those who suffered from the effects of trauma were trying, and ministry leaders were telling them to try harder. Without knowing the cause or understanding the effects, the hurting people we were called to help were shamed and judged. They either buried their pain, as I did, or left, which I also did eventually. The result was an outwardly spiritual group of Christians who knew how to follow rules but dared not reflect too deeply on their inner turmoil.

Those who did look deeply within began to deconstruct this lifeless faith and heal their pain. When I chose to heal, I did not realize that I was embarking on the most important spiritual experience of my life. It was hard and messy. Few understood why I chose to walk away from a career and lifetime of service within the church and church-related educational settings. I gave up everything to spend three years living in an RV while walking through the process of trauma-based healing. As a result, I now believe that I am worthy of God's love and that the turmoil was never a spiritual problem. What the traumatized world needs is the message that healing trauma can enable them to access the abundant life that Jesus promised.

FINAL THOUGHTS

While I have only highlighted three of the major areas of trauma that have had an impact on our churches, communities, nation, and world, it is not an inclusive list by any means. In just the past three years, we have added social and political unrest, the death of millions during the pandemic, mass shootings, and an increasing mental health crisis. There is no one on this planet who has escaped some form of trauma.

Becoming trauma informed is the path to transforming the faith community's messages in ways that can bring hope to those who suffer. The church can become the place that embraces and supports the healing of trauma. The skepticism of many ministry leaders about anything other than scripture being *the* answer to a problem has caused many to fear trauma-informed therapies and other healing practices that could have given them hope for healing. Changing this skepticism requires ministry leaders to grasp the life-altering effects of trauma. It requires the paradigm shift that becoming trauma-informed, sensitive, and responsive can provide.

Chapter 3: Leadership Reflection Questions

- Had you previously considered how prevalent trauma is in the lives of those who attend any ministry in which you lead? What new insights did you gain from reading the chapter?
- When considering the demographics of your church, in what ways might the trauma of war, racism, or religious trauma be most likely?
- Are there ways that you or those in your ministry might be unintentionally discounting the effects of historical trauma in the lives of those you serve?
- How aware are you of the personal and ancestral stories of those you lead? What is an example of how knowing someone's story assisted you in ministering more effectively?
- How might previous experiences of religious trauma be affecting the individuals within your ministries? Is there freedom to share these previous experiences in ways that bring healing?

Section Two

ACKNOWLEDGING THE IMPACT OF TRAUMA ON SPIRITUAL PRACTICES

Nathan and I were once again sitting on the porch with our cups of coffee. I was still enjoying the fact that he could say that he liked himself. It had been a long journey to that statement. My question this time resulted from hearing so many survivors say they couldn't believe God loved them. "Do you believe God loves you?"

There was silence for a moment. Then he said, "I believe it, but I have a hard time accepting that God loves me."

I pressed no further. It made sense for several reasons. First, knowing something is true and feeling like it is true are two different things because they reside in different parts of our brain. It has been prevalent for church teaching to pit emotions against mind, solid doctrine, and/or faith itself. Most sermons I heard said to ignore feelings, and "Stand alone on the word of God." Ministry leaders have often vilified the very emotions God created, even though the Bible is passionate and filled with raw emotion from cover to cover.

Many who have experienced trauma have a distorted or damaged relationship with their emotions, with physical sensations, or with making sense of their pain. Many times, all of the above. Trauma has an insidious way of shattering people at their core, pitting mind against body, feeling against understanding. Where would Nathan feel God's love if he could? In a traumatized body that had learned *not* to feel? Was it possible to grow close to God without feeling? Teachings that diminish the importance of feelings lack an understanding about how essential it is to experience God's love in all aspects of our lives and bodies and have further confused the spiritual growth of so many. In fact, I believe this distorted teaching has reinforced the negative impact trauma has on our lives.

While it is generally accepted that the primary focus of ministry is to help people draw closer to God, growing up in a pastor's home helped me understand that many parts of ministry do not seem related to this focus. There is usually much activity in the church, but how much of that effort actually facilitates growing closer to God? Are we depending on programs, projects, and event-planning while avoiding the more difficult self-reflection necessary for spiritual growth? Perhaps so, perhaps not. Nevertheless, the church claims to be in the service of growing closer to God, and so, on the most fulfilling days, this is what we believe we accomplish by the sheer output of our combined energy.

But let's focus on the ministries that *have* made an intentional effort to deepen our experience with God. Since participating in spiritual practices has been presented as one of the most essential methods of spiritual growth, I began to ask myself a question: "Why do people struggle with spiritual practices?"

This was when *Celebration of Discipline* reentered my life. I say reentered because the concepts in this book had permeated the thousands of sermons I had heard over the years. A low estimate of the number of sermons I listened to over my life would be close to 10,000. The memories of these sermons were embedded in my mind in both positive and negative ways.

While there were many other authors who have written on the topic of spiritual practices, I chose to focus on Foster's work as that which would have been influential to many church leaders during my adult life. Richard Foster *never said to try harder.*

If this was true, then what did he say? I also wondered if his intent was compatible with trauma-sensitive spiritual practices.

With these questions in mind, I began exploring Foster's work through a trauma-informed lens. The day I settled in to get started was a warm July day—thankfully not heatwave warm, just comfortably so—in my Pacific Northwest home office. The window was open, the birds were chirping, and a squirrel was jumping from tree to tree in the lush wetland space outside my window. It was a perfect day to begin writing. And then I realized I was stuck.

How could that be?

My excitement about the project vanished. I looked at my copy of *Celebration of Discipline* sitting next to me, and all I could see was one word: discipline. What did that word mean to me? What did it mean to others? Did it have anything to do with the challenge I was going to discuss? For some reason, the word discipline did not feel trauma informed.

Was the very word discipline *blocking me from writing?*

It made little sense. I had spent years explaining the word discipline to future teachers. "You are to be a guide. Classroom discipline should look like Jesus leading the disciples." In my doctoral work, I gravitated to the leadership style of servant leaders who lead in relational ways. In my trauma-informed advocacy work, I discuss therapeutic parenting and trauma-sensitive strategies for the classroom—which are relation based. In my personal life, I believe God is my loving guide. Yet my gut feeling was that my conception of the word discipline, now staring at me from the book cover, was the reason my progress stopped.

My thoughts sent me to Facebook to ask my friends about what picture or image the word discipline brought to them (an overview of their responses is located in Appendix 2). I realized my hesitation about the word was well-founded. At the end of this unexpected but informative day, I reflected on how our views about discipline have been affected not only by prominent voices in the Christian community who have espoused punitive discipline models but also by the "try harder" approaches to spiritual practices.

The Spiritual Disciplines proposed by Foster were meant to be a guide to spiritual growth. Sadly, they have sometimes been used to shame those whose spiritual practices do not meet an unreachable standard of perfection. I would grow to understand that this is the opposite of their purpose!

The question I asked my friends revealed the degree to which our ideas about discipline cause us to be uncomfortable—even for those who did not experience abuse as children. It is essential to unwind the punitive ideas of the word discipline that cause these knee-jerk responses to the terminology. I realized that while the spiritual practices were meant to bring order and direction to our spiritual life and require us to build habits, they should feel neither punishing nor painful. This reflection led me to predominantly use the term "spiritual practices" unless specifically referring to or quoting Richard Foster's work.

My reflections on the effects of trauma on spiritual practices follows the framework used in *Celebration of Discipline*, though his is not the only framework available. His three categories: inward, outward, and corporate Disciplines do provide a structural outline that has stood the test of time. All three of these categories present challenges for those who have experienced trauma, especially trauma that occurred during childhood. The specific challenges are as unique as everyone's story but make sense when viewed through the lens of the neurobiological and psychological effects of trauma.

At some level we can all relate to the challenge of spiritual practices because the struggle is often a result of being human. Building habits of any kind is inherently challenging, but it

> Building habits of any kind is inherently challenging, but it should not be impossible. In my own life, it *was* often impossible, but I never understood why until I began to un-layer my childhood trauma.

should not be impossible. In my own life, it *was* often impossible, but I never understood why until I began to un-layer my childhood trauma. The effects of trauma go far beyond the conceptual understanding of self-discipline. Are the spiritual practices challenging because of a lack of self-control, or does it go much deeper? It is time to answer this question.

Section Two: Leadership Reflection Questions

- Do you ever hear those who struggle spiritually express feelings about not feeling God's presence? What practices do you suggest for helping them? How are these practices either effective or ineffective? What have you believed the problem to be if not helpful?

- Have you read the book *Celebration of Discipline*? How were you introduced to the book and how have you utilized in in your personal faith and/or ministry?

- What have you utilized to become more familiar with spiritual formation practices? What resources have you found helpful?

- What is your gut-level reaction to the word discipline? Did the perceptions of others shared in the text or in Appendix 2 surprise or not surprise you? Is it possible that the word may be standing in the way of some within your ministry embracing the idea of practicing Spiritual Disciplines?

PART ONE

WHY DO THE TRAUMATIZED FEAR OPENING THEMSELVES TO GOD?

As a child, I refused to sing "Jesus Loves Me." Telling my Sunday school teacher that I was bored with singing the song too often wasn't the real reason. I simply did not believe the song was true—I didn't believe Jesus loved me. Often children who experience abuse, especially if it's sexual in nature, blame themselves and feel unworthy of God's love. I was no exception. Yet, I fully believed that God loved everyone else.

In what ways does childhood trauma affect the capacity to open our inner life to God? The feeling that many who have experienced trauma express is that God feels distant from them. The truth is that trauma and the resulting shame cause the traumatized to separate themselves unconsciously and sometimes consciously from God and others.

Questions abound in the minds of children and adults alike: *How could God love me after what happened?* This is often embedded in the minds of the traumatized. *If God loved me, why wasn't this awful event prevented? Why was I all alone in this pain?*

The following is not an exhaustive description but does offer a foundational understanding that helps explain how the effects of trauma cause spiritual practices to be difficult to access: Relational trauma damages the attachment relationships involving trust and security. It also creates false internalized messages of shame and a deep need for validation. Identity formation is hindered and the individual struggles to find a sense of self.

The basis of all of these struggles is neurobiological and affects all areas of behavior and learning. The effects of trauma, we will learn, affect every area of an individual's life. Most who were abused as children have felt the effects of every item mentioned above. Each will be addressed by the specific manner in which a particular spiritual practice is affected, but first it is important to understand the implications of ignoring the pain from traumatic childhood events.

HOW DOES CHILDHOOD PAIN AFFECT PARTICIPATION IN SPIRITUAL PRACTICES?

My own story proved to me that it was possible to function outwardly while struggling inwardly. Not all can hide the inner pain as well as I did—though it wasn't healthy. How the effects of trauma are exhibited in people's lives depends on the support they received, the extent and type of trauma, their age at the time, and how often the trauma occurred. Taking all this into account, appearing functional is possible for many people who have been impacted by trauma. It is a survival skill—a way to go under the radar so no one will discover what happened. They do not want anyone to know they are not okay. As children, they were often shamed if they did.

It is shocking when someone dies from suicide without showing any outward signs of distress. These stories tell us that while it is possible to hide our distress, it is not healthy. In hindsight, many did show unrecognized effects of trauma. In *The Body Keeps the Score*, Bessel van der

> How the effects of trauma are exhibited in people's lives depends on the support they received, the extent and type of trauma, their age at the time, and how often the trauma occurred.

Kolk stated: "Most of our conscious brain is dedicated to focusing on the outside world: getting along with others and making plans for the future. However, that does not help us manage ourselves. Neuroscience research shows that the only way we can change the way we feel is by becoming aware of our inner experience and learning to befriend what is going on inside ourselves."[17]

Living outwardly functional lives, while necessary for successful adult living, should not involve ignoring the pain of childhood. All who experienced childhood trauma and desire to fully thrive must do the deep work of healing their inner child who still calls out for help.

Without healing, many have misapplied church teaching and describe the hurting child inside themselves as an inner demon or their "sin nature." The emotions of children who have been impacted by trauma can feel out of control, much like a frightening monster. It is often essential for children to unconsciously separate themselves from this pain, but as van der Kolk says, "Pushing away intense feelings can be highly adaptive in the short run. The problems come later."[18] Often these problems are viewed as spiritual struggles by the individual and others.

When individuals suffer from unresolved childhood trauma while living outwardly functional lives, they often have little concept of the peace that passes understanding. This was how I lived my life. None who knew me suspected the level of trauma I eventually acknowledged. After reading my first book, a few of my friends recognized some of the trauma symptoms, but most asked me how I lived the life I did. The answer? With my childhood dissociative coping strategies that distanced me from the turmoil. I described this as living at two levels, something that became apparent when I tried to access any spiritual practices that involved reflecting deeply on my inner world.

The fear of inner emotions caused the more reflective spiritual practices to be unattainable. Opening my inner space to myself or God felt terrifying, both consciously and unconsciously. When those who suffered trauma as children talk with me about beginning therapy, they often express fear about what they might uncover, or even that they might be making stuff up. This fear is the *knowing unknowing* of trauma. I never hear anyone whose traumatic memories surfaced, say, "I was so surprised something bad happened to me as a child." We may not have remembered exactly what happened but knew something had—even though we longed to believe it wasn't true. This was true of my friend Lillian.

> When those who suffered trauma as children talk with me about beginning therapy, they often express fear about what they might uncover, or even that they might be making stuff up. This fear is the *knowing unknowing* of trauma.

Lillian called me after her therapy appointment. I was watching for her call and had told her I would be available if she needed me. We met when she was a student in one of my college courses and had kept in contact through the years. When she read *Brave*, she messaged me. "I think something happened to me. Am I just making it up because I read your book?"

She was not the first person to ask me this question, so I asked, "Did you ever sense this might be true before reading *Brave*?"

"Yes, and I think I need help," she answered like so many others had. I agreed, and we worked together to locate a therapist.

After several sessions, she began to piece together the fragmented parts of her story. She knew how old she was (six), where she was (a neighbor's house), who was there (the neighbor's teenage son), but not what happened. My sense that this would be the day her subconscious would release the memory was correct.

She sobbed as she began to tell the story. "In some way I knew this but could not consciously accept it. He did terrible things and threatened that if I told anyone he would kill my family. I never told anyone. I asked to go to their house, so I thought what happened was my fault. I kept going to the altar during services and asking God to forgive me, but I never told anyone what happened. I knew, but then I didn't remember. How is that possible?"

Lillian could not remember because God created us to survive. Sometimes our mind must distance itself from traumatic memories so that we can live. It is a myth that "If it was that traumatic, you would remember it." Sometimes that may be true, but in the case of children, the opposite is usually true. Repressed memories are real. I know this is true in my life because so many inexplicable triggers began to make sense as my traumatic memories surfaced. Triggers are clues, and we avoid those things that trigger us because it is too close to the memory we are consciously or unconsciously trying to forget.

It is no great wonder that opening our inner world up to God is challenging when that is the place where we have unconsciously sequestered the inner child—or teenager, or young adult—whom we cannot love and possibly loathe. In unconsciously blocking this part of us, we also block God from entering and transforming our inner spaces. Without healing from trauma, the inward Spiritual Disciplines of meditation, prayer, study, and fasting can be difficult to access. The following thoughts on trauma-sensitive spiritual practices align with this framework while exploring how trauma affects the spiritual lives of so many.

Section Two Part One: Leadership Reflection Questions

- Are you familiar with the therapeutic healing term "inner child work?" Did the material in this Introduction to Part One connect, enhance, or add to your thoughts about the application of that work to spiritual growth? If so, in what ways?
- How does the traumatized individual's fear about feelings or sensations inhibit access to spiritual practices? Can you give an example of an individual you worked with who seemed to distance themselves from childhood experiences? Why might pressuring these individuals to do spiritual inner work be counter-productive?

Meditation Through a Trauma Lens

S taring intently at my therapist, I said, "Wait, my mother was trying to protect me from being abused again?" How could this be true? My lifelong narrative was one of being shamed for attention-seeking behaviors as a young child. As I worked through this memory involving my mother, it was now clear that she was telling me I might get hurt again.

"She approached this in all the wrong ways and caused so much shame, but I can accept that she was trying to protect me," I said. It was a dramatic change in perspective.

In *Celebration of Discipline*, meditation is framed as a practice that, "Sends us into our ordinary world with greater perspective and balance."[19] My therapy sessions fulfilled this description. It was a process that took me deep inside my memories with the assistance of EMDR (Eye Movement Desensitization and Reprocessing).[20] Then, with my adult ability to process, it was possible to reflect on what took place at the deepest levels of my emotional brain. Though it was difficult to sense at the time, I do not doubt that God was present. Many attest to deeply spiritual experiences during EMDR therapy sessions. These perspective-changing sessions fulfilled the purpose of meditation.

EMDR (EYE MOVEMENT DESENSITIZATION AND REPROCESSING)

There are a growing number of trauma-informed therapy modalities now being used to assist in healing. EMDR was the primary modality used during my healing. While I have only included information on EMDR, it is not the only modality that is effective in healing trauma. There is a growing understanding that modalities that only focus on changing behaviors with cognitive strategies cannot adequately address the effects of trauma being held in the body. While the effects of trauma appear psychological, the treatment must necessarily also focus on helping the client process the trauma held in the body. This isn't only true in therapy. I will include many ways that somatic or body-based experiences that aid in the healing process can be included in our spiritual practices.

EMDR: "A psychotherapy that enables people to heal from the symptoms and emotional distress that are the result of disturbing life experiences. Therapist directed lateral eye movements are the most commonly used external stimulus, but a variety of other stimuli including hand-tapping and audio stimulation are often used. EMDR therapy facilitates the accessing of the traumatic memory network so that information processing is enhanced, with new associations forged between the traumatic memory and more adaptive memories or information. These new associations are thought to result in complete information processing, new learning, elimination of emotional distress, and development of cognitive insights. After successful treatment with EMDR therapy, affective distress is relieved, negative beliefs are reformulated, and physiological arousal is reduced."[21]

It is crucial to remember that the purpose of Christian meditation is to commune with God and find direction through listening. The challenge for those impacted by trauma is to hear God's loving voice and not mistake the shame-based messaging in their heads as that voice. God's voice is loving and nonjudgmental. Shame tells them there is something horribly wrong with them; that they are unworthy of God's love.

HOW DOES SHAME DEFEAT A RELATIONAL CONNECTION WITH GOD?

At the center of every story of trauma is shame, which settles deep into the mind and body of the traumatized and blocks healthy relationships. From the beginning, the Bible provides examples of God seeking relationships with humans The first of these examples was the relationship between God and humans in the Garden of Eden. It is a beautiful picture of fellowship until shame entered the picture. At that point, humans began hiding from God.

Probably one of the most defining characteristics of shame is our very denial of it in our lives. I remember the day I told my therapist that I didn't believe I was suffering from very much shame. What I should have said is, "I don't allow myself to feel the shame that is coursing through my body all day long at the slightest provocation."

In his book *The Soul of Shame*, Curt Thompson explained shame as an "interpersonal neurobiological event."[22] He perfectly described the feeling as "the unexpected shearing effect of shame."[23] I now understand this feeling was pervasive in my life. My powerlessness as a child deeply embedded a sense of never being

> I remember the day I told my therapist that I didn't believe I was suffering from very much shame. What I should have said is, "I don't allow myself to feel the shame that is coursing through my body all day long at the slightest provocation."

enough into my psyche. Every public, private, or imagined mistake set off a chain reaction of stress chemicals in my body.

Thompson's description fit my body's reaction exactly: "[The] arousal is precipitously unhinged, like so many colliding railway cars piling up behind the mind's engine as it has come to a screeching halt."[24] Everything in my life was built upon the absolute necessity to either avoid or disengage from this feeling.

In the religious world, this biological sensation is often mistakenly called "conviction." My subconscious response to this false idea was to keep God at an arm's length, just as Adam and Eve did in the Garden of Eden. I cannot remember any teachings that distinguished guilt over wrongdoing from this horrible train-wreck sensation of shame and unworthiness that is ever present in the bodies of the traumatized.

Shame in its most basic form—embarrassment—does help us recognize appropriate or inappropriate behaviors. In a healthy form, normal feelings of embarrassment help young children understand how to live in the world. Shame usually becomes unhealthy because our mistakes or childlike behaviors are punished either physically or through isolation. We believe we are bad instead of understanding our behavior was incorrect. The emphasis is the punishment of our "sinful behavior" instead of receiving relational instruction.

In the biblical story, Eve's realization that she was tricked (not smart enough) was the beginning of shame. Both she and Adam hid from God, the very one who could relationally help them. This is still the narrative lived out by many.

Relationships are the antidote for shame. Our fear of relationship with God and other humans affects every spiritual practice. In hiding our shame, we are inhibited in our efforts to interact with God, just as children become inhibited in expressing emotions to adults and others.

HOW DO FALSE INTERNALIZED MESSAGES AFFECT MEDITATION?

How do these false messages of shame originate? Childhood trauma is more than a bad thing that happened; it is what individuals come to believe about themselves. In *The Body Keeps the Score*, Bessel van der Kolk explained the complicated web of trauma in a child's mind and body. "Most of them suffer from agonizing shame about the actions they took to survive and maintain a connection with the person who abused them. This was particularly true if the abuser was someone close to the child, someone the child depended on, as is so often the case. The result can be confusion about whether one was a victim or a willing participant, which in turn leads to bewilderment about the difference between love and terror; pain and pleasure."[25]

The words of abusers often play in a loop in the brain of a child, remaining there until adulthood. "You wanted this," is the most predominant loop for all types of sexual abuse. When this negative-message loop is mistaken for the judgment of God, the deep feelings of worthlessness are overwhelming. These are the voices that demand attention when the adult survivor of childhood trauma is still.

Religious teachings based on original sin often feel true to those with these deeply embedded false messages—some that occur so early in life that they lack language. False internalized messages, and the self-loathing that accompanies them, fit well with these theologies. An emphasis on sin makes sense if they incorrectly blame themselves for their abuse. Richard Rohr, in *Trauma*, asked, "Could this be what mythology means by the 'sacred wound' and the church meant by an 'original sin,' which was not something we did, but the effects of something that was done to us? I believe it is."[26]

Sadly, in this scenario, meditation can become a time for the those impacted by trauma to reflect on their feelings of worthlessness. They can either avoid it or wallow in it. In both cases it blocks the purpose of meditation which involves hearing the voice and words of a loving God. If those impacted by trauma are to ever believe themselves as worthy of God's love, it is essential that our messages move away from the view of a God who is punitive.

A friend who has been on this journey of healing wrote me and said, "One of the first verses I ever remember being comforting when it comes to salvation was 2 Corinthians 5:14 about the love of God convincing us. After all the hell, fire, and brimstone preaching I'd heard, the fact that God's love is what convinces us to follow him—that was earth-shattering."

Yes, once the survivor can understand themselves as blameless and God as loving, they can then begin to fulfill the true purpose of meditation. God has always desired this. God never turns away from or leaves the hurting alone in their pain and suffering. Abusers' voices can drown out the voice the wounded most need—the voice of the God who loves them.

WHY IS SILENCE SO DIFFICULT?

Like most who have experienced severe trauma, I unconsciously devised numerous strategies that separated me from my inner turmoil. If I was not reflecting too deeply about my internal state, it was possible to believe the story I told myself about my own life—a story that either ignored or repressed my childhood trauma. I was well versed in distancing myself from the turmoil. Yet, if asked to be still, meditate, or pray silently, there was little doubt that a very troubled part of me existed deep inside.

Early in my healing journey I tried the Eastern form of meditation that focuses on an emptying of the mind and immediately knew it was not a good plan. It felt very similar to times of silent prayer during church services. Though the Eastern form of meditation is not the form Foster promoted as a path to hearing and obeying God's word, both can have a similar effect. All forms of meditation that involve stillness and reflection can be problematic for those impacted by trauma.

The difficulty with silence does not negate the value; it does require healing and/or less traditional paths, such as silence while walking in nature. Silent walking was essential to my own healing. The newly found quietness in my mind was profound, and nature was at its most beautiful. Walking made the experience of communing with God accessible. In addition, walking aids the healing of trauma because it involves bilateral stimulation, which helps integrate information in the two hemispheres of the brain.

Therapy is a deep, demanding form of meditation—one that many fear. When those impacted by trauma begin healing and are willing to enter into this form of meditation, God meets them there. This happened to my friend Amy.

After several years of healing, Amy chose to complete an intensive therapy session, and when finished, she decided to stay at a hotel before driving home the next day. It was a rough night of releasing—shaking off—trauma and reflecting on new perspectives gained from the session.

The following day, she took a wrong turn and entered a driveway to turn around. The driveway went up a hill, and at the top, she noticed an open grassy area with benches circling a cross in the center of the circle. She wrote the following message to me upon returning home and included a picture of the cross with blue sky and clouds in the background:

"I was not going to stop and get out, but I felt like I needed to. I couldn't decide if I was mad at God for this or thankful. I sat there for forty-five minutes just talking to him about everything—the good, the bad, and the ugly. It was grounding to sit in the sun and feel the sun beaming on me. It was very comforting and exactly what I needed. It was just so God, so ironic, and so a part of my journey to have gotten lost and turned around at a cross after struggling so much in the night! There are a lot of things I'm not sure of anymore regarding faith, but there are core things that don't waver and have been consistent through trauma and healing. Those are the things I know are real about God. They make up the basics of faith and are enough for anyone who needs hope."

Knowing my friend's story, a time of meditation that centered on the cross was an example of God creatively entering into her processing. Opening her inner world through meditation was an integral part of healing. It is the most beautiful and difficult path anyone could ever choose to follow. As Amy experienced, God is ever present and working toward a loving relationship.

FINAL THOUGHTS

The culmination of my healing process fulfilled the purpose of meditation in enabling me to think differently about my experiences and live differently as a result. In truth, my three-year-long and ongoing healing conversation with God has enabled me to step out into my life in ways I never dreamed would be possible. I am not the only one who has found this to be true. In facing painful pasts, those impacted by trauma can return to a place of childlike faith. This faith is the kind Jesus says we need in order to enter the kingdom.

While traveling across Idaho, we stumbled upon the Sacred Heart Mission just outside of Coeur d'Alene. I was completely transfixed with the simplicity inside the sanctuary. Except for a few rows of chairs, it was empty. For some time, I was alone. In those moments I felt complete stillness inside of me and knew God was smiling. My hard work enabled me to stand before God quietly. This inner stillness began a new phase of constructing an inner sanctuary in the now-open spaces. Meditation was now readily available.

Chapter 4: Leadership Reflection Questions

- In *Celebration of Discipline* Foster stated, "Meditation sends us into our ordinary world with greater perspective and balance." Can you give an example of a time when your perspective was changed either during meditation or during therapy?

- What is the difference between shame and guilt? Can you give an example of each from your own experience or from someone you supported in ministry?

- How are shame and conviction alike and different? How might they be confused in ourselves or perceived incorrectly in others?

- If relationships are the antidote for shame *and* the traumatized struggle with establishing relationships, how does this stand in the way of building community in the church?

- What is an example of a false internalized message that you have helped someone overcome, or overcome yourself? Were you able to connect it to childhood experiences?

- How can the inner turmoil and false internalized messages seem like an inner demon or "original sin"?

- How does silence frighten many who have been traumatized? What precautions should be taken when encouraging meditation that involves silence for extended periods of time?

Prayer Through a Trauma Lens

"I was out running," Ryan began. "I was angry at God, but that didn't seem right. Who was I to be angry with God?"

I kept listening, knowing exactly how he felt. Ryan and I had been introduced by a mutual friend who realized we were both working to bring trauma-informed information to faith communities. During a Zoom meeting, while working on a project, we had begun sharing parts of our healing journeys.

Ryan continued. "I just kept running faster and faster until I just couldn't run anymore. Then all my anger exploded out of me. I began yelling at God—actually cussing at God."

I involuntarily giggled—not good form as a listener, but Ryan laughed too. Cussing at God seemed so uncharacteristic of this ministry leader. "Did it feel healing?" I asked.

"It was! Suddenly I felt the presence of God and was deeply impressed that God was thanking me for finally being honest. Right there on the path, I began crying and collapsed to the ground. *God wanted me to be honest.* It was life-changing and the beginning of what has become a remarkable ongoing conversation with God. Now I understand there isn't anything that can't be expressed."

Though we had talked many times, this was a part of Ryan's story that I did not know. His very authentic and honest faith now made complete sense. It was a result of a relationship with God in which he could be vulnerable and express true emotions.

HOW DOES EARLY TRAUMA AFFECT THE BELIEVER'S PRAYERS?

Ryan's story reminded me of the day in therapy when my anger at God exploded out of me. My therapist's calm acceptance mirrored the acceptance Ryan felt from God. The purpose of prayer is to communicate with God, as Foster describes relationships with loving human fathers: "Openness, honesty, and trust mark the communication of children with their father."[27] Sadly, this is not always what children experience with their fathers as Ryan's experience demonstrates. Many adults were shamed as children for emotional outbursts—or worse, physically punished or abused. They project that fear of being shamed or hurt onto God and stop themselves from experiencing the openness and honesty that would be a path to healing. While healing, their prayers need to be raw outpourings of their pain. If this does not feel acceptable, many who have suffered trauma as children will believe they must leave God behind in order to express their very legitimate pain. There are healing communities where expressions of pain are accepted and even encouraged. God wants churches to be among those communities.

It requires a great deal of trust to openly express emotions to other people or to God. The ability to trust forms within early attachment relationships. Attachment is the foundation of life. All children enter the world needing the one with whom they were intimately connected before birth. A child's need for this attachment relationship is rooted in survival. In my mind there is no stronger human drive. When the mother holds the child to her chest after birth, there are many benefits for both mother and child. The child and the mother physically need each other.[28]

When this cannot happen for medical or other reasons, then care-givers must be very intentional in building an attachment relationship.

> All children enter the world needing the one with whom they were intimately connected before birth. A child's need for this attachment relationship is rooted in survival. In my mind there is no stronger human drive.

Even children adopted at birth can experience a sense of loss which often can't be understood or expressed since it is preverbal and sensory. Attachment-focused therapeutic therapy can provide the guidance and support for this process.[29]

Curt Thompson, in his book *The Soul of Shame*, stated, "Secure attachment is also highly correlated with the maturation of several functions of the prefrontal cortex, including body regulation, at-tuned communication, emotional balance, fear modulation, response flexibility, empathy, insight, and intuition."[30] Human development and modulation of the fear response is formed in relationships that are preverbal and lived out only as emotions. When attachment goes wrong, for any reason, the lifelong effects can be devastating. Since attachment wounds occur so early in life, the effects may feel like it's simply their personality. Many explain these effects as an empty ache that cannot be described or soothed.

The attachment relationship is the barrier of protection be-tween a child and the difficulties of life. All children experience trauma to some degree. It is nurturing relationships that make the difference between healthy healing and maladaptive coping. We are wired for the connections that will enable us to survive.

The attachment relationship lays the foundation for trust. In cases where the biological mother cannot provide this relationship, an attuned caregiver can make a difference. What is critical for the infant is an affirmative answer to these questions: If I cry, will someone come to care for me? If I need a hug, will someone hold me? If I am hungry, will someone feed me?

These needs cannot always be readily met, but if adults work to repair the relationship, this process builds resilience. If the answers to the above questions are most often yes, a child learns to trust. Trusting caregivers doesn't guarantee being able to trust and openly communicate with God, but it is certainly a good foundation to build upon.

HOW DOES TRAUMA MAKE ASKING DIFFICULT?

What happens when a child who cannot trust adults reaches out to an invisible God? Many tell me stories of how they begged God to help them as children, to no avail. Without an understanding of free will and evil, children's views of God can be deeply warped by abuse. They will need many safe relationships (attachments) to repair this damage.

On the other hand, many tell me that they felt God with them even during abuse. This sense is crucial in being receptive to trusting God and believing in prayer. Once again, every story is different. Those who seek faith must at some point come to terms with God's role in their suffering. Sometimes it is this struggle that helps them begin conversations with God in raw emotional ways that bring healing and an attachment relationship with God. Only then is it possible to ask and receive. The call to always remain spiritual and positive interferes with this necessary process.

Many who suffered trauma or neglect as children find it almost impossible to ask for anything. Their needs were ignored, and now asking and not receiving feels like rejection. Also, the internalized mindset resulting from not having needs met as children—and often being shamed for very natural human needs—causes many to feel selfish for any request they might make. Sometimes this affects how they read scriptures about prayer. For example, the following verse felt like everything I dared asked for was selfish: "When you ask, you do not receive, because you ask with wrong motives, that you may spend what you get on your pleasures."[31] Why would I ask?

The common outcome for Christians who have experienced trauma and neglect is an others-focused prayer life. This type of prayer life does not accomplish inner transformation. Because of this, it may appear that there is an unwillingness to change, but I propose that for many it is not an unwillingness. There is nothing that Christians impacted by trauma desire any more than change, but their intense desire to change what they cannot understand about themselves often drives them to pray without ceasing in a manner that lacks attachment to God. Believing that God *wants* to answer their prayers would be transforming, but instead they doubt themselves and fear asking for what they need. For many, the Christian phrase, "If it is God's will..." feels comfortable, since they believe it probably is not God's will—for them, anyway.

> There is nothing that Christians impacted by trauma desire any more than change, but their intense desire to change what they cannot understand about themselves often drives them to pray without ceasing in a manner that lacks attachment to God. Believing that God *wants* to answer their prayers would be transforming, but instead they doubt themselves and fear asking for what they need. For many, the Christian phrase, "If it is God's will..." feels comfortable, since they believe it probably is not God's will—for them, anyway.

Understand that most of this internal conversation is unconscious. In my own life, I could barely ask a family member to get me a glass of water and rarely asked God for anything unless the need was desperate. It surprised me when my prayers were answered, and I wondered if God was irritated by my asking and simply answered out of frustration. What a tragic view of God.

HOW DO THE TRAUMATIZED BELIEVE THAT PRAYER EVEN MATTERS?

With all the confusion that trauma causes in prayer lives, the ultimate question is, does prayer matter? Richard Foster offered a resounding yes to this question. He said, "We are working with God to determine the future! Certain things will happen in history if we pray rightly. We are to change the world by prayer. What more motivation do we need to learn this loftiest human exercise?"[32] This view of prayer is similar to that of Mark Gregory Karris in the following description of what he calls conspiring prayer:

"Conspiring prayer is performed with God rather than to God. Conspiring prayer is a form of prayer where we create space in our busy lives to align our hearts with God's heart, where our spirit and God's Spirit breathe harmoniously together, and where we plot together to subversively overcome evil with acts of love and goodness."[33]

Prayer does matter, though this did not resonate in my soul until I healed and began to partner with God to change my world. These conversations with God led to actions, and through this process, trust and attachment have built the relationship for which I long desired.

This verse helps me the most: "If you abide in me, and my words abide in you, ask whatever you will, and it shall be done for you."[34] Abiding feels less like a rule-bound structure and more like a relationship. God and I did wander the paths of my life together in a relationship, though it seldom involved me consciously asking—*because I couldn't.* Yet, when the answers came, I sensed that God understood my unconscious *asks* that could not be verbalized. I have seen this in the lives of many who suffered trauma. God meets those who suffer where they are and hears the pleas they cannot voice. Slowly, as they begin to trust and find their voice, they can ask and believe that God cares about their needs.

CAN THE TRAUMATIZED BELIEVE THEY HEAR GOD'S VOICE?

Owen sat across from me, shoulders drooping and eyes averted. "I was convinced I was right," he quietly said. "I prayed about it and knew that she was cheating on me. All I could hear was the voice that asked me if I was going to let this happen to me again. Somehow, I felt my anger was righteous anger, and God was telling me to confront her."

I felt very sad for Owen. He ended the relationship over a suspicion that proved to have no foundation. What was tragic was that it wasn't the first time this had happened. After the last time, I begged him to seek professional help. His fear of being abandoned again, as his mother had done to him when he was small, was destroying his life.

I murmured something compassionate, but he went on. "I know, you really want to tell me that I should have gone to therapy. But I thought that I understood the connection well enough that it wouldn't happen again. Just like before, it welled up inside of me, and what felt like prayer was really me hearing the same old message that no one will ever love me enough to stay."

I tried to choose my words carefully as I replied. "Owen, you understood the connection logically, but emotions require deeper healing. Therapy could help you to open those hurting places and heal the deep wounds that keep sabotaging you. You couldn't remain regulated when that hurt was triggered. You reacted without reflecting. With help, you can heal the wound and be able to reflect before acting. Spiritually, we would say that when you are triggered, you need to spend time with God meditating about the situation and praying in a manner that calms your anger, and then ask for wisdom in dealing with the problem appropriately. That is extremely hard to do with this wound inside of you. Yes, therapy would help."

"Do you think if I get help it would be possible to repair what I did?"

I hoped this would be possible.

Owen's story demonstrates the importance of meditation as a precursor to effective prayer, which requires the ability to hear the voice of God and distinguish it from our pain narratives and internalized messages.

If meditation is reflection, prayer takes us one step closer to action and that is where it can get complicated for those who have experienced trauma. Owen was consumed by anxiety and overwhelmed with anger when he confronted his girlfriend. In other words, he was triggered. The first step he needed to take was deep inner reflection where he might have felt a sense of misgiving about the confrontation and stepped away from the trigger. These emotions that caused him to judge without all the information were a sure indication that it wasn't God leading him. It was, instead, his unresolved trauma.

Many misguided prayers may grow out of a lack of the kind of meditation that brings us into a relationship with God, one that helps all of us to know what God would and would not ask us to do. It is also possible that many damaging actions that people claim as "following God's voice," result from inner turmoil that has not had the benefit of healing. From their deepest inner pain, they can easily spew anger and judgment. Sadly, I can see many places in my life where this happened.

DISCERNING THE VOICE OF GOD

In the book, *Healing Shame and Guilt: A Guide for Ministers, Therapists and Spiritual Directors*, Janice Morgan Strength provided a thorough discussion of discerning the voice of God and distinguishing it from the voice of Satan. She wrote, "God's Spirit described as the Holy Spirit, convinces people of truth about themselves (John 16:7–17), reminds them of their position as children loved by God (Romans 8:16), comforts and encourages them (John 14: 16, 26), and prays for them (Romans 8:26–27)."[35]

Through meditation and prayer, God allows people to see themselves as they are seen—as the beloved. While I do not discount the powerful force of evil in our world, the false internalized messages of shame narratives are the fodder. Many blame the internal strife on "the accuser" who seeks to "devour us," and this places the solution outside themselves and leaves them powerless. Healing illuminates these false messages caused by deep pain, and, in doing so, robs "the accuser" of the primary weapon that is used against them.

FINAL THOUGHTS

Jesus instructs that we become like children. That describes the condition of being unlayered from the difficulties of life, especially trauma. Many who experienced childhood adversity or emotional neglect never knew this kind of relationship. I have watched God woo them into relationship and stand in awe when they express their prayers as talking to Abba (Daddy) Father. The childlike prayers of my friends who are survivors of familial abuse may be the very strongest evidence of the greatness and power of a loving God.

While healing, I often wrote conversations between my child self and God (some are in my previously published books). There is power in these childlike prayers that Foster recognized: "Children also teach us the value of the imagination. As with meditation, the imagination is a powerful tool in the work of prayer."[36] When healing brings the wounded to childlike imagination in their prayers, they can believe anything is possible, even when the stories of their lives tell them something very different. This is the very essence of spiritual strength.

Chapter 5: Leadership Reflection Questions

- Have you ever experienced a time when your anger with God exploded out of you similarly to how it happened with Ryan? How was that experience similar or different from what Ryan experienced? What important understanding emerged from that experience or while reading the chapter?

- Often attachment is discussed when explaining adult attachment styles. How does the understanding of the ways trauma affects children add to those discussions? How does it affect our relationship and communication with God?

- How might trauma be an explanation for the "other-centered" and "fear of asking" that permeate the prayer lives of so many? How might you, as a ministry leader, develop a culture of asking within your ministry?

- Do you have an example of a time when someone (or yourself) might have mistaken a false internalized message as the voice of God? In what ways could this be avoided?

Fasting Through a Trauma Lens

J erry looked at the list of chapters in my preview and sighed deeply. "Oh, good, you are going to talk about fasting. It's a big deal at our church, and I hate it."

I appreciate the fact that my friends and family feel they can be honest with me. It is rarely necessary to use the phrase, "So, what do you *really* think?"

Instead, I asked, "Why do you hate it?"

"This is going to sound bad, but I hate fasting because it feels like I must suffer and beg God for things. Like if I haven't suffered enough, then God isn't going to give me what I need. I don't even believe that about God. I wonder where it came from?"

My mind wandered back to a time in our lives when my husband and I believed the same thing. Maybe more for myself than Jerry, I asked, "Was fasting taught this way, or was it just another one of those things we somehow picked up by the prevailing practices of 'the more spiritual'?"

Jerry shrugged. "Once, when our family was desperate for an answer to prayer, I fasted and begged God to bring a solution to the problem. Yet, the problem wasn't solved for years. Well, come to think of it, maybe it was solved but not until we lost a lot of money. That didn't feel like an answer. Fasting seemed like suffering for no good reason."

"Begging God for something" seemed a far stretch for a practice intended to bring people closer to God. Jerry's personal story of neglect during childhood probably made this fasting experience feel like one more time when no one, not even God, was listening. How courageous to even try!

HOW ARE TRAUMA AND PHYSICAL HEALTH CONNECTED?

Before discussing fasting as a spiritual practice, it is necessary to understand how trauma affects the body. The ACE (Adverse Childhood Experiences) research[37] demonstrated that the greater the number of adverse experiences children face before the age of eighteen, the greater their chances of specific health risks as adults. Two of those risks that relate to the following discussion of fasting are obesity and diabetes.[38]

Current research is making significant progress in understanding the body and brain connection, and this connection became apparent to me after my husband's diagnosis of type 2 diabetes several years ago. For many years he has controlled his diabetes through diet, but we became aware that his symptoms seemed to increase during PTSD episodes. (Yes, two traumatized people married each other.)

My overactive sense of smell can detect when his blood sugar is high and very closely pinpoint the level even before he completes a glucose strip test. My hypervigilant brain can also identify when he is experiencing a flashback. One day, in a moment of God-sent wisdom, I connected the two. We began to check his blood sugar and track his flashbacks. This most often occurred in the night when the scent of his high glucose levels would wake me. During this time, he began working with a therapist to develop strategies to remain grounded when triggered, which is difficult when asleep or waking in terror. Remarkably, as he learned to regulate the PTSD, his glucose levels stopped spiking so dramatically.

> The field of medicine is beginning to recognize childhood adversity as one root cause of many medical conditions, along with genetics, epigenetics, diet, environmental concerns, and so on.

Because of this experience, I have followed the growing research on the metabolic processes that may play a part in PTSD.[39] Since PTSD is pervasive in those who have experienced trauma, it needs to be added to the list of conditions that require caution and the need to seek medical advice before fasting—diabetics, expectant mothers, heart patients, and others.

The field of medicine is beginning to recognize childhood adversity as one root cause of many medical conditions, along with genetics, epigenetics, diet, environmental concerns, and so on. During doctor visits, I now explain the effects of my childhood trauma to medical personnel. Increasingly, they find my sharing informative and helpful as they continue to connect the dots between childhood trauma and disease.

WHY IS FASTING DIFFICULT FOR THE TRAUMATIZED?

There is also a connection between diabetes and depression. Once thought to be caused by the stress of living with diabetes, depression is now seen as the result of changes in the areas of the brain that control emotions.[40] My lifelong struggles with depression were exacerbated when attempting to fast, the exact opposite of using the practice to draw closer to God. The body and brain cannot be thought of separately.

We are wonderfully made. Yet, when trauma occurs, the ways our body helps us survive often turn against us. I could not fast even though I wanted to. The fasting affected my propensity for depression and made me aware of sensations in my body—sensations I had learned to ignore or dissociate from.

It came as a great surprise to me, past the age of sixty, that feelings could be felt as sensations in the body. When asked, "Where do you feel this?" I said, "In my head." I didn't *feel* my feelings; I *thought* about my feelings. My attempts at fasting never brought me closer to God because the body sensations of hunger caused traumatic memories and false internalized messages to surface. These negative internalized messages drowned out God's loving voice.

What is the purpose of fasting as a spiritual practice? In my church experiences, it was explained as a way to focus on God and deny self. To me that meant that it was a way to prove that I could control my body. Foster concurs: "More than any other Discipline, fasting reveals the things that control us."[41] Controlling my body was what I did and therefore fasting should not have been a problem, but it was. Fasting did not help me bring my body under control; the effects were quite the opposite. It released emotions and body sensations I could not tolerate. It caused me to loathe my body even more.

I had no problem relating to the apostle Paul's words, "No, I strike a blow to my body and make it my slave so that after I have preached to others, I myself will not be disqualified for the prize."[42] This probably was not a good word picture for someone who hated her body. One Sunday, while learning to *not* control my body in unhealthy ways, I sat in the morning service and watched one of the pastors demonstrate what it meant to flog oneself into submission. It was graphic and disturbing; I will never understand why it was necessary. As I watched, my hatred of my body and how "spiritual" it felt became clear.

It took many therapy sessions to even begin considering my body as a vital part of me, let alone the beloved creation of God.

Fasting resulted in increased loathing of my body and this was the last thing I needed. It was also not the purpose of spiritual fasting. Controlling ourselves to practice spiritual pursuits is never the answer. Foster said, "Fasting must forever center on God. It must be God-initiated and God-ordained."[43] That is the definition of those things we undertake *with* God, versus forcing ourselves to obey.

FASTING AND EATING DISORDERS

For many who struggle with eating disorders, an emphasis on fasting as a necessary spiritual practice can be life threatening. Several women volunteered to share their experiences with fasting. The following demonstrates the complexity of one woman's desire to be involved in a spiritual practice that very easily triggered the same cycles involved in her eating disorder (ED).

"The few times that I participated in fasting, either corporately or individually, it produced cyclical feelings of control, pride, then shame similar to when I'd restrict my diet during periods of my previous ED. When I would control my eating, I became better at suppressing hunger, and could go for longer and longer periods without 'feeling' hungry. I'd usually feel a sense of pride and accomplishment, followed by shame when I would eat or feel hungry.

"I'd feel similarly during fasts, even when I had recovered from my ED. I'd feel accomplished when I wouldn't feel hungry, attributing it to God. Then, I'd recall other times I felt similar, and it'd remind me of the high feeling I'd get when I would restrict my eating in the past. It felt so nice to control something in my life. Soon after the feeling of accomplishment set in, I'd feel ashamed for seeking control instead of relying on God. I'd then feel ashamed I was hungry and ashamed that I wasn't a 'good enough' Christian to fast. As I'd fall back into controlling my hunger I would stop fasting and feel disappointed in who I was. I avoided fasting after a few instances of this."

Another explained much the same thing when she said, "As I recognized my restrictive patterns in eating, it became hard to engage in fasting without also triggering some of the restrictive thinking and habits again."

This was echoed by another woman. "I had eating disorders as a teenager—mostly bulimia and binge eating, with periods of being very restrictive. It's therefore very hard to fast without triggering those thinking patterns."

Much the same as the trauma-responsive fasting, explained later, one woman said, "If I want to do a spiritual practice that brings me closer to God, and it had to involve food, it would be whatever the opposite of fasting is. Unfortunately, my ED thoughts are still present enough that even though I'm in recovery, I can still be triggered when feeling hunger."

Another gave examples of her own experience with this. "I decided to do something instead of fasting, such as reading the Bible once a day, or journal prayers once a day. Or otherwise, sometimes I would fast doing certain activities. Fasting social media, for example. That wouldn't trigger the disordered eating behavior."

It is important to listen to these voices as they sincerely desire to participate in spiritual practices as a way to draw closer to God. This was evident when one of the women said, "I wish I could fast as a way to seek spiritual intervention or offer sacrifice and learn spiritual discipline. I accepted long ago that not all disciplines are for everyone, and there are others I can practice instead." Knowing our limitations and providing the necessary self-care should not feel like a spiritual failure.

HOW CAN FASTING HELP THE TRAUMATIZED HEAL?

Explaining fasting—giving up those things that control us—as a healing practice requires a personal story about standing in the pantry with a stack of Oreos in my hand. I *could not* remember what brought me to the kitchen. "Oh! Water!" I said loudly. Laughing at myself, I poured a glass of water and headed back to my writing with cookies in tow. My justification was, "No one wants cookies that were touched."

While enjoying the cookies, I considered how this could be prevented in the future. In my childhood story, food *was* the answer. My trips to the pantry appeared to be a physical problem I could control; in reality, it was a childhood coping strategy that walked me to the kitchen. Cookies weren't a healthy strategy, but control and self-condemnation weren't either. The root of this strategy went deeper than hunger.

The ways abused or neglected children or adults learn to cope, create neural pathways in their brains. Even the act of "not doing" reinforces the pathway—often making it even stronger. If I tell you not to think about something—like Oreos in the pantry—it will make you think about it even more! For these embedded "addictions," the answer requires building new pathways. Dr. Bruce Perry, a leading trauma researcher, explained it this way: "Therapy is more about building new associations, making new, healthier default pathways. It is almost as if therapy is taking your two-lane dirt road and building a four-lane freeway alongside it. The old road stays, but you don't use it much anymore. Therapy is building a better alternative, a new default."[44]

> My trips to the pantry appeared to be a physical problem I could control; in reality, it was a childhood coping strategy that walked me to the kitchen. Cookies weren't a healthy strategy, but control and self-condemnation weren't either. The root of this strategy went deeper than hunger.

In other words, the only way to stop a strategy that was embedded in us as children is to build a new and better freeway. I asked myself, "What need was being served by going to the pantry?" Finding a way to meet the need was the key to building the freeway. Hunger was not the reason I went to the pantry. My neural pathway from childhood said, "The answer is in the kitchen." What I wanted was attention from my mother. The kitchen was her domain, and I was not allowed in.

Oddly, my need for a conversation often results in going to the kitchen for food. Keep in mind, I did not consciously realize my desire for a conversation was why I headed to the pantry for Oreos. Pathways created in childhood are usually not logical, until you understand the story. Now it is clear to me that I often wander to the kitchen for nothing more than conversation.

How do we build a new neural freeway? My freeway requires me to have a village of those who engage with me, both professionally and personally. This reduces my snack habit by ninety percent. My brain can think of thirty new things before I get out of bed in the morning. My need to express these ideas has been evident since childhood. Both writing and work are better with conversations; cookies are not the answer.

Healing can turn fasting—controlling what controls us—into a process of replacing old, unhealthy neural pathways with new ones. This will later be discussed as a trauma-sensitive fast from "doing." Self-compassion helps those who are healing to understand that the old road is still there and sometimes, under stress, their brain decides to do a bit of off-roading. In my case, off-roading usually looks like a package of Oreos.

FINAL THOUGHTS

If the purpose of spiritual practices is to draw closer to God, my conversation with Jerry demonstrated that this wasn't always what fasting accomplished. After sharing the content of this chapter with Jerry, I asked him what he thought.

"I spent some time thinking about it. The idea of drawing closer to God wasn't a part of what I was doing. Understanding this helped me. We do have things that control us. Like what you wrote about heading to the pantry," he said with a grin.

Jerry's feelings about fasting began to make sense as he shared how he would go for days without food as a child. "I hoarded food and telling myself to stop hoarding made me angry toward the part of me that hid food in my room in case no one fed me. Fasting reminded me of how that kid felt."

With this revelation, I was sure Jerry would never attempt fasting again. Then, to my surprise, he said, "I have been working on a new neural pathway to listen carefully to my body and do small mini-fasts. I feel God caring about what happened to me whenever I feel hungry. We both love on that kid when it happens. My love for the amazing kid who figured out how to survive is a new freeway; my anger and fear no longer control me."

With self-compassion and awareness, Jerry could begin accessing a trauma-informed process for fasting. For most everyone, when fasting feels safely accessible, then yes, absolutely participate in this spiritual practice. Do it with caution, self-compassion, and someone to walk beside you who understands how trauma can affect the process. The ineffective ideas regarding fasting in the "rule book" of spiritual practices are problematic for many who may try to solve their inner turmoil but unintentionally make it worse.

My approach for this chapter was unexpected even to me. My goal was not to replace the more traditional views on fasting for those who find them to be accessible. The content has been a wrestling match as I reached into this unexplored area of my own story. My choice to explore why fasting was inaccessible to me took me in directions I never planned. At the same time, it confirmed what I firmly believe. We can understand the reasons we do the things we do.

In the book *Why You Do the Things You Do*, Clinton and Sibcy provided insights that encourage and help readers to do the deep work of understanding themselves. They wrote that "The first step to knowing which path of life to take is to look honestly at ourselves and at what brought us to where we are."[45] Not everything individuals do is unhealthy. Some of what they do is personality, but unhealthy coping strategies usually result from childhood experiences. This is especially true for those who find habitual patterns so hard to break. No wonder the inner reflection of meditation as a basis to prayer, fasting, and all other Disciplines is so significant. Without it, many feel like failures in all the spiritual practices. Once again, being trauma informed helps all of us to understand that the struggles are not a spiritual problem.

Chapter 6: Leadership Reflection Questions

- How are all the practices of meditation, prayer, and fasting similar in how they affect those who have experienced trauma?

- There is a concern when working with traumatized individuals that they will become flooded with emotions that they can't regulate. Have you ever seen this happen during church services? Is your perspective of that event changing in any way? How?

- How is the practice of fasting approached in your ministry setting? What precautions do you have in place when or if you emphasize this spiritual practice? What other precautions would you add after reading the chapter? (Specifically address Eating Disorders).

- The focus of fasting is often control of self. In what ways is this counter-intuitive for those who have experienced trauma? How is the perspective of building new neural pathways different from this? How are the end results the same or different?

Study Through a Trauma Lens

Peter was one of my most brilliant college students. It would not surprise me if he read through half the library while completing his degree. We had many engaging intellectual conversations over the years. Then one day after he graduated, he asked if we could meet for lunch. He needed to talk.

Midway through our meal and conversation, he said, "I have the hardest time expressing emotions." I knew this about Peter but did not see this admission coming. "I want to have relationships, but when I go on dates I always end up explaining something like quantum physics. I know, it's awkward."

He had never talked about his childhood, so I asked, "Did anyone ever express emotions in your home?"

Peter laughed. "No, we just sat around talking about quantum physics. The only way to get anyone to talk to me was by saying something super intellectual. That was how we talked about the Bible too. We never talked much about personal things. Now when I look back on it, I realize how expressing emotions was shamed."

It was evident Peter had been using his remarkable brain to try to answer his dilemma. My next question came directly from my own story. "What would happen if you cried?"

It was a telling question. Peter's face flushed as he struggled to keep from bursting into tears. Probably crying was the very worst thing he could imagine doing in a restaurant. I changed the subject to allow him to gather his composure.

Once composed, Peter asked, "Is there a book I could read?" Then, realizing what he had asked, he laughed and said, "Reading a book is my answer to everything! It seems like what I really need to do is cry."

Often our intellectual efforts are a mask for the feelings we cannot tolerate. Peter, like me, gravitated to intellectual pursuits to avoid his feelings. In contrast, many who experience childhood trauma must overcome how it devastates their ability to learn. When this happens, the spiritual practice of study becomes inaccessible. We will return to Peter's story again, but let's look now at how trauma affects learning.

WHY DOES TRAUMA MAKE STUDYING DIFFICULT?

Comparing the brain scan of a child raised in a nurturing home with the scan of an abused child leaves no doubt concerning the effects of trauma. Trauma causes structural changes in the brain.[46] A friend who suffers from the effects of Fetal Alcohol Syndrome (FAS) and was trafficked by her family as a child expressed it this way: "They didn't just steal my innocence; they stole my brain."

NEURODIVERSITY

The concept of neurodiversity began with the work of sociologist Judy Singer in the 1990s. She believed that some children's brains learned, thought, and processed differently than the brains of neurotypical children and believed that this should not be viewed through a deficit lens.

Neurodiversity moves away from identifying disability and approaches treatment from a strength-based perspective. Neurodivergent people "experience, interact with, and interpret the world in unique ways. That can sometimes create challenges. But it can also lead to creative problem-solving and new ideas—things that benefit everyone."[47]

The four main types of neurodiversity are ADHD, Autism, Dyspraxia, and Dyslexia. Various advocates of neurodiversity have expanded what is included beyond these four types—all involve brain processing. Fetal Alcohol Syndrome (FAS), which is caused by prenatal alcohol exposure, shares some of the same characteristics and challenges as Autism. Both are considered spectrum disorders.

Many a time, the effects of trauma mimic the challenges faced by neurodiverse individuals. Also, trauma and neurodiversity often occur together. It is necessary to be cautious not to make assumptions about those whose behaviors do not fit into societal norms. It is especially important to not place spiritual judgements on those who are challenged. Generally, their faith possesses a simplicity and strength worth celebrating!

One of the topics I address when speaking to teachers is how trauma affects a child's ability to learn mathematics. As a college liberal arts and developmental math instructor, I witnessed various learning issues long before I understood that many could be trauma related. There are other causes for learning disabilities, and these are always important considerations, but when listening to the students' childhood stories, there were usually traumatic events of some type.

When I asked these Bible college students, who were noticeably stressed about taking a math class, when they began to believe they could not do math, most answered, "Well, I couldn't memorize my math facts in elementary school."

My next question seemed unrelated. "How do you do in your Bible classes?"

"I love my Bible classes, but I can't memorize scripture," was a typical response.

"So, the problem is with memorization?" Then I watched them slowly make the connection between memorizing and their difficulties with math. Most had never connected their struggles in both math and Bible memorization. I would smile and say, "My star chart for memorization in elementary school never got completed either."

I wish I could go back to those students and explain what I now understand about the effects of trauma on learning, specifically memorization. When allowed to access the tools they needed, such as calculators, they were capable math students.

My memorization issues plagued me academically. Graduate work that was less dependent on memorization was much easier for me than my introductory college courses. There was a workaround for everything that most would accomplish by memorizing. One of those was knowing how to use Bible study tools to trace down the verses I only remember in pieces.

One day my therapist said, "You really do know your Bible." It was a surprise to me, but she was right—just not in traditional ways. My workarounds likely taught me much more than reading and memorization could have.

Sustained reading is also problematic for many who have experienced trauma. During my healing process, I realized how hard it had always been for me to read. Suddenly, without forcing myself in unhealthy ways, I could barely read five pages of a book at a time. My head would start buzzing, my anxiety would consume me, and soon I was not able to comprehend anything. Healing has helped, but I had to work hard, and still do, to read for any length of time. I have great compassion for those who struggle. Telling someone who is struggling with trauma-related learning deficits to read a book is usually not helpful. There is a reason why simple psycho-educational memes and infographics are so popular on survivor-based social media pages.

EFFECTS OF TRAUMA ON LEARNING[48]

1. Metacognition: Internalized trauma narratives interfere with the development of self-talk, which is necessary for self-regulation, higher-order thinking, and problem-solving.
2. Memorization and Information Retrieval: Structural changes in the brain, including reduced hippocampal volume, affect the ability to encode new information, retrieve long-term memories, make associations, and integrate new concepts.
3. Automaticity: Immediate retrieval of basic skills and information is difficult and slow. It prevents reaching higher levels of thinking unless memory tools are utilized.

WHAT PREPARES THE TRAUMATIZED FOR STUDY?

Peter was right in saying he needed to cry—something our society has made unacceptable, especially for men. Tears provide many physical and emotional benefits. I doubt anyone ever cried as many tears as I did while healing; it felt like my eyes would fall out of my head. I became an unashamed crier with this verse as my guide: "You have taken account of my wanderings; Put my tears in Your bottle. Are they not recorded in Your book?"[49] I told Peter and continue to tell others, "You need to allow yourself cry." This is especially true for those whose emotion-avoidant minds try to intellectualize everything.

Foster provided a helpful distinction between meditation and study that is crucial in understanding how many either struggle or excel with studying—specifically in studying the Bible but also books in general. "Meditation is devotional; study is analytical. Meditation will relish a word; study will explicate it. Although meditation and study often overlap, they constitute two distinct experiences."[50]

It is possible to study without becoming emotionally engaged. Neuroscience helps us understand this. Cognitive higher-level thinking takes place in the prefrontal cortex while emotions reside within a middle area, the limbic system. While meditation might be difficult because it engages the emotions, study can often be done without emotional complications. Unless, of course, the brain has been affected by trauma which will often trigger emotions while reading.

Reading about trauma is part of the healing process, but the content often makes those who have experienced trauma uncomfortable. Many who would benefit from reading *Brave* tell me that they are afraid to read it. I understand; it is self-protective for those impacted by trauma to avoid what triggers them. If viewed as emotional clues, triggers can help them know there is something they have not yet processed; something that would benefit them by accessing professional help. The books I suggest as resources are written in a style less likely to trigger, but nothing is ever trigger-free. Reading along with someone—or listening to the audio with them—is a great way to provide a sense of safety during the practice of study for someone who has experienced trauma. Reading one page is more than no pages. Healing is not a race; it is a process.

HOW DOES RELIGIOUS ABUSE AFFECT STUDY?

It is also important to consider those like me, whose abuse occurred within church-related contexts. Scripture triggers many people because they hear the voices of their abusers who both taught them and abused them—sometimes using scripture to justify their heinous acts.

During one of my first opportunities to speak about the effects of trauma, a religious-based organization invited me to participate in an interview. One of the prepared questions was to share a verse that helped me during my healing journey. I had a long conversation with God because my religious trauma ran deep, and scripture couldn't be part of my healing. I told God, "I just need to think of a verse! No one will understand if I try to explain."

God's answer was, "Be honest."

That seemed like a lot to ask, so I came up with a verse, but when the question arose, I blurted out, "There isn't one. Scripture is a trigger for me." The podcast host was gracious, yet I still drowned in shame for days.

I consoled myself much like Brené Brown did after her TedTalk, "The Power of Vulnerability,"[51] in which she said that she experienced a breakdown. She told herself not many would watch the TedTalk. I thought the same of my webinar, but for both of us, this wasn't true. I watched in horror as the view count edged over 4,000. Then, to my surprise, some who also experienced church-based abuse thanked me for being honest. I realized that God understood that the very thing I was avoiding was something they desperately needed to hear.

As I took down protective strategies while healing, it became clear how dissociating from my pain allowed me to live without acknowledging how much of what I did triggered me. I studied the Bible, spoke in chapels, taught Bible studies, and so on—always distancing myself from the inexplicable inner chaos. I did what was necessary to survive and meet the spiritual expectations of others. On the day of the webinar, I was finally honest. God has honored me for that vulnerable response.

If childhood or adult abuse occurred within a church context, the

> If childhood or adult abuse occurred within a church context, the abused must unwind how scripture may have been misused to assert control.

abused must unwind how scripture may have been misused to assert control. There are helpful books on this subject, but reading can sometimes induce fear if the material includes ideas that were not part of a parent's or pastor's "approved" reading list. Many were taught that if they listened to other views, they could lose their faith. Those who face these fears usually find themselves in a process of deconstruction. However, it is possible to come to the other side with a deeper faith. The resources that are included in Appendix 6 provide guidance for reconstructing faith—one should not have to leave faith behind to heal. Though it may be necessary for those who experienced religious abuse to leave the toxic environments that caused the damage, it is also possible for them to build a far stronger faith that is based on a freeing relationship with God.

RELIGIOUS TRAUMA

There is abundant research that addresses the mental health value of spirituality; there is also a growing research-based understanding of the damage caused by unhealthy religious practices. Distinguishing between healthy and unhealthy spiritual practices can be a subjective minefield without an understanding of and ability to recognize the effects of trauma. Recognizing elements of my church experiences as religious trauma felt like a betrayal of my heritage without this understanding.

Religious trauma runs the gamut from the unintentional effects of common religious practices to clear abuse involving sexual abuse or cults. Without deep reflection, every church has the potential to cause religious trauma in the lives they are called to serve.

The North American Committee on Religious Trauma Research (NACRTR) states that, "Religious trauma results from an event, series of events, relationships, or circumstances within or connected to religious beliefs, practices, or structures that is experienced by an individual as overwhelming or disruptive and has lasting adverse effects on a person's physical, mental, social, emotional, or spiritual well-being."[52]

In addition, Dr. Marlene Winell defines Religious Trauma Syndrome (RTS) as "The condition experienced by people who are struggling with leaving an authoritarian, dogmatic religion and coping with the damage of indoctrination. They may be going through the shattering of a personally meaningful faith and/or breaking away from a controlling community and lifestyle. RTS is a function of both the chronic abuses of harmful religion and the impact of severing one's connection with one's faith."[53]

There is sometimes a thin line between "authoritarian, dogmatic religion" and cults. Dr. Janja Lalich offers a helpful checklist that can be used to evaluate patterns that are cause for concern. The following four stood out to me as red flags that I ignored in order to belong.[54]

- Questioning, doubt, and dissent are discouraged or even punished.
- The group has a polarized, us-versus-them mentality, which may cause conflict with the wider society.
- The leadership induces feelings of shame and/or guilt in order to influence and control members. Often this is done through peer pressure and subtle forms of persuasion.
- Members are expected to devote inordinate amounts of time to the group and group-related activities.

Bessel van der Kolk spoke to the draw that authoritarian cult-like religious groups have for the traumatized.

> Many traumatized people find themselves chronically out of sync with the people around them. Some find comfort in groups where they can replay their combat experiences, rape, or torture

with others who have similar backgrounds or experiences. Focusing on a shared history of trauma and victimization alleviates their searing sense of isolation, but usually at the price of having to deny their individual differences: Members can belong only if they conform to the common code. Isolating oneself into a narrowly defined victim group promotes a view of others as irrelevant at best and dangerous at worst, which eventually only leads to further alienation. Gangs, extremist political parties, and religious cults may provide solace, but they rarely foster the mental flexibility needed to be fully open to what life has to offer and as such cannot liberate their members from their traumas. Well-functioning people are able to accept individual differences and acknowledge the humanity of others.[55]

DOES WHAT I DO QUALIFY AS STUDY?

With or without the severe effects of trauma, every person has those areas where they are strong and others where they are less capable. It is crucial for those affected by trauma to focus on compassionate, strength-based spiritual practices and honestly accept those areas that pose challenges. Layering shame on top of trauma prevents both healing and growth. It is important to know that God meets us where we are and helps us take baby steps.

Some who have experienced trauma have still found robust ways to study, while others find it impossible. Neither is a determiner of faith. The strain of meeting others' expectations kills the joy that can be found through study. Healing is one path that can help many to calm the mind and access study. For some, the damage goes far beyond the need for healing. No one should feel less than because of this. Many have felt shame for learning disabilities throughout their childhood and beyond. It is easy to forget the challenges some face as we recommend books.

Most who face pressure and unrealistic expectations for maintaining spiritual practices are unlikely to understand the trauma-based reasons for their inconsistent use of the practices. Some find unique avenues to accomplish the practice of study but may not believe their methods are spiritual. Others simply double down and force themselves to practice study, often living out an intellectual faith with little emotion.

For the spiritual practice of study to be effective, one must set aside the "rule book of acceptable reading." It is crucial to read material with which we both agree and disagree. It is difficult for those who have been impacted by trauma to hold two contradictory things in mind at the same time. This showed up for me in the overwhelming number of times I said the words *always* and *never*. It is easy to believe that anyone who does not agree with us one hundred percent is the enemy, but both agreeing and disagreeing with an author is healthy. Censorship arises from this inability to accept the value of disagreement.

Studying a variety of views and topics helps everyone to both broaden their understanding and affirm what does and does not align with their core values. It is difficult but necessary to not feel threatened by those who think differently. The need to belong makes this challenging. Many strongly-held beliefs are fear based and not grounded in the life Jesus intended for us to live. When those who hold these fear-based beliefs only interact with others who believe exactly the same, it leads to us-versus-them narratives.

FINAL THOUGHTS

Whatever way we can help those who have experienced trauma to open themselves to God will allow them to reap untold rewards in spiritual growth. For those who have experienced trauma, this must begin with self-compassion and a belief in a compassionate God. They also need others who understand the effects of childhood trauma to help them. God's grace includes the incredible amount of knowledge we now have about the brain, the effects of trauma, and methods of healing. God has provided the knowledge about healing trauma that is necessary to alleviate the suffering of many, but trauma often stands in the way of fully accessing this information.

Whatever stands in the way of study will limit growth. This is true academically, psychologically, and spiritually. Foster explained, "Many are hampered and confused in the spiritual walk by a simple ignorance of the truth."[56] You can't know what you don't know. Some may be unable to access the information in this book without the support of others who understand the effects of trauma. Those who cannot access the spiritual practice of study will be limited in their understanding of both the scriptures and what researchers have learned about the effects of trauma on our brains and bodies.

Chapter 7: Leadership Reflection Questions

- How does an understanding of the cognitive (pre-frontal cortex) and emotional parts of the brain (limbic brain) help explain how intellectual efforts are a mask for the feelings we cannot tolerate?
- Review the box that explains the effects of trauma on learning. Can you identify spiritual practices that would be difficult for those whose brains have been affected by trauma? Can you think of adaptations that might enable all to access these practices?
- Are you aware of any within your ministry who have experienced religious abuse? Has anyone mentioned that he/she struggles to read scripture? What alternative study methods could you suggest?

- How might counselling that is entirely focused on spiritual healing be problematic?
- Are members of your ministry encouraged to read books that allow them to wrestle with various views on a subject? Are there platforms or groups available for open discussion? Are ground rules provided for civil discourse?
- How can psychoeducational material that helps church members understand trauma and its effects be included in various ministry programs or practices?

PART TWO

WHY DO THE TRAUMATIZED FEAR THE WORLD AROUND THEM?

Abigail slid into the aisle chair in the back row of the classroom. Glancing at the door each time another student entered, she looked relieved when they sat down in a different row. I tried to gain eye contact with her, but she would not look up at me.

I seldom assigned seats in my classes because I intuitively understood why the Abigail's needed to choose their own. I mentioned this to the students and added that I would do my best to only call on students who volunteered to speak, with the hope that everyone would participate. Planning learning activities that allowed students to prepare an answer in advance of speaking was helpful to those who, like me, often shut down without a script. I did my best to help Abigail but knew she would eventually need to present a lesson.

Knowing Abigail would require encouragement, I did my best to help her through what seemed to be stage fright, but on the day of her presentation, she froze. As she stared blankly at the other students, I was sure she would faint. Thankfully, she didn't, but she did run from the classroom, drop the class, and change her major. Abigail would not talk with me about what happened and eventually left college.

Before that day, Abigail shared that she had wanted to be a teacher since she was little; she was doing her best to fulfill that dream. This occurred before I began to understand trauma, but looking back, the hallmarks of someone who was terrified of living were evident. Today, her inability to make eye contact, hypervigilance, choice to sit close to the door, and frozen fear response would make sense.

HOW DOES TRAUMA AFFECT LIVING IN THE WORLD?

In what ways does childhood trauma affect how the traumatized live their lives? The following aspects will once again be used as a framework for helping explain how trauma blocks the spiritual practices that involve living out in the world: Relational trauma damages the attachment relationships involving trust and security. It also creates false internalized messages of shame and a deep need for validation. Identity formation is hindered and the individual struggles to find a sense of self.

A defining characteristic of those impacted by trauma is hypervigilance, or the more technical term hyperarousal. The opposite is hypoarousal. Hyperarousal involves the fight and flight responses, while hypoarousal causes the individual to freeze, just as Abigail did. Then she fled. All of these reactions are the result of the brain's fight, flight, freeze response to threat.

Educators see these trauma responses when children explode in anger (fight), run from the room (flight), or shut down (freeze). These behaviors are natural fear responses in all human beings but are overwhelming for the traumatized. According to van der Kolk, trauma "produces actual physiological changes, including a recalibration of the brain's alarm system, an increase in stress hormone activity, and alterations in the system that filters relevant information from irrelevant information."[57]

To Abigail, everyone who entered the classroom was unconsciously a potential threat, and she needed to be near the door should it be necessary to flee from danger. She was hypervigilant from the moment she walked into the room—probably during all moments of her life.

I asked the followers of a trauma-focused Facebook page how hypervigilance felt. Their responses flooded my laptop computer screen. My heart hurt as I remembered the many years their words were my life experience. One mentioned a meme that likened hypervigilance to having forty tabs open in the brain at one time. I thought everyone lived that way! Along with this response were dozens of others that described overwhelming brain activity:

- "Amazing awareness! Like your brain is on fire."
- "I can't keep my eyes focused on one thing; I survey my surroundings constantly."
- "Like walking into Walmart hearing every step, seeing every person's facial expression, hearing every conversation, anticipating their moves, emotions, etc."
- "Noticing every little thing that is going wrong even when no one else notices it."
- "Always aware of every nuance in my surroundings and self—exhausting, yet informative."

Many responses revealed the physical reactions involved in hypervigilance:

- "When you can feel every hair on your body."
- "Always feeling anxious, can't even relax. Can't be still."
- "It causes tingling all over me (anxiety)."
- "Never shutting down, never stopping being on alert, constantly feeling like a buzzing live wire, always feeling this building up."
- "Like being electrically shocked, flinching, and jumping every few seconds."
- "Screaming at any little thing. I jump back and scream!"

Many responses described a sense of being in constant threat of danger:

- "High alert—danger. Always waiting for disaster."
- "Ready to protect. Impending doom."
- "Constantly on guard and looking for danger."
- "Feeling like I can die at any moment. Always waiting for the other shoe to drop."
- "Constant exhaustion from always anticipating others' moods."
- "Hyperaware and ready for what is and what could be."
- "Impending fear from the minute you wake until you fall asleep."
- "Constantly on guard and always looking over your shoulder."
- "Ready for war. Like Armageddon is happening every day."

One response was particularly telling: "Anticipating the absolute worst at all times despite no evidence it's even going to happen." In other words, it is possible to cognitively know in the prefrontal cortex that there is no actual danger and still have a sense of danger reside in the middle and lower brain regions—the limbic system and brain stem.

Positive thinking and spiritual admonitions are seldom fully effective because they do not reach the root of the problem in the emotion-driven

> Positive thinking and spiritual admonitions are seldom fully effective because they do not reach the root of the problem in the emotion-driven regions of the brain. Positive thinking says, "Walk away from the feeling," but the only way to process the fear response is to sit with it while using self-regulation tools.

regions of the brain. Positive thinking says, "Walk away from the feeling," but the only way to process the fear response is to sit with it while using self-regulation tools. These tools are often not readily available to those with a history of childhood trauma. Sitting with our emotions is fertile ground for a panic attack.

This introduction to hypervigilance, a primary characteristic of trauma, provides the essential knowledge for addressing the challenges of the outward Disciplines. It is no wonder that survivors often struggle with simplicity, solitude, and submission. Many, like me, gravitate to service—a place where it is possible to stay busy and find purpose in helping others. The risk is burnout because our inner well is often empty of the peace that would sustain us. It is filled with inexplicable turmoil instead. A common thread in many of the Facebook responses to my query was exhaustion. Yes, constantly being on high alert is exhausting, especially when they have good reason to believe the world is a dangerous and frightening place.

WHY IS EMOTIONAL REGULATION IMPORTANT

Will the healing processes involved in the inner spiritual practices discussed earlier automatically accomplish taking the inner peace into the outer life? Sadly, the effects of trauma make it way more complicated. Healing inwardly did not magically change how I was walking around in the world. All my coping strategies fought against it. The inner healing created space for new patterns of living, but the call to old coping strategies is tenacious because there are neural pathways in our brain that are difficult to change. Remember, it is a new freeway and the desire to go off-roading is strong!

In a recent meeting, a friend explained a surprising realization about himself. He had started reading a book the day before and completely missed an important meeting. Upon reflection, he realized that reading was how he escaped as a child. Something unsettling had occurred earlier in the day and he picked up a book, began reading, and missed the meeting. He understood what he needed to do was process the unsettling event and find a solution. Instead, he unknowingly slipped back into childhood coping strategies.

My friend's vulnerable confession prompted one of my own. I explained how I also escaped into books as a child and how it caused me problems while raising my children. I often did not hear their repeated attempts to get my attention. He and I discussed how reading wasn't a bad strategy—not like taking drugs would be—but both were escapes. Reading was definitely more socially acceptable and unlikely to destroy our lives.

Neither of us received adequate help in learning effective ways of processing emotions as children. Without realizing it, we were still escaping by using our childhood strategies. Reading a book is a good plan for relaxing. It is not healthy if it's consistently used as is a means of disengaging with life.

Those who experienced trauma as children often unconsciously continue to cope with a world that frightens them by using the same coping strategies that they did as children, usually with more adult versions. They missed essential building blocks of development. Without the necessary help to develop healthier coping strategies, they unconsciously cling to the only methods that have proven effective—their survival-based approaches.

FINAL THOUGHTS

We have the basic human need to create some version of felt safety in our world. The absence of danger is very different than feeling safe. Our surroundings can be free of danger, but the effects of trauma—not being safe—do not allow us to *feel* safe.

The spiritual practices discussed next depend on inner transformation. Thus, inner fears and survival-based coping strategies are shifting sands upon which to live a spiritual life. Simplicity and solitude seem counterintuitive to survival and often feel frightening, while submission recreates a sense of powerlessness. Service is an answer, but often gravitates toward seeking validation, though, at a conscious level, the desire and intent to serve others is sincere.

The solution to all of this requires building the missing developmental pieces from childhood. Few can do this without assistance. Understanding how trauma affects the way faith is lived out in the world is essential in giving spiritual guidance that does not create additional shame.

Part Two: Leadership Reflection Questions

- How can an emphasis on positive thinking be ineffective and possibly harmful for those who have experienced trauma?
- On the other hand, how can dwelling on negative events and emotions also be harmful?
- Review the descriptions of hypervigilance. Explain ways that these individuals who responded to my query might struggle with traditional church services. Can you think of options that might help?
- What is the basis for self-regulation? How can an emphasis on self-control increase the effects of trauma, creating hypervigilance or hypovigilance?

Simplicity Through a Trauma Lens

Addie sat across the lunch table from me. She was probably twenty years my senior, but as part of our church's women's ministry mentoring program, she asked for a mentor and was assigned to me.

"Were you able to get any decorating done this week?" I posed the question with all the optimism I could muster, though the answer would probably be no. Addie hated her house. Any pictures or decorations she owned were still in the boxes piled in every room. I suggested finding one photograph of her grandchildren to hang. Decorating new homes always helped me deal with the chaos of moving, and I could not imagine living with boxes in corners.

The problem not only affected Addie's house, it affected every aspect of her life. It was an inward problem that was disturbing how she lived in the world. She was depressed, and my mentoring was possibly more damaging than helpful. By understanding the effects of my trauma, I would have recognized that my obsessive need to set a house aright was a fight response to the chaos of my many moves as a child and adult. Addie coped with her stress by shutting down—a freeze response that exhibited as depression.

We both needed help, but there were no answers in the world we lived in, and we weren't vulnerable enough to share our stories in a fashion that would have built relationships. Addie was probably suffering from the effects of trauma much like I was. Both of us were longing for answers that no one could give us. If, as Foster said, "the Christian Discipline of simplicity is an *inward* reality that results in an *outward* life-style,"[58] then my obsession gave the appearance of having the inward reality—it was a coping strategy I learned as a very young child. In truth, both Addie and I were inwardly troubled but outwardly, our struggles looked very different. My greatest strength was making dysfunction look stellar—until I collapsed. Maybe Addie was the same, and what I saw *was* her collapse. I will never know. She died from cancer a few years later.

WHY IS SIMPLICITY SO DIFFICULT?

Around the time that I was meeting with Addie, my husband worked as a truant officer for our local school district. He came home with stories of the houses he visited to check on absentee children. Many rooms in these houses only had trails winding through overwhelming stacks of newspapers, trash, and odd collections of items. We started watching a television show about organizers who were invited into homes to help people make order out of chaos. During the show, the "hoarders" would tell their stories; it usually involved some level of trauma and often included neglect and food insecurity. The individuals often became agitated (fearful) and angry (protective) over giving up their possessions.

While these people knew they needed help—they did allow the show to enter their chaos—they were often dead set against releasing anything as if their life was threatened. Because of the effects of their trauma, it did feel life-threatening. The anxiety they displayed was palpable and could easily be misinterpreted as an obsession with worldly possessions. In reality, it is the result of the traumatized working hard to feel safe in the world they create for themselves—even though it is often the exact opposite of simplicity. When a child believes they are the only one who can or will meet their needs, the methods they use to get their needs met carry over into their adult lives, and the result is usually counter to simplicity.

WHY ARE POSSESSIONS SO IMPORTANT?

The television show's host worked hard to help individuals connect their inner struggles over possessions and their own traumatic stories. Those who understood and faced their traumatic experiences were often able to begin releasing the stranglehold on their possessions. For many this wasn't possible.

The loss of possessions is a common theme in many of the stories shared with me. Sometimes it is by fire or another natural disaster. Often it is through an escape from an abusive situation. Many children in foster care arrive without any possessions. Sometimes children lose cherished possessions as a punishment. It is no wonder the trauma of loss results in the unconscious drive to gather possessions. The same holds true in the case of food insecurity.

These examples are extreme, but many can look around at the things they collect or have in excess and trace them back to their childhood stories. My dad lived through the Depression era, and even when I bought him reams of paper, he tore open envelopes to use as writing paper. We laughed about it, but the scarcity mindset of those who suffered deep trauma is tough to overcome. Yet only in changing this mindset can the abundant life accessed through simplicity be achieved. How can this happen?

If physical and emotional needs go unmet during childhood, many are often unconsciously driven to fill their lives with unfulfilling possessions. Foster wrote, "The inward reality of simplicity involves a life of joyful unconcern for possessions."[59] This unconcern is based in trusting God to provide. Since trusting God grows out of our earliest attachment relationships, those impacted by trauma as children often lack this foundation and find it difficult to trust in God's provision.

Many of the challenges faced by those who have experienced trauma compete against the following areas of simplicity identified by Foster (rephrased):

- Choose useful over trendy
- Recognize and seek to heal addictive habits
- Be generous to others
- Ignore the lure of unnecessary possessions
- Enjoy all that the world offers freely
- Choose nature as the path to enjoyment
- Avoid unnecessary debt
- Be honest and keep your word
- Avoid anything that comes as a result of the oppression of others
- Avoid being distracted by good when it overshadows God

Once again, all of this is what many children learn as they grow up in nurturing homes. Those who do not have this privilege cannot easily step into these practices without guidance. Simplicity is not an easy path for those with unmet childhood needs.

ARE POSSESSIONS A SOURCE OF VALIDATION?

What are personal possessions if not a path to validation? My false internalized messages of unworthiness cried out for validation and acceptance. I collected possessions, built a career, and achieved academic success, but none of this kept me from the mental health tsunami that precipitated my headlong fall into simplicity after retirement. Few knew the backstory; my Facebook feed was a carefully disguised adventure. My need for validation that motivated me toward success now fully consumed me with shame. The danger of feeling rejected seemed to be everywhere in my life and career. I was overwhelmed with feelings of not being enough.

Curt Thompson described this shame narrative: "...as an undercurrent of sensed emotion, of which we may have either a slight or robust impression that, should we put words to it, would declare some version of *I am not enough; There is something wrong with me; I am bad; or I don't matter.*"[60] My survival depended on no one knowing this truth.

It is easy to understand how this search for validation can motivate many to walk down paths that fight against simplicity. Our modern culture is obsessed with consumerism. This obsession is equally true inside and outside of faith-based communities because salvation alone does not remove the internalized message of shame that says, *I am not enough.* Those living with internalized shame messages fight against the gnawing sensation that they are not enough in all the ways survival requires. Accumulation of wealth and possessions is a strategy to calm those fears.

When Jesus told his followers to not be anxious about what they would wear, where they would live, and if they would have food, he was speaking to a traumatized nation. I imagine many of the listeners had lived at the edge of all these catastrophes. They weren't even thinking about wealth; they were trying to survive. They knew the feeling of not being enough and Jesus was saying, "It is okay to not be enough; you are enough to me, and I've got this one." What a beautiful message to those who are living in survival mode.

> Our modern culture is obsessed with consumerism. This obsession is equally true inside and outside of faith-based communities because salvation alone does not remove the internalized message of shame that says, *I am not enough.*

IS SPIRITUALITY A SOURCE OF VALIDATION?

The accumulation of possessions is the most common manner by which modern culture encourages us to seek validation. Once again, the need for validation arises from the unmet childhood needs that cause many to feel that they are not enough. It becomes a false message that repeats on a loop throughout their life, and there is no better method to achieve validation in the church than to be there every time the doors open.

While an overdependence on validation is a problem, the need for validation itself is a healthy human need. Gaining validation makes life comfortable and rewarding, but it will not solve the problem of being enough. My solution to the problem of validation was academic and career success. I was convinced that putting a PhD after my name would finally help me feel like I was enough. It was a disappointing day when what Thompson described as "the undercurrent of sensed emotion" did not instantaneously vanish. No matter what I accumulated, be it wealth, awards, or degrees, it would never change the internalized message of not being enough.

Those who receive adequate validation as children are better prepared to not depend on it as adults. They, in turn, are more able to give it to others. There is no shame in needing validation. Oprah Winfrey once commented that everyone wants to know if they did a good job after an interview—even presidents. She learned to tell everyone something good about how they did.[61] Everyone needs validation. Those with unmet childhood needs more desperately seek validation as adults, and they will often do a lot more than they should to ensure it is received.

As Christians, wearing a mask of spirituality is often a valiant attempt at confirming our enoughness. When children come to believe they are not enough, they often grow into adults who need other Christians to believe they are spiritual. When they do seek help because of this deep sense of not being spiritual enough, the answer is usually "try harder." This answer only reinforces the belief that they can never be enough to God. It is a cycle in which they do try harder, do more, and try to please everyone in their attempts to be validated. This spiritual busyness fights against simplicity.

Coming to terms with the reasons for seeking validation in unhealthy ways is a crucial part of healing through simplicity. The question is: Will it ever be possible to feel like we are enough? The fact that putting PhD after my name wasn't enough proved that this question was at the center of my struggle. Nothing I could ever own or do would fill the void created in me as a small child.

The only way I could ever be enough would be to believe that God *created* me to be enough. This healing truth of enoughness often runs into a snag within faith communities that look at self-affirmation with suspicion. Many years ago, after catching a glimpse of how much God loved me, I told a friend, "I think God delights over me!"

"That is a dangerous path," this friend responded. "We should not think too highly of ourselves. God views us as sinful."

To my credit, I refused to accept that God was not delighted in me, but I realized this wasn't a view I should express in that church setting. In faith communities that embrace this view of God, it is almost impossible for those who suffer to ever believe they are enough. And without believing this, the unconscious drive for validation refuses to settle for simplicity. Sadly, many believe that God's creation is inherently not enough, and that embracing this view is somehow spiritual.

FINAL THOUGHTS

At some level, the spiritual practice of simplicity is a challenge to everyone in a society where our belongings seem to go into the closet and multiply. We could all learn from those who seem completely satisfied with less. Some of these people are living in nursing homes. They are the ones who have kept only things that have meaning to

Janyne McConnaughey, PhD

create a comfortable environment. They enjoy your visit but are content when alone. Their secure base is internal. This describes my father. I am thankful that his quiet, contented presence was still with me as I tumbled into unexpected simplicity. He set a perfect example.

To accept being enough, I had to release all the methods I was using to prove my enoughness. I must tell you that simplifying my life by discarding the many ways I sought validation felt very much like free-falling. Anyone on this path should seek support and take it slow. It is counterintuitive to humans that becoming the person they long to be will most often require them to stop doing many of the things they thought would get them there.

Simplicity grows from accepting that validation is not the goal of life and does not determine worthiness. In remembering that everyone is enough to the loving God who longs for a relationship, it is possible to drop the human need for validation. God longs for a relationship with imperfect humans, and there is nothing anyone can do or not do to change this. We are all imperfect human beings who are enough in God's eyes. Healing allows the wounded to become enough for both themselves and God.

Jesus's descriptions of the kingdom of God involve a life not bound by all the conscious and unconscious means by which humans seek validation. Setting aside the nonessential things that distract from healing is a refining process that removes this overwhelming need. Sometimes that means not doing many things expected of a church member, a good friend, or an over-the-top employee. Like Paul says in Hebrews, Christians must set aside those things that hinder them from obtaining the prize, which in this case is healing. It is essential to believe that healing *is* the work that leads to a life of simplicity.

Chapter 8: Leadership Reflection Questions

- As illustrated by the story of Addie, the effects of trauma can exhibit in very different ways. Can you think of instances in your church when you witnessed fight, flight, or freeze responses?
- How do the protective mechanisms of trauma fight against the spiritual practice of simplicity?
- While needing validation is normal, how does childhood adversity hijack this basic human need?
- How does the marketing of advertisers easily trap those who are seeking validation through possessions?
- How are the need for validation and spiritual busyness connected? How does spiritual busyness fight against simplicity?

Solitude Through a Trauma Lens

Everyone described my coworker Joseph as an extrovert. If there was a gathering, he was there—and most likely the center of attention. He was good-looking, intelligent, and funny. Everyone was glad when Joseph showed up at a party. Everyone, that is, except Joseph, who was exhausted by the end of the day or evening. Like many, he had fine-tuned being the person everyone wanted to be around so he would not be alone.

Working alongside Joseph could be frustrating. Pinning him down to a meeting was like catching a butterfly. Everyone laughed and said, "That's just Joseph." But was it? I wondered. I understood my own need to be the funniest person in the room. I did not want to be left sitting alone at a banquet table; there was no surer way to feel less than.

It is the fear of being alone—without connection—that drives many trauma-related behaviors. Juxtaposed to this fear is the opposite fear of being *with* others. The answer is never to be alone and to always be in control of social situations. Being funny accomplishes this quite well.

Much of the social anxiety we feel resides in inadequate early attachment relationships. Children who are securely attached to a parent or caregiver are content when left alone because they know someone will return and care for their needs. A child whose needs were ignored or only met intermittently has no such guarantee. For them, being alone comes with a sense of abandonment.

When Joseph's exhaustion became overwhelming, he sought help from a therapist. He slowly began to understand how his severely depressed mother was often unable to meet his needs when he was a small child. He felt abandoned emotionally despite cognitively knowing she loved him. At a young age he learned to fend for himself and make connections with others to fill the gap. Anytime he was alone he was overwhelmed by intense feelings of loneliness, a sensation he could not describe to anyone, not even himself.

WHY IS SOLITUDE SO CHALLENGING?

Often ministry required me to be an extrovert. Like me, Joseph wasn't an extrovert, and that was why the social gatherings were exhausting. My clue to this truth came after joining a colleague during a round of after-graduation celebrations. At every stop, she became more energized as I became increasingly exhausted. In contrast to her enjoyment of being with others, she often talked about how renewing the spiritual practice of solitude was. I found this practice inaccessible and frightening. Now, after my healing journey, I understand that solitude and silence could have been a spiritual strength if it wasn't for the profound effects of attachment wounding and trauma that caused me to need constant human interaction.

One of my earliest fleeting memory sensations that surfaced with the help of EMDR was of sitting in a crib and watching dust particles dance in the sunbeams coming through the vertical blinds. I was alone and content. This contented feeling was not part of my memories that occurred after my abuse and my mother's emotional abandonment. After the abuse, being alone felt increasingly threatening, though dissociation was a helpful coping strategy as a child.

UNDERSTANDING DISSOCIATION

Dissociation can be thought of as lying along a continuum. At one end are the normal healthy coping strategies we utilize to deal with everyday stressors. Daydreaming is one example. At the opposite end, in cases of extreme trauma usually occurring during early childhood—long-term physical, sexual, or emotional abuse—the coping mechanism of dissociation takes more extreme forms and affects the individual's ability to function in healthy ways.

Those most affected by the fear of being alone have likely also experienced the loss of emotional connection. This is especially true when the primary caregivers are the source of abuse. Early childhood relational trauma decimates the first three levels of Maslow's hierarchy of needs—physiological needs, safety needs, and love/belonging needs. The primary ways that children learn to feel safe, even when alone, are replaced by survival strategies.

One of the essential jobs of parenting is to help the child learn to self-soothe through coregulation. It begins with the mother or other caregiver's gaze. Jonathan Baylin and D. A. Hughes, in *The Neurobiology of Attachment-Focused Therapy*, described it like this: "The kinds of communicative signals that are strong releasers of oxytocin are mutual gaze, certain tones of voice that are similar to child-directed speech or 'motherese,' and certain qualities of touch."[62] It is in these interactions that the child learns to self-soothe.

To coregulate, a parent must be self-regulated. Parents who themselves did not have attuned caregivers often struggle to be attuned to their children. This pattern can easily transmit from one generation to the next. Hypervigilance can result from overt trauma and neglect but also the more subtle lack of attunement to the child's emotional needs.

Individuals who experience healthy attachment relationships as children learn how to calm themselves and can more easily find the pause space between a trigger and reaction. They also generally feel safe and are less likely to be on constant alert to their surroundings. They are well equipped to embrace the spiritual practice of solitude as adults.

> Parents who themselves did not have attuned caregivers often struggle to be attuned to their children. This pattern can easily transmit from one generation to the next. Hypervigilance can result from overt trauma and neglect but also the more subtle lack of attunement to the child's emotional needs.

Without healing, individuals' attachment to and trust in God is hindered by their attachment wounds and the need to control the world around them when their needs were not being met. The attachment relationship is a building block that affects every spiritual practice.

WHY IS HAVING A SECURE BASE IMPORTANT?

I enjoy sitting in parks and watching young children interact within healthy attachment relationships. If the park is a new experience, a child will stay very close to their mother, or another caregiver, before timidly venturing out. Often, the mother will play with the child for a few minutes. Eventually, most adults who are hoping for a break step back to see if the child will continue to play. When the child realizes this, they may run back to the mother—their secure base. Sometimes it takes several tries, or trips to the park, before the child feels secure enough to arrive and immediately run off to play. It is a process.

If caregivers immediately urge the child to go play, it seldom works. The urging works against the process. The child must feel safe. Only then can they choose to explore, knowing they can return if they need to. The mother is a secure base. During healing, the process of attachment and eventual independence from my therapist looked much the same. Every human, young or old, who feels safe will choose to explore.

What does it feel like to venture out without a secure base? Recently, my husband and I were driving down a country road. The heavy traffic slowed us down enough to notice things we would have normally missed. We saw a sign for an RV park and decided to explore.

The road took many turns and got narrower as the surrounding area became increasingly unfamiliar. The farther we drove from the main road (the safe base), the greater my anxiety. I mentioned being uncomfortable and my husband said, "I will keep you safe!" That should have reduced the level of my anxiety; he is a great protector. I wondered why it did not work. When we turned around and followed the road back, I could feel the tension leave my body. We strayed too far from the main road—the secure base where I felt safe. The sensation of anxiety felt no different than all the other times I experience anxiety, which told me the problem is the lack of a secure base.

The examples of the child in the park and our country-road exploration demonstrate the basic human need for a secure base. We all need dependable relationships and safe spaces. Relational trauma, a form of abandonment, robs the traumatized of both, and the turmoil it causes in their bodies prevents them from feeling safe, even with themselves.

Thinking back to the small children and caregivers in the park, I appreciate the process required for encouraging independence and exploration. This is how healthy development happens. When relational trauma interrupts this process, children are left to figure life out the best they can. Part of the healing process is to fill in the missing developmental pieces that can reduce the fear of living in the world. In therapy, the therapist can become the secure base that helps those who have experienced trauma to develop the healthy coping strategies they did not learn as children.

WHEN IS SILENCE HEALTHY?

Silence is inherent in the spiritual practice of solitude. Both are extremely challenging for those who have experienced trauma. Both were central to my sense of failing spiritually. While reading Foster's chapter on solitude, the reasons for this became clear and provided a path for self-compassion.

For those without a trauma history, solitude and silence are far less threatening. Children caught in abusive situations are often kept silent with threats when they should speak. If they do speak up, they are often shamed or not believed. They learn to keep an unhealthy silence. Maya Angelou aptly said, "There is no greater agony than bearing an untold story inside you."

One of the core relational challenges for those who have experienced childhood trauma is knowing when to talk and when not to talk. This makes what Foster described as silence extremely challenging. "If we are silent when we should speak, we are not living in the Discipline of silence. If we speak when we should be silent, we again miss the mark."[63] What a complex challenge this is for someone who was silenced as a child!

> For those without a trauma history, solitude and silence are far less threatening. Children caught in abusive situations are often kept silent with threats when they should speak. If they do speak up, they are often shamed or not believed. They learn to keep an unhealthy silence.

What does a survivor tell and not tell? There were no easy answers. As I wrote in a blog that discussed the process of *Brave*, "Sometimes, in the process of sharing a piece with someone I trusted deeply, I understood it was not a part I would ever share publicly. I value the relationships that provided safety during this phase. Yet

I also learned the value of caring for myself by *not* telling. I also learned that choosing not to tell is not the same as hiding."[64]

Those who are healing need safe listeners as they learn when and where to share. The Discipline of solitude enables those who are healing to sit with themselves and honor parts of their stories that are better left unsaid. Freedom is in knowing the difference between vulnerability and oversharing. It is both complicated and precarious. When listeners flinch, judge, or diminish them, the healing process stops.

When the hurting are fully heard, it is then possible to begin sitting in silence and solitude. While healing, I came across this quote by Peter A. Levine: "Trauma is not what happens to us, but what we hold inside in the absence of an empathetic witness."[65] I put the quote on my phone and reflected deeply on its truth. I understood that after almost sixty years I had finally been heard—and believed. Being heard by an empathetic witness transformed me.

Another complexity of trauma is illustrated by Foster when he said, "One reason we can hardly bear to remain silent is that it makes us feel so helpless."[66] I agree. I also struggle, but do not necessarily disagree, with the sentence that follows the one above: "We are so accustomed to relying upon words to manage and control others. If we are silent, who will take control? God will take control, but we will never let him take control until we trust him. Silence is intimately related to trust."[67] I would say yes to healthy silence; the silence that we choose. It is a silence born in trust and not fear.

The effects of trauma are evident in the following paragraph in which Foster explains our need to defend ourselves: "A frantic stream of words flows from us because we are in a constant process of adjusting our public image. We fear so deeply what we think other people see in us that we talk in order to straighten out their understanding. If I have done some wrong thing—or even some right thing that I think you may misunderstand—and discover that you know about it, I will be very tempted to help you understand my action!"[68]

The root cause of my overexplaining was shame—a feeling of being less than or unworthy. It kept me in protective mode and compelled me to explain my actions and intentions—often to random people like store clerks whose opinion of me did not matter! None of this was my fault, and it was life-giving when Foster said, "One of the fruits of silence is the freedom to let God be our justifier. We don't need to straighten others out."[69] It took much healing to get to that point! What most would think is simple is often very complex for those who have experienced trauma of all kinds but most specifically childhood trauma.

HOW DOES CHILDHOOD ABANDONMENT AFFECT SOLITUDE?

I was the youngest child in my family, and when I reached high school my parents began to enjoy their independence. They would often go eat at their favorite restaurant located about an hour away and then do some shopping on the way back. They did not always tell me they were doing this, but I wasn't surprised if I came home to an empty house. I usually found something to eat and read a book until they showed up.

One evening, they were a couple of hours later than usual because they decided to make an extra stop. Without any way to communicate with them, I was overwhelmed and frantic by the time they arrived. Looking back on this, I now realize that most teenagers would not have been in such a dysregulated state.

My sense of abandonment as a young child surfaced with all the big feelings of a small, frightened child. I felt powerless to help myself and my imagination turned catastrophic. I was convinced I missed the rapture. Hell was not nearly as terrifying as abandonment. My parents were astounded to come home to a distraught teenager who exploded into sobs and raging anger.

In her book *Fear Traps*, Dr. Nancy Stella described this experience: "When caught in a fear trap, we relive our past trauma. We can think and behave at the age we were when the trauma occurred."[70]

I was about three years old emotionally when my parents arrived home. They began leaving notes after that, at least most of the time.

Foster correctly stated that "The fear of being left alone petrifies people."[71] We are relational beings and are born into this world seeking to attach to someone who will watch over and care for us. Once again, we return to the attachment relationship as the foundation for all future relationships.

The importance of attachment has been mentioned several times, but the spiritual practice of solitude requires an even deeper look. Curt Thompson stated, "Technically, attachment refers to the process by which the immature infant brain accesses and utilizes the strengths of the mature adult brain in order to learn how to organize and regulate itself."[72] It is how infants learn how to calm themselves—how they learn to feel safe when alone. For the securely attached who believe that the world and the people in it are generally good and kind, this is not a huge leap of faith to feel safe while alone because they internalized this belief during their early interactions with safe adults.

HOW CAN SOLITUDE HELP US HEAL?

As much as I would prefer this to only be about the joy of healing, that would deny the depth of work necessary for healing; work which requires the individual to sit in solitude—something I came to describe as "aloneness." For me, it was the most difficult part of healing.

Many begin therapy, but when this phase sets in, they run from it. Some of my friends wondered if I had taken on too much, gone too deep. I wasn't sure I disagreed with them. Foster described this process the following way: "When God lovingly draws us into a dark night of the soul, there is often a temptation to seek release from it. . . Recognize the dark night for what it is. Be grateful that God is lovingly drawing you away from every distraction so that you can see him clearly. Rather than chafing and fighting, become still and wait."[73]

When talking about how dark my solitude truly was, I do so because I never heard the darkness described as a process of healing. Before reading the previous description, all I had ever heard was that the darkness was an "attack of Satan" and a place to be cleansed of *my* sin. An acceptance of sin as the cause of turmoil was assumed. In contrast, for those who are healing from abuse, the darkness is a place of healing from the sins committed against them. A place where God draws close to help them heal their deepest wounds.

During the solitude of healing, I stopped attending church services. It may have looked like I was leaving God, but in truth, it was the only way to find Him. I needed friends to walk beside me outside of the context of church involvement. The relationships were more important than attendance as I passed through the darkness in the healing practice of solitude. When churches and ministry leaders focus on church attendance, they miss this important time of ministering to those who are healing. The greatest gift to someone who is walking through this process is to encourage professional help and then to act as a secure base for them.

> During the solitude of healing, I stopped attending church services. It may have looked like I was leaving God, but in truth, it was the only way to find Him.

Sometimes the best form of solitude is a friend who comes to sit with you without the need to talk. We should certainly not be like Job's friends who blamed the struggle on sin. Job was sitting in solitude to recover from the trauma that arrived through no fault of his own. Job needed a trauma-sensitive friend who understood the effects of trauma on his life.

Sitting in solitude opens the door of healing. There is no denying the process, nor should we deny the challenge of this practice for those who suffered in silence as children. Reflecting on the spiritual practice of solitude affirmed how deeply spiritual my healing process actually was!

FINAL THOUGHTS

Some years later, while attending an event, I saw Joseph sitting quietly on the other side of the room. He smiled as I made my way toward him.

"Hello," he said. "I read your book."

Surprised, I thanked him. "What did you think? It probably wasn't the book you expected me to write."

Joseph laughed. "No, it wasn't, but it made me face my story and go for help. I was exhausted from living a life that didn't even feel like me. I just couldn't stand being alone or not the center of attention. I am sure you noticed."

Now it was my turn to laugh. "Yes, I did notice. We were alike in many ways. I wondered if you also had a story."

"I did. Thank you for telling yours. With help, I can now enjoy a quiet life and walks in the woods near my house. I realized how much I enjoy being alone and listening to the sounds of nature. God talks to me there. I enjoy people, but I enjoy being by myself also."

"Me too." We both settled back to observe the busyness all around us.

For most of my life, the larger the crowd of people, the more alone I felt, but being completely alone was even more terrifying. Healing has enabled me to be more comfortable in solitude and crowds. Foster wrote, "Solitude is more a state of mind and heart than it is a place. There is a solitude of the heart that can be maintained at all times."[74] This state of mind is the healing effect of the spiritual practice of solitude.

Chapter 9: Leadership Reflection Questions

- How is solitude connected with and different from silence?
- What does the term co-regulation mean? How is this foundational building block essential for the spiritual practice of solitude?
- What does it mean to have a secure base in childhood? How does the disruption of this developmental phase affect the adult's spiritual practice of solitude?
- In what ways is the fear of being alone connected to early attachment relationships? In what ways can a child experience feelings of abandonment?
- Why is solitude an important element in healing? How might the solitude of healing be misinterpreted by ministry leaders? How can individuals be supported during this phase of healing?

Submission Through a Trauma Lens

S
tanding in my office doorway, Sarah asked if I had a minute to talk. My door was always open for students, though I do confess to inwardly sighing on that day. Not because of the student but because of the piles of grading I could not seem to conquer.

We talked for several minutes about the struggle she was facing because a roommate wanted her to go to an out-of-town event over the weekend. She wanted to go but had conflicted feelings about it. I suggested what seemed like a simple solution and she said, "Okay, I will check with my father."

I had heard Sarah say this before, so this time I queried, "Check with your father?"

"Yes," she responded. "He insists I run these kinds of decisions by him and my mother."

I was confused. "Sarah, you know you are in college now and can make these decisions on your own, right?" The fear in her eyes told me to press no further.

Over the following months Sarah came to my office more and more often. She seemed desperate for me to understand how important it was for her to submit to and honor her parents. I was surprised when Sarah began to consider if it might be possible to not return home at the end of the semester. This fleeting idea was immediately followed by an explanation about how going home would honor her parents. She often told me how respected they were in her church and community.

WHY IS SUBMISSION CHALLENGING?

Sarah's story demonstrates the damaging effects of an incorrect view of submission. Those who have suffered from abuse as powerless children are the most vulnerable to the abusive and incorrect teachings on submission. This may seem counterintuitive. It seems they would want to live in a fashion that allowed them to make choices. Maybe, but it is not always possible.

The type of parenting that Sarah experienced was described by Brian D, McLaren in *Faith After Doubt*. He stated, "In the framework many of us were taught, parenting was all about discipline (which, in that context, meant punishment). Parenting was all about instilling in our children unquestioned submission and obedience to authority (which, in that context, meant our children agreeing to be dominated)."[75]

The neural pathways for submission are deep grooves in the roadways of the mind. Submission, even coercive submission, seems normal for many. Often the unconscious need to control our outer world is merely the opposite side of the coin of forced submission.

HOW ARE SUBMISSION AND CONTROL DIFFERENT?

Releasing control goes against every survival instinct. Many of those with histories of trauma never felt they had control over any part of their lives. Now, as adults, they long for control and are also not good at setting boundaries. These facts cause them to distrust those who deserve it and be vulnerable to those who seek unhealthy control. They often feel powerless in the face of authority. In obedience, they become exactly what powerful leaders demand. It always involves submission.

When power uses religion, those who sincerely desire spirituality often become ensnared by authoritarian leaders—both in religion and politics. While longing for control over their lives, they unconsciously walk-through doors that lead to being controlled.

My strength of character tells me one thing. Without a history of trauma, it is impossible to explain

> Anytime a decision is forced—often by the threat of loss of respect, love, or support—the agreement is not freely given submission. Capitulation (forced choice) is not the same as submission (free choice). The first is power based, the second is relation based.

my capitulating to nonsensical rules while living within legalistic circles. Following rules that made no sense was *not* how I was raised, even though it was part of the culture, and does not fit who I now understand myself to be. Authority, especially religious, and the unconscious drive for belonging are formidable forces in the lives of those who have suffered trauma.

What Sarah believed was submitting on her part was instead capitulating to her parents' control. If there had been a discussion about decisions—for example, the weekend outing—Sarah could have expressed her desires and her parents could have explained their own. Sarah could have listened and chosen to follow their guidance. She also could have chosen to not follow their guidance without fear of loss of love or punishment. This type of relational submission was not available to Sarah.

Anytime a decision is forced—often by the threat of loss of respect, love, or support—the agreement is not freely given submission. Capitulation (forced choice) is not the same as submission (free choice). The first is power based, the second is relation based.

123

HOW DO SUBMISSION AND SURVIVAL CONFLICT WITH EACH OTHER?

In explaining the freedom which results from submission freely given Foster explained it as "... the ability to lay down the terrible burden of always needing to get our own way."[76] The unconscious drive to get our own way is born in the unmet needs of childhood. As mentioned before, instead of the adults meeting the child's needs, the child was left to find a way to meet those needs. The resulting behaviors are often deemed manipulative. It is a survival skill.

For a powerless child, many situations involving unmet needs, lack of protection, or abuse can feel life-threatening. Often trauma survivors will react to a situation in a manner that seems unreasonable, as if it were a life and death situation. For an adult, whose childhood needs were not met, or if they experienced abuse or neglect when asking, the determination to have things go the way they want, at an unconscious level, can truly feel like a matter of life or death.

The need to be right is also unconsciously equal to the need to survive. In Foster's following statement, I have substituted "self-preservation" for "self-will": "Only submission can free us sufficiently to enable us to distinguish between genuine issues and stubborn [self-preservation]."[77] Children are determined in their fight for life! Yet fighting for everything does not serve them well as adults.

Also, many children impacted by trauma *are* submissive (coercively controlled). What looks like submission for the traumatized is most likely the autonomic freeze response. It is the safest choice, but forced silence is never healthy.

HOW CAN SUBMISSION PREVENT FORMING AN IDENTITY?

While healing, I began to catch a glimpse of myself as who God created me to be, not as the powerless self my childhood trauma produced. I was intrigued by these two competing selves and began to take personality tests. I could either take the test as the authentic me or the powerless, traumatized me. I realized that many questions on the tests were more trauma based than actual indicators of core personality traits.[78] I also realized that when I showed up as the true me in a legalistic world that demanded submission, it did not turn out well. Twice it ended in being fired.

While we all play different societal roles, I now understand I can be the same person no matter what role I step into. Why do so many wear masks within circles and on social media? Is it because of our fear of not belonging? The fear of abandonment? Those impacted by trauma often unconsciously submit to Christian peer pressure and lose themselves in the process.

The desperate need for connection says, "Tell me who to be, and I will become that person." This is especially true of those traumatized or neglected as children. They usually did not have many of the foundational experiences which would have provided a secure identity; it feels comfortable to be told who they should be. The loss of identity looks very much like submission.

The loss of identity connects to the almost ubiquitous self-loathing experienced by trauma survivors. The so-called "worm theologies" prey upon this false message (*worm* refers to "wretched worm" in the song "Amazing Grace"). The message is that self-denial and submission to God require us to believe we are unworthy. Those who survive childhood abuse already believe they do not deserve love. Self-denial and self-loathing are used interchangeably and confirm the false messages of the trauma. I appreciated that Foster differentiated between the two. "Self-denial is not

> The loss of identity connects to the almost ubiquitous self-loathing experienced by trauma survivors. The so-called "worm theologies" prey upon this false message (*worm* refers to "wretched worm" in the song "Amazing Grace"). The message is that self-denial and submission to God require us to believe we are unworthy.

125

the same thing as self-contempt. Self-contempt claims that we have no worth, and even if we do have worth, we should reject it. Self-denial declares that we are of infinite worth and shows us how to realize it."[79]

The incorrect interpretation of self-denial becomes a trap for those impacted by trauma because their sense of self has been decimated or unformed. How is self-denial possible if there is no sense of self to deny? Only in finding the self that trauma buried can one truly experience what it means to enter the self-denial that is the cornerstone of submission.

When Sarah looked inside herself, she could only find who she believed was a horrible little girl who constantly displeased her parents. She later said that she always wanted to get rid of this part of herself. At that point I encouraged her to seek professional help.

Sadly, Sarah was rejecting the part of her that was the child God created and trauma harmed. Trauma turned the innocence of childhood into a complicated web of extreme emotions that frightened Sarah as an adult. She could not see who she was without the effects of the trauma caused by coercive submission standing in the way.

Our identity is not lost in healthy submission but for most who suffered early life trauma, their identity never had much of an opportunity to grow. To practice a healthy form of self-denial the seething subconscious pool of self-loathing requires the process of healing. Without healing, those who outwardly live spiritual lives may still live an inward life that feels not much different than before salvation.

Incorrect understanding of self-denial is the breeding ground for shame. The "worm theologies" are built upon the belief that God despises his sinful creation and so should we. It makes sense to the wounded that God hates the traumatized self they mistakenly loathe. In hating themselves they believe that God feels the same. There is nothing that could be further from the truth! God deeply loves them and hates the evil actions that wounded them. Who they are is not defined by their actions. Thus, even when the effects of trauma result in choices they regret, it does not define who they are. They are God's beloved creations.

WHY IS SUBMITTING WITHOUT HEALING A PROBLEM?

Over the years, without a healthy sense of identity, I watched both myself and others transform to fit expectations. We said the right words, did the right things, and pursued the correct paths, often surrendering to ministry. Sometimes the change was strikingly obvious, especially when new Christians began attending church. Everyone applauded the changes without wondering who these people might be aside from their submission to the powerful influences of authoritarian leaders.

The call to submission and loss of self are not always overtly apparent. Feelings of powerlessness, combined with a desire to belong, can make attending a church with an authoritarian leadership style feel like finding a home. The rules are clear and the community structure is less chaotic than the ofttimes tumultuous former lives of survivors. Attempting to live differently outwardly without the inner transformation of healing defines the lives of many traumatized Christians who have not accessed healing. They are searching for something or someone to help them live less chaotic and more peaceful lives and are perfect targets for legalistic views of submission and obedience.

At the core of unconscious dissociative survival strategies is a distancing from a part of oneself. This includes memories, body sensations, and ultimately, the sense of self. In my story and the stories of many who share with me, who we are depends on what fits best with our need to belong/survive. Without a clear sense of self—who I am at the core and what I will do or not do—individuals told to "find their identity in Christ" often miss the true nature of Christ and depend on authoritarian or charismatic church leaders to define themselves.

The following description of submission brought me to tears because it is so clearly *not* what was demonstrated by legalistic authoritarian leaders during the years when I needed relationally safe submission to leaders who valued me as an equal. Foster stated:

> In submission we are at last free to value other people. Their dreams and plans become important to us. We have entered into a new, wonderful, glorious freedom—the freedom to give up our own rights for the good of others. For the first time we can love people unconditionally. We have given up the right to demand that they return our love. No longer do we feel that we have to be treated in a certain way. We rejoice in their successes. We feel genuine sorrow in their failures. It is of little consequence that our plans are frustrated if their plans succeed. We discover that it is far better to serve our neighbor than to have our own way.[80]

A hierarchal or authoritarian leadership model cannot generate communities in which both leaders and followers share the power. Also in this description is a crucial element of healing: loving others unconditionally. This unconditional love during childhood enables the child to develop a secure sense of identity. It is what every adult who did not know unconditional love as a child needs from those who lead them.

My healing resulted from God's leading and lots of hard work along with the unconditional love/regard from therapists, my family, and close friends who walked alongside me. All of us needed to accept the messiness of healing. Being able to receive help from others should define submission, and this is not possible if the help is offered with judgment. Any sign of judgment creates more shame and shuts down the healing process.

Submission becomes healing when the basis is a relationship of equals. This results in freedom—something that is counterintuitive to most who have experienced relational trauma. Sometimes during therapy, I became frustrated because my therapist would *not* tell me what to do. In my mind she was the authority. I was still living within the powerlessness of my childhood and looking for someone to tell me who I was and what to do. In a paradoxical twist, those impacted by relational trauma must learn what it means not to submit. Only then can submission be a choice.

> Submission becomes healing when the basis is a relationship of equals. This results in freedom—something that is counterintuitive to most who have experienced relational trauma.

HOW ARE SUBMISSION AND BOUNDARIES CONNECTED?

A consequence of abuse is the effect it has on a child's ability to set boundaries. Sarah did not know where she began and her parents ended. She believed her father's mood was caused by what she did or did not do. Making sure she always did the right thing was how Sarah protected herself. Even away at college, she was controlled by the overwhelming need to please both her mother and father. This led Sarah to check in with her parents more than necessary. It never went well, and she had to learn to set boundaries to protect herself.

Learning to set appropriate boundaries is a key to healing through relational submission. Most who experience relational trauma as children do not know it isn't healthy to feel every emotion in the room and that it isn't healthy to feel responsible for the emotions of others. While some are naturally more sensitive to the emotions around them, in the extreme, many characteristics attributed to empaths sound much like the effects of trauma. Adults raised in homes where the quality of their life depended on being able to "read" the grown-ups in the room, struggle to separate the emotions of others from their own.

A survivor without a strong sense of identity easily adopts the emotions and identities of others. This may feel like healthy submission for a time but will eventually dissolve into resentment. They must learn healthy relational submission that does not force them to change who they are or what they are doing. Healthy submission chooses to make appropriate choices that do not feel coerced. It is impossible to live in relational submission without a clear and secure sense of self. Without this, individuals will constantly be on the defensive, protecting a self that feels in danger. To not be secure in their identity and ability to set boundaries results in a mix of powerless vulnerability and defensive fear.

Relational submission is another expression for the word "vulnerability." Shame, our sense of not being enough, is the enemy of vulnerability as it destroys the ability to submit to one another. Curt Thompson wrote, "Healing shame requires our being vulnerable with other people in embodied actions. There is no other way, but shame will . . . attempt to convince us otherwise."[81] When healing occurs and these individuals impacted by trauma no longer need to live defensively, protecting their inner self that has been wounded by shame, they can then experience mutually submissive relationships.

Understanding submission as a relationship between equals is essential for those who have been abused by the powerful. Submission does not require open access by any who would cause harm, either physically or emotionally. This is not submission; it is abuse. Being secure in who they are will allow the traumatized to recognize healthy relationships, set boundaries, and gladly serve one another.

FINAL THOUGHTS

It would be years before I understood the full story that brought the look of fear to Sarah's eyes. She was coercively taught to submit, but she eventually realized she had been a powerless child that capitulated from fear of rejection and abandonment. As a result, she developed no identity outside of what her parents expected her to be. This was a great loss because she was a brilliant and talented young woman.

Over many years, she accessed healing and began searching for opportunities to use her God-given talents. Watching her break free from the stranglehold of her oppressive home was both inspiring and difficult. Her service to her family and God became richer as she better understood herself and freely chose to give care and support to others.

Through this process, Sarah learned what relational submission did and *did not* require. She changed generational patterns and set her family on a different trajectory. Not all stories end on such a positive note, but I have confidence it will become more common as younger generations change the stigma around seeking help for mental health.

I have witnessed many like Sarah who suffered from coercive submission as children seek healing in various forms and mature into adults who truly live out relational submission. It is also true that many people change outwardly while still suffering. They know they want their life to be different but are unable to love themselves with the same nonjudgmental compassion they offer to others. This was true in my life for many years.

My ultimate submission was to follow God's prompting and vulnerably walking into a therapy office to begin healing. It was there that I grew to understand my identity outside of the effects of trauma and how to both accept and develop boundaries within relational submission. In this process, the words of Jesus came to life. "He who finds his life will lose it, and he who loses his life for my sake will find it."[82] This verse perfectly describes the healing spiritual practice of relational submission!

Chapter 10: Leadership Reflection Questions

- How are unhealthy submission patterns developed during childhood? How is this connected with the need to control as an adult?

- How can controlling parenting practices that demand submission place the child in danger? Does your ministry assist parents to develop non-punitive relational parenting practices? Are you familiar with resources to share with parents that explain their child's emotional and physical development, specifically brain development?

- Why do adults who experienced childhood trauma often seem to over-react to situations? How can understanding their story provide a better understanding of their reactions?

- How can the need to be right be connected to childhood trauma? Why do the traumatized gravitate to tightly controlled church settings? How is this both helpful and harmful?

- How are self-identity, boundaries, and submission connected? In what ways does emphasizing that "our identity is in Christ" prevent the traumatized from building a sense of self not developed in childhood?

- How do you understand the role of submission in faith communities? Positively or negatively?

Service Through a Trauma Lens

M any years ago, on a warm September Sunday, a new couple joined our church. Everyone was abuzz with how fortunate we were to welcome them into our congregation. Allen and Hallie had attended for several weeks, charming both the staff and members. Their energy was contagious. I was preoccupied and never asked where they came from or why they came. I still don't know those answers.

Soon after joining the church, the couple set their sights on the music ministry, loudly proclaiming how their talents could transform the program. The problem was that the other members were all happy with the worship music and deeply loved the current worship leader. As my engagement with the couple increased, my keen radar for those who could potentially cause a rift sounded an alert. And then they were gone. Rumor said the pastor, in no uncertain terms, told Allen their worship talents were not needed. Those in the know said there was quite an explosion.

HOW CAN SERVICE TRAP THE TRAUMATIZED?

If healthy submission is giving up control, then unhealthy service is taking control. It was exactly what Allen and Hallie attempted to do. I recognized how this looked when reading the following statement in *Celebration of Discipline*: "Self-righteous service comes through human effort. It expends immense amounts of energy calculating and scheming how to render the service."[83] Now, with a trauma-sensitive lens, I am curious as to why they were so driven to serve. Was it self-righteousness or a need to take control of life?

> If healthy submission is giving up control, then unhealthy service is taking control.

Once again, we need to look compassionately at those who were powerless as children and survived by trying to control their world. Was this Allen and Hallie's backstory? I will never know, but I do know that in my own story, though more subdued, gaining recognition was a significant unconscious driving force.

The following excerpt from my memoir, *A Brave Life*, demonstrates this type of over-zealous service:

> I was a worker and loved being at church. I would help with anything and had my hand in everything. All this helped me feel like God loved me a little more than uninvolved people. Then one day my thumb started hurting. Silly discomfort. I blamed it on an old injury, wrapped it up, and went on. Then not just one thumb hurt; the other thumb hurt too. My knuckles began swelling and before long, my elbows hurt so badly they couldn't rest on a table. Scott helped me cut my sandwiches in half; I opened doors by leaning on them; cafeteria trays became too heavy to carry; I had to make several trips to my classroom because the stack of books became

too heavy to carry all at one time. This made life complicated.

Soon, exhaustion set in, and I began to take naps every day. The doctors ran inconclusive tests, but when they said, "Whatever the problem is, it isn't going to kill you," I quit spending money at their offices and rested—the only thing that helped.[84]

My life was fraught with these intermittent collapses, usually with physical ramifications, which the ACE research has since helped me understand. The earlier descriptions of hypervigilance explain why these collapses occurred—my body was on constant alert.

Internalized messages of shame—unworthy of God's love—explain the unconscious motivation that drove me to the point of collapse more than once. After this episode, I began quitting everything. I had pushed myself too far. Years later, while healing, there were many days and weeks when I was unable to leave my home and ended up back in bed despite my best efforts. It wasn't depression as it had been during much of my life—I was just done. After showing up for family, church, and jobs my entire life, it wasn't possible anymore. Serving drove me to the point of collapse.

When service is based on extrinsic motivation, as Foster stated, "It needs to know that people see and appreciate the effort."[85] This very possibly describes how unappreciated Allen and Hallie felt when they stormed out of the church building. They weren't necessarily wrong about this; everyone in that situation needed a better understanding of what drives the need for recognition and/or control.

HOW IS SERVICE A SURVIVAL STRATEGY?

Service was one of my carefully crafted survival strategies. Therapy was disconcerting because I had nothing to offer except for payment.

This caused many awkward attempts at doing something to validate my existence. Gifts of any significance were not appropriate. I could not go help my therapist pull the weeds in her yard. My strong need to serve was like an elephant in the room. Because of my therapist's boundaries, I slowly realized my unhealthy need to serve was embedded in my childhood trauma. Without this learning experience, I would be writing books to make myself valuable to God and others. And desperate for recognition.

What were the external rewards I was seeking? To become so valuable that I would not be abandoned—not by my therapist, not by my friends, not by my church, and not by God. The energy I exerted to accomplish this was stunning. My traumatized body and mind lived my life as a small, sexually abused child in a hospital room, stuck at the instant when my mother became so distressed because I could not stop crying that she walked out, and my father followed to care for her. It was a horrific family tragedy, and no one had the resources to help me. At the age of three, I learned abandonment was possible and how it felt. That event unconsciously influenced many choices in my life.

There is no fiercer survival need than the need to belong. A human infant left unprotected has little hope. The unconscious drive to belong is strong. In those who have survived trauma, it is overwhelming. In the book *What Happened to You?*, Bruce Perry offered this description of the drive to belong: "The brain is continually scanning the social environment for signals that tell you if you do or don't belong. When a person gets the signals—many of which are subconscious—that they belong, their stress-response systems quiet down, telling them they're safe. They feel regulated and rewarded. But when they get cues that they don't belong, their stress-response systems are activated."[86]

In faith communities, there is only one way to be sure you belong—service. As Perry stated, belonging does calm the stress response. I can vouch for this. No one served with greater devotion than I did while raising our children. The sense of belonging provided by working alongside my friends who were also raising children was crucial to my survival. My inability to say no due to fear of abandonment led to the physical collapse described earlier.

I admit the difficulty anyone would have had distinguishing my overzealous trauma-based involvement from true service. My point is not to stop serving or stop others from serving but to help them find a place where their gifts can be utilized and not ask them to serve indiscriminately. No one should feel they have to do *everything* to belong. While writing this section, I had a conversation with a friend whose church leaders gave her a recognition award for "doing everything." She realized what she was doing when God impressed on her that she was never asked to do everything.

Ministry leaders need to recognize how easy it is to gravitate toward those who cannot say no. When staff members are overworked, it is easy to unintentionally fall into the trap of preying upon the vulnerability of those who so desperately need to belong. While sitting in a staff meeting, someone mentioned a need and another staff member said, "Oh, Ruth will be glad to do that." There was an awkward silence because Ruth was not on staff and was already doing everything no one else wanted to do. Value the Ruths with restraint!

How much of my service was self-righteous? As someone who survived atrocities inflicted on me by church members as a child, I say none. I was doing the best I could and now understand my need for belonging, my fear of abandonment, and that service was not the answer. May we as church leaders encourage healing so all can reap the benefits of service, find the balance, and know that God never abandons anyone. Belonging does not require service.

> Ministry leaders need to recognize how easy it is to gravitate toward those who cannot say no. When staff members are overworked, it is easy to unintentionally fall into the trap of preying upon the vulnerability of those who so desperately need to belong.

WHAT DOES SERVICE LOOK LIKE
DURING A PANDEMIC?

While watching several of my friends struggle to fight through the brain fog left by COVID-19, I knew it would be crucial to stay healthy. There were more books in my future; writing depended on keeping my brain in working order. So, I chose isolation. What I did not realize, until considering the spiritual practice of service, were the ways that the abrupt ending of my plans would turn into unexpected gifts.

What was unexpected was the many technology advances that enabled me to serve from my bedroom. While recently visiting Denver, we turned a corner and ended up in front of one of Zoom's global offices. I took a selfie with the Zoom sign. Zoom was my unexpected pandemic companion that provided an avenue of service.

It was in my office/bedroom that I embraced the truth in Foster's explanation that, "True service comes from a relationship with the divine Other deep inside. We serve out of whispered promptings, divine urgings. Energy is expended but it is not the frantic energy of the flesh."[87] In the isolated quiet of the pandemic, it was possible to better listen to those promptings. It also opened up a new world of opportunities.

Through Zoom and other similar applications, I attended conferences; board, committee, and publisher meetings; webinars; and therapy sessions. Three college roommates and I began a monthly roomie Zoom chat, and I returned to an online version of my beloved Colorado City Carnelian Coffee book club (left behind when I moved). It was a rare day when I was not rearranging my bedroom for some type of meeting. In truth, I probably made more connections during those two years than could have possibly happened by traveling.

Between the meetings were Zoom chats with friends, followers, other trauma-informed advocates, and readers from around the world. Now I realize that my use of Zoom, email, Facebook

Messenger, and the like developed a lifestyle of service. As frustrating as social media could sometimes be, God used it to prompt me to reach out and care for those who were struggling. While this may get more challenging in the future, it is a part of my life that grounds me. The pandemic isolation transformed me without consciously realizing this was true. How could I have known that my plans had to crash to understand how to embrace a quieter walk with God on this mission to bring hope to the world?

FINAL THOUGHTS

Those who have healed are the best emissaries for bringing hope to the world. They can serve in faith-based communities and organizations that support healing. They can become therapists and can also tell their stories and encourage others. Their service is a powerful force of hope. It may be impossible to be completely free of the effects of trauma, but it is possible to rewire and develop necessary tools to use under stress.

It is also true that healed trauma survivors must continue to be cautious to not allow opportunities to serve steal the time for continued self-reflection and healing. Their service to others can only be as effective as their service to themselves. With this awareness, the spiritual practices of inward reflection can be encouraged as an important part of continuing healing and service. For ministry leaders, it is an important caution to not jump to readily to encourage the healed trauma survivor to get involved in serving. While it feels good to serve others, it does not feel good when service causes them to return to old survival habits because they have exhausted their inner resources.

Chapter 11: Leadership Reflection Questions

- In what ways did the story of Allen and Hallie demonstrate the need for validation and control? How can these be explained as effects of trauma?
- How can the survival need for belonging trap those who experienced trauma into serving to the point of collapse? Do you have an example of a church member who suddenly resigned from serving in various capacities? What was the reaction of leadership and members of the church?
- In what way does the human need to belong drive many to overzealous service? In what way is this connected to the common thread of abandonment felt by many survivors?
- How does the church unintentionally encourage those who over-serve? What precautions can be set in place to ensure that members do not work to the point of collapse?

PART THREE

WHY DO THE TRAUMATIZED FEAR THE CHURCH?

N o one who knew Nathan as either a child or adult would have suspected that his life story included the trauma of childhood sexual abuse. While reflecting on this fact after one of our porch conversations, I realized how well he had hidden his trauma while sitting in the pews of the churches he attended.

At various times, Nathan had served on both the church board and staff at a large church in the city where we lived. He taught an adult Sunday school class for many years, and all knew him as a kind, hardworking man who loved his family.

Nathan owned his own business, but as the children grew and family needs increased, he often worked additional jobs. When approached about a position in a company owned by another church member, he jumped at the opportunity.

A few weeks into the job, things did not seem right. Nathan felt some of the decisions made by his new boss were not the best ones, and mistakes were being covered up instead of addressed. Finally, when a significant mistake was made, the boss blamed it on Nathan and fired him.

Reeling from the shock, Nathan went home, cleaned the workspace for his business, and then set out on a thirty-mile walk across the wilderness area near his home. When the police came across

Nathan and took him home, he was nearly incoherent. It would take many years to fully understand how the self-loathing caused by his childhood trauma nearly destroyed him after this incident.

Nathan resigned from teaching the adult Sunday school class; his change in demeanor was a topic of conversation among the class members. Most seem to believe the owner of the company was in the right. The pastor asked Nathan to come to meet with him and the business owner for a time of reconciliation and forgiveness. In the meeting, there was no opportunity for Nathan to share his side of the story. The assumption of guilt only made things worse. His downward spiral continued, and the family eventually moved their membership to another church.

HOW DOES TRAUMA AFFECT LIVING IN FAITH COMMUNITIES?

Everyone experiences difficult life circumstances—how we are supported or not supported in the aftermath is crucial. The lack of understanding surrounding the following effects of trauma will again be used as a framework for helping explain how trauma blocks the spiritual practices involved in participating in faith communities: Relational trauma damages the attachment relationships involving trust and security. It also creates false internalized messages of shame and a deep need for validation. Identity formation is hindered and the individual struggles to find a sense of self.

Once Nathan's loss of his job triggered his childhood trauma, life began to spiral. There seemed to be no end. Though Nathan and his wife did not fully understand the effects of trauma in his life, they thought psychiatric care might help. His wife's health insurance covered a minimal number of sessions, but when her faith-based employer asked for a letter explaining why the psychiatric care was necessary, the shame created by this request led to the decision to discontinue the therapy before using the allowed number of sessions.

Many years later, Nathan experienced a similar incident by another faith-based employer who he learned had not been truthful in their communications with him, resulting in a job loss again. This betrayal by those in positions of trust dragged Nathan back to the turmoil of his childhood. This time, he was in the process of healing from his trauma. Once again, Nathan reeled from the betrayal, but now he knew the overwhelming pain was connected to his childhood trauma.

Nathan also realized how the "worm theology" taught in the churches he attended connected to the false internalized messages created by his trauma. All of this confirmed his deep sense of shame, feelings of unworthiness, and intense self-loathing. While his early trauma was not faith-related, his adult trauma was. Incident after incident, he felt rejected and misunderstood. It all felt much the same as his childhood abuse. It was as if a landslide of trauma began during childhood and never stopped.

Nathan finally concluded that church had nothing to offer him—except to remind him of his worthlessness. He is statistically part of the decline in church attendance displayed in membership trends.[88] Nathan remains connected with a church community that has been encouraging during the pandemic, supports them financially, and does odd jobs to help when he can but will likely never again engage deeply within a faith community.

HOW DOES TRAUMA LEAD TO JUDGEMENT IN FAITH COMMUNITIES?

The book description for *Celebration of Discipline* states that "The corporate Disciplines of confession, worship, guidance, and celebration bring us nearer to one another and to God."[89] While the inward and outward Disciplines focus on the individual, the corporate Disciplines inherently require community. When the community does what it is supposed to do—loves one another—it can be a place of healing. When it fails, as it did for Nathan, it robs individuals of the opportunity to draw closer to God and one another.

So many assumptions were made about Nathan's situation. When humans do not have all the facts, *we make things up*. This was part of the problem. We all do this. It leads us to believe that we are right and that others need our wisdom about how to live. The assumption in Nathan's case was that his struggles were an indication of guilt and not the effects of trauma. They thought they knew exactly what the problem was, and that the solution was confession of guilt. They were wrong.

> When humans do not have all the facts, *we make things up*. This was part of the problem. We all do this. It leads us to believe that we are right and that others need our wisdom about how to live.

Several years ago, while sitting at a table with various ministry leaders and spouses, I asked the question, "What if we didn't make rules? Could God tell people how to live?"

It was quiet and then one of the spouses said, "Oh, no, people don't know what to do or not do unless someone tells them. We can't just leave this to God."

No one in the group disagreed with her. I quietly looked around the table at everyone before walking away. They all seemed to agree that they knew what was best for everyone.

In the same way, the staff and members assumed they knew Nathan's story and what he should do—apologize to the boss and reconcile. They were all faithful Christians, but as a community of faith, they failed him by assuming they knew the truth and never considering his side of the story.

There are thousands upon thousands of stories like Nathan's. Over the years, as Nathan's friend, I often said, "Oh no! Not again! Why can't others care about Nathan the way he cares about them?" It seemed like there was a target on my friend's back. This is true of many who have experienced severe trauma as children. They are misjudged and don't recognize the warning signs to get out. The unconscious drive to belong blinds them to potential dangers.

When Nathan saw the careless business practices of his boss, he should have walked out. Walking out seemed impossible because of the effects of "learned helplessness" in his life. Survivors generally stay to be hurt another day. They only leave when the damage is so devastating that it is impossible to stay. Or they are dismissed. The emotional turmoil during these challenging experiences often gives others more fodder for judgment. This is when those impacted by trauma most need the unconditional love of the corporate body of Christ.

I would imagine every reader knows a similar story—whether it's their own, a family member's, or a friend's. We know both church leaders and members fail. Many of us also know we have been part of this failure in various ways. Sometimes ministry leaders step back from those who are suffering because they lack understanding and words. Sometimes we all just flat-out judge others, spoken or unspoken. Sometimes, in trying to do good, we unwittingly cause more damage.

HOW CAN UNDERSTANDING TRAUMA HELP REFRAME JUDGEMENT?

What is remarkable about Nathan is that he avoided the potential dangers that could have resulted from his severe trauma. The ACE research tells us his health and behavioral risks were astronomical. How tragic that those who judged him did not realize the incredible human being who lived among them. His ACE score did not predict his life outcomes, but it did put him at risk for both mental and physical challenges, in large part because of the lack of support.

After years of healing but before digging deeply into the ACE research study, I thought I had a clear picture of the role of choice in my life and the lives of others. It was a rather black-and-white version of what was done to me (not guilty) and what I chose of my own free will (guilty). Still, like most Christians, I erroneously believed people were the cause of their own problems.

Then I came across a series of bar graphs showing the increased chance of risky health behaviors that rose in lockstep with the number of ACEs an individual experienced. These behaviors included smoking, alcohol and drug addiction, promiscuity, and suicide. As I stared at the graphs, it began to sink in—the church traditionally called all these behaviors "sin." In truth, they are all survival-based forms of self-regulation, as discussed earlier—suicide is the result of finding no other option to calm the inner storm.

> Simply calling these behaviors "sin" and admonishing those who struggle to "just stop it" only creates an atmosphere in which the behaviors go underground and become a petri dish for the growth of shame narratives of failure.

In his book *In the Realm of Ghosts: Close Encounters with Addiction*, Gabor Maté stated, "It is impossible to understand addiction without asking what relief the addict finds, or hopes to find, in the drug or the addictive behaviour."[90] Often those who come to salvation hoping to find relief for the effects of trauma soon fall back into old soothing behaviors because the problem was not spiritual, it was physical. Maté went on to explain the biochemical basis for addition:

> All addictions—whether to drugs or to non-drug behaviours—share the same brain circuits and brain chemicals. On the biochemical level the purpose of all addictions is to create an altered physiological state in the brain. This can be achieved in many ways, drug taking being the most direct. So, an addiction is never purely 'psychological'; all addictions have a biological dimension.[91]

Without going too deep into the neuroscience of addiction, suffice it to say that simply calling these behaviors "sin" and admonishing those who struggle to "just stop it" only creates an atmosphere in which the behaviors go underground and become a petri dish for the growth of shame narratives of failure.

It is profound and nearly miraculous that Nathan did not turn to addiction to numb his pain. Did the tight constraints of legalism provide a buffer that helped him? Possibly, yes. It did not address the inner turmoil, but it did provide structure and control. Only healing would have prevented addiction *and* assisted in developing healthy coping strategies.

FINAL THOUGHTS

I recognize how a compassionate, trauma-informed, and sensitive faith community would have hopefully reacted differently when Nathan's demeanor changed so dramatically. The pastoral staff would have understood that the job loss was traumatic for him and not pressured him to reconcile. Maybe they would have asked for his side of the story and not assumed the boss was the one telling the truth—or the whole truth.

There should be no assumption that people are in turmoil because of their sins. I am not saying there is a human being alive or deceased who has never sinned, but not everything religion labels as sin is a deliberate rebellion or turning away from God. In addition, not all the sins which affect us are our own. We suffer most from the sins others commit against us.

It is not sinful for a someone who has experienced trauma to struggle. Yet almost one-hundred percent of the sermons I have heard on the topic of sin, and remember, I have listened to thousands, start from the premise that the listeners must point directly at themselves. If the sins of others are mentioned, it is still their problem if they cannot leave the sins perpetrated on them in the past. Leaving pain in the past is the eventual goal, but the method must be healing, not forced forgiveness of those who hurt them.

The question is, how could an understanding of the effects of trauma—both Nathan's understanding of his trauma and the understanding of the leaders and members of the faith community—have helped this story be different? It is hard to imagine that those impacted by trauma will flock to our churches when the message doesn't compassionately see their suffering as anything but sin. Also, how could an emphasis on healing have woven through the corporate Disciplines of confession, worship, guidance, and celebration in a manner that would have transformed Nathan's spiritual life?

Why do those who have experienced childhood trauma fear the church? Sometimes it is because of childhood experiences connected to the church, but it is often because church communities unintentionally inflict more harm in their efforts to "fix" those who struggle from the effects of trauma, usually having no idea of the story behind the behaviors. If I could rewrite this story, Nathan would have received the relational care that would have provided a safe space to share his story. The listeners would have immediately known to help him seek professional trauma-based care and supported him during the messy process of healing. It would have transformed his life.

Part Three: Leadership Reflection Questions

- At the end of Nathan's story, he concluded that the church had nothing to offer him. Why do you believe he felt this way? In what ways did his experiences lead him to this conclusion?
- When considering someone who left your ministry, how aware were you as a leader of their childhood experiences?
- Addiction was used as an example of how understanding trauma can reframe judgment into compassion. Can you think of other addictive behaviors that those in your ministry struggle with? Would understanding the root cause as trauma suggest different approaches to supporting them? How so?
- What other behaviors might be trauma related? Can you think of some that you have considered healthy or "not unhealthy," but have the hallmarks of addiction?

Confession through a Trauma Lens

Looking around at the shocked faces of the other women in the Bible study group, Cassandra knew she'd made a judgment error. During the years she attended the group, she'd enjoyed the fellowship, learned many biblical truths, and appreciated the prayers of her friends. Cassandra was also beginning to understand—and sometimes even believe—that God might love her, and maybe always had.

Cassandra had shared some of her spiritual struggles with the group but never mentioned her date rape at the age of fifteen and how her parents decided she should have an abortion. She always felt thankful for their decision, but she now knew she should not have expressed this sentiment in the group.

The group leader gathered herself and said, "I am sure God will forgive you for the abortion." Cassandra realized she hadn't sounded repentant. The uncomfortable sensation of shame enveloped her as she mumbled how it wasn't her choice, but now she was sure that she needed forgiveness. The women gathered close and prayed for

Cassandra with sincere, heartfelt words, believing she would receive God's forgiveness.

As Cassandra shared her story with me some years later, it was clear she never freed herself from the cloud of shame that descended on her that night. She continued attending the Bible study and said that no one brought up the subject again.

"I didn't grow up in a home that believed abortion was wrong," she told me. "The women didn't seem to understand, I was pregnant because of rape, and the abortion was my parents' decision. What they said to me made it feel like I was the one who did something wrong. After that night, I was afraid that everyone in the church thought I'd committed some horrible sin. I never felt guilty about it until that happened, and then after that, I never felt forgiven. From then on, I was always on guard."

WHY IS THE SIN NARRATIVE A PROBLEM?

Childhood trauma turns traditional church narratives upside down because the assumption is that the church is a gathering of imperfect and forgiven sinners. This belief permeates the sermons, music, and programs, but childhood trauma never fits the paradigm.

The women in Cassandra's Bible study prayed for her forgiveness. They assumed the abortion was her choice and the result of an indiscretion. Cassandra, so consumed with shame, could not correct their error. She began to doubt her understanding of what happened. Now in her late twenties, she sat holding her newborn baby in her arms. The shame embedded by the incident overwhelmed her.

"How could I have killed a baby no matter how it had come to be?" She was struggling to understand the situation from the perspective of her traumatized fifteen-year-old self, who had no choice in the decision. She needed help from others who could see her as the fifteen-year-old and not the adult sitting in front of them. What they saw as sin was completely out of Cassandra's control.

Faith communities who embrace the sin narrative as the principle that binds them together find it difficult to offer unconditional love. Assumptions of guilt get in the way and result in loving others *despite* their story, instead of loving them with their story.

From this sin perspective, the tendency is to view others' stories as failures instead of recognizing the strength involved in overcoming them, including still being alive. When others see failure, the traumatized also believe it to be true. They either hide their truth or share it as a confession of weakness and sin. Those impacted by trauma, specifically relational trauma, can always find a reason to blame what happened on their own sin, even when they were sinned against.

> Childhood trauma turns traditional church narratives upside down because the assumption is that the church is a gathering of imperfect and forgiven sinners. This belief permeates the sermons, music, and programs, but childhood trauma never fits the paradigm.

CAN CORPORATE CONFESSIONS BE SAFE?

The testimonies (confessions) of those impacted by trauma often focus on their responsibility for the pain in their lives. Some recovery programs make this a required step for healing. I do not discount accountability, but for what? For the effects of trauma?

A trauma-sensitive recovery program will always lead the participant to heal childhood wounds so they can understand what *was* and *was not* their responsibility. Once, when asked to speak at a church-based recovery program, I mentioned that I would talk about ACE research and how the effects of childhood trauma are not the fault of the person or a spiritual problem. The program leader decided that my presentation wasn't a good fit. Since then, I have set a boundary to only present to recovery groups that focus on strengths and helping participants heal from the effects of childhood trauma.

Group confessions are not always safe. Between the first and second job-related betrayal, Nathan sought help through an organization that provided courses and support groups. The leaders did not recognize that there was an underlying story to Nathan's turmoil and managed to add another layer of shame by focusing on sin-based group confessionals. Nathan never revealed his childhood story, and though he ended up in a corner in a fetal position weeping uncontrollably one evening, they did not assist him in seeking professional help. Cassandra's misstep in the Bible study group was similar. The assumption that the turmoil is caused by sin can be a damaging and possibly dangerous mistake.

The traumatized need others to understand the effects of trauma and recognize that there is an untold story beneath their mental health or behavioral challenges. This is not to say that excessive probing is an appropriate plan of action, but no one ever asked Nathan or Cassandra, "What happened to you?" For Nathan, this did not occur until he walked into a therapist's office twenty years later. It was there that he finally felt safe enough to participate in what I now understand as trauma-sensitive confession that set him on a path to healing.

WHAT DO WE SEEK WHEN CONFESSING?

For many years, "altar calls" were weekly events at my churches. I watched some members walk the aisle regularly. As a teen I also made many trips to the altar during camp and camp meetings. What was I looking for? Peace. Maybe the other frequenters of the altar were longing for peace also. I thought the path to this was confession and forgiveness.

While filling out the therapy intake form forty-plus years later, it asked what my desired result of therapy would be. I wrote the word "peace." It was my lifelong desire. Now I understand my visits to the altar were a plea for peace. For those impacted by trauma, peace only comes through healing. We might feel God's love at the altar but walk away without peace—especially if we believe the problem to be sin. I asked for forgiveness again and again, but the inner turmoil would not leave. I was begging God to forgive me for the effects of my childhood abuse. Frequent confession is a cry for help.

What type of confession *will* bring peace? For most who experienced trauma as children, it is the act of finally telling their truth during therapy. This is an act of confession, but not the type of confession based on the sin narrative. For those who survived atrocities, their sin is not the stumbling block that keeps them from growing closer to God. It is the sins of others, which were inflicted upon them, along with the false internalized messages of shame.

> Healing does not require multiple retellings of the trauma; in fact, we now understand this works against healing. Repeated confessions create deeper neural pathways in the brain.

Healing does not require multiple retellings of the trauma; in fact, we now understand this works against healing. Repeated confessions create deeper neural pathways in the brain. As van der Kolk stated, "Repetition leads only to further pain and self-hatred. In fact, even reliving the trauma repeatedly in therapy may reinforce preoccupation and fixation."[92]

As a child, I was curious about the church members who testified by recounting a long list of sins. Now I recognize that many repeat confessors were stuck in a trauma loop of self-loathing and needed professional help to build a different neural pathway.

WHAT ARE HEALTHY CONFESSION AND LISTENING?

How is confession in therapy different than confession in a church setting? There are many similarities but in trauma-based therapy there are additional practices that specifically address trauma. The confession (sharing) is similar if the listener is attuned and nonjudgmental. Being trauma-informed and sensitive helps the listener be both.

Most who knew me over the years believed I was an open book. In reality I neither consciously remembered nor told much of my story of sexual abuse. One part of the story was different—I did remember and one day when deeply troubled by it, I chose to tell my pastor's wife. To my absolute surprise, she said, "Why are you blaming yourself? He was a perpetrator! It makes me so angry this happened to you. Good thing I don't know him." This heartfelt moment of anger on my behalf held me steady for the next twenty years until trauma-based therapeutic help arrived. This is an example of confession *and* attuned listening.

Most survivors of childhood trauma feel responsible for their abuse—unconsciously or consciously. I was surprised to find this false sense of guilt and shame buried deep inside me, despite what my pastor's wife said. I told many of those who shared with me that they were not responsible for their abuse while burying my own shame. Healing from this embedded false message is not an easy process!

As I contemplated the spiritual practice of confession, I wanted to believe that it could be a path to transformation. Some experiences that did not turn out as well as that of my pastor's wife made me hesitant to trust the practice of confession. Yet, since it is the secret-keeping that causes the most damage to the traumatized, this feels correct. There is great freedom in telling our stories—in safe spaces.

In church meetings, I have listened when those who were experiencing mental health issues asked for prayer. The silence was deafening. It felt as though the air was sucked out of the room. Most often, people do not know what to say in response to this type of confession. After sharing my own story, some have told me that their story was so close to the surface that they avoided saying anything that would disrupt their own tightly controlled emotions. In the face of this deafening silence, I have had to learn that their silence was not about me; it was about them.

We are vulnerable beings and have difficult life experiences. We build layers of protection, and shame tells us no one could possibly love us if they knew the truth of our story. Shame also tells us we are unworthy of God's love. Only when everyone is willing to be vulnerable can we avoid the silence that sucks the air from the room. When we are unwilling to be vulnerable, those who do share openly about their trauma cause us to feel uncomfortable. If we are silent in our discomfort, we miss the opportunity to provide support to those who are healing.

> We are vulnerable beings and have difficult life experiences. We build layers of protection, and shame tells us no one could possibly love us if they knew the truth of our story.

DOES CONFESSION INCLUDE ACCOUNTABILITY?

My emphasis so far has been on freeing ourselves from needless shame and guilt. Does this mean we do not hold ourselves or others accountable? Absolutely not.

It is possible to understand that the root cause of addictive behaviors is because individuals did not learn healthy self-soothing strategies as children *and* stress the importance of accountability. This is not excusing; it is promoting healing. What is needed is compassionate accountability, something many did not receive as children. Accountability based on relational care is very different from judgment or control.

When accepting the responsibility of hearing the confessions of those impacted by trauma, we must do the inner work necessary to maintain self-regulation. One of my favorite sayings is, "No one ever calmed down by being told to calm down." We usually tell someone to calm down because their emotions are unsettling to our own. It is easy to escalate a situation when emotional triggers are involved. This type of interaction helps no one. Accountability does not involve holding power over another. We teach others to be accountable by being accountable ourselves. This is the power of mutual confession, which can also be defined as vulnerability.

HOW DO WE SAFELY RECEIVE CONFESSIONS?

To help Cassandra through the painful memory of the Bible study, I shared my teenage experience at an altar where a church member accosted me. I was trapped in an abuser's web of deceit and begging God to help me. The woman, with a one-sided glimpse of the situation, incorrectly interpreted my halting prayer for help. She decided I was confessing sin and judged me. The fleeting feeling that God was crying over me vanished as the shame caused by this woman's attack consumed me. Cassandra listened closely, knowing that I understood the grip that shame held over her.

Recently, I learned how the woman who accosted me had helped another friend through a very turbulent time in his life. Much interactional pain is not done by evil people whose intent is to harm. Hearing this information was God's gentle reminder that we all make mistakes. My intent is not to judge but to encourage us all to do better. When we understand the effects of trauma, we are much less likely to misjudge others.

I asked Cassandra, "What did we both need?" After talking for a few minutes, we decided we needed others to listen without judgment. We needed them to fully grasp that our distress was not a confession of guilt. We were being vulnerable before God and others about a painful life event over which we had no control. We needed others not to assume our guilt.

The following addition to Foster's quote is a simple way to become more trauma-sensitive in our thinking: "We are sinners [and/or traumatized humans] together. In acts of mutual confession [vulnerability] we release the power that heals. Our humanity is no longer denied but transformed."[93] I regret how my own traumatic story was unconsciously hidden—even from myself. I spent my life listening to others vulnerably share their own painful stories without ever showing any sign that I also experienced childhood trauma. To now be able to sit with another in mutual vulnerability is transforming for both of us.

Adding the concept of vulnerability to the spiritual practice of confession makes it accessible to both those who are hurt and those who hurt—that includes all of us. Without it, we focus on all the ways we have fallen short and miss the blessing of healing the deep wounds of our painful childhood experiences. Our buried stories of the sins against us are as damaging to our spiritual growth as any hidden personal sin we may have committed.

Foster ended the chapter on confession with this paragraph. (I again have taken the liberty to exchange the word *vulnerability* for *confession*.) "The Discipline of [vulnerability] brings an end to pretense. God is calling into being a Church that can openly [be vulnerable in] its frail humanity and know the forgiving and empowering graces of Christ. Honesty leads to [vulnerability], and [vulnerability] leads to change."[94]

FINAL THOUGHTS

In practicing confession, faith communities hold the fragile hearts of the traumatized in their hands. Empathy and understanding are especially needed for those who have been sinned against and are suffering the effects of trauma. Not all who fear being vulnerable do so because of the sins they have committed. It may also be true that it is the sin of others that the person is unable to share and may erroneously believe they caused. While I agree it is important to speak these truths, proceed with caution. Many have been encouraged to open their wounds too quickly, without professional care, sometimes with devastating results.

Churches would do well to devote resources to train their ministry staff and laity in how to be trauma sensitive and responsive. Creating a ministry for the traumatized is rather ludicrous since, at some level, the entire congregation would be attending. Being trauma sensitive is just as much about understanding and healing our own story as it is about helping anyone else. We are all in this together. We all must be mutually vulnerable if we are to create safe spaces in our churches. As in the relational practice of submission, we are also equals in our confessions.

Chapter 12: Leadership Reflection Questions

- In Cassandra's story, the assumption for the need to repent was incorrect. Can you think of times when similar assumptions may have unintentionally hindered the healing care someone needed?
- What potential harm can come from the practice of corporate confession or vulnerability? What safeguards could be set in place to prevent this?
- Have you had some that you serve repeatedly seek forgiveness? How can understanding the effects of trauma help you to minister more effectively to these individuals?
- How can modeling mutual vulnerability enable the body of Christ to address the ways that the difficult stories of others cause us to feel uncomfortable?
- When someone confesses something that you would traditionally call "sin," how comfortable are you with holding non-judgmental space for them without offering admonition or instruction? Is it possible to balance unconditional acceptance and accountability? How?

Worship Through a Trauma Lens

N athan was in town visiting family and we sat on my front porch to talk. I asked him, "Do you remember a time of worship when God felt close?"

He thought for a few minutes. "No, I really don't. I always felt like God was watching me and waiting for me to do something wrong. As a kid, I never attended church, but one summer my dad sent me to a Christian camp. The woman who taught at the camp said God was watching us all the time, so we needed to be sure we were good. I knew horrible things were happening to me, so it frightened me. I just always felt that way."

Remembering that Nathan attended concerts at Calvary Chapel when he was a young adult, I asked him about his experience at the concerts.

"Calvary Chapel had Monday night concerts that I went to for a while. The music was uplifting."

When we began playing one of the songs from the concert, I recognized it immediately and began singing along. I remembered how the lyrics of the song had captured my feelings of hopelessness at that time.

While listening to the song's words, I wondered if the concerts were, as Foster stated, "God's efforts to initiate, restore, and maintain fellowship with [Nathan]."[95] It wasn't too long after attending the concerts that Nathan was invited to another church. It was there that he met his wife and made many life-long friends. Unfortunately, the legalistic church culture took them both down a path that stole the relational connection God was creating. In the new church, it felt as if God was judging their every move. This seemed familiar to Nathan because of what he had experienced as a child, so he accepted their view of God. Still, he remembered the connection he felt at the concert.

Nathan continued to reflect. "The songs at the concert had so much hope in them, and while there, I didn't have to pretend to be anything but me. It was so different."

"Yes," I said, "hope and authenticity were what you needed! I think that is part of what worship offers us. Maybe you were worshipping without realizing it."

HOW DOES SERVICE BLOCK WORSHIP?

Nathan and his wife's involvement in churches over the years involved much serving and minimal worship. Many serve to the extent that they seldom attend a service to simply worship. They don't realize they aren't worshipping; they believe their service *is* worship. Though Nathan was involved in various elements of corporate worship, going to church focused on serving. When his world came crashing down and he could no longer serve, church involvement lost its purpose.

In a church I once attended, one gentleman spent his entire Sunday morning in the Sunday school office. While, admittedly, I was judgmental at the time, I now would sit and talk with him. I am sure he had a story. Leaders must become compassionately aware of those who serve too much, others who watch the exits for escape routes, and still others who seem not actively present during worship. They deserve to be honored for showing up and not condemned if they don't. They also deserve to be part of a corporate community that believes in the spiritual practice of healing, gently holding space for them during worship experiences that can bring deeply painful emotions to the surface.

It is a great disservice to those impacted by trauma when their eagerness to serve and please others robs them of opportunities to grow closer to God through worship. It is even more tragic when the stress of their constant service depletes them to the point of collapse and causes them to no longer feel valued in the church. What people need to know is that they are worthy of God's love simply because they exist. This sense of worthiness can only happen if everyone participates in community and worship without being valued only because of their contributions.

WORSHIPPING WITH THE WHOLE BODY

At this point, it feels redundant to speak of the ways trauma affects our ability to access spiritual practices. I can almost hear readers saying, "Oh, she is going to talk about quieting the mind again." Yes, I probably am and rightly so because each practice depends on one basic premise—the quieting of the mind before the presence of a loving God.

It is also the case that our entire physical body needs to be included in worship experiences, especially since this is a problem for the traumatized, whose bodies are always on high alert. All the constant movement they unconsciously use to deal with the inner turmoil stands between them and God. The trauma is in every cell of their bodies. As mentioned before, the term "mental health" is a misnomer. Worship is often a shallow experience when they feel it is necessary to be still by pressing down feelings of shame that rumble internally. The methods with which individuals impacted by trauma unconsciously protect themselves from experiencing emotions, fights against the release of emotions necessary for worship.

When some have difficulty accessing worship, the admonition to "try harder" is particularly ineffective. Take a minute and reflect on what your body feels like when trying harder to do something—anything. It is how I feel when I raise the weight level at the gym—braced and ready for action. Now think about what it feels like to reach the ocean, sit down, and breathe in the air. This is worship. Trying harder does not work.

I fail to understand why the church at large that is so committed to spiritual practices, seems to have missed the emphasis Foster made by saying, "The point is that we are to offer God our bodies as well as all the rest of our being. Worship is appropriately physical."[96] Christianity, for the most part, took the rhythms out of the church. When the drums returned, the outcry was very vocal. I welcomed the drums; they felt regulating to my overactive trauma responses. I understand there are traumatized people for whom the loud music and lights cause a sensory overload—also those with sensory processing disorders. Once again, every trauma response may have similar root causes but varying triggers.

Over the years, I have watched traditional services become less and less participatory and listened to judgmental comments about "more lively" churches. Because trauma resides within the body, involving the entire body in worship is essential. Foster suggested, "God calls for worship that involves our whole being. . . Often we forget that worship should include the body as well as the mind and the spirit."[97]

The release of trauma—held as stress hormones and energy—requires movement. This movement can be internal, such as during a massage, or external, as in dancing. The important point is that the body must move in order to heal. This understanding has led the medical field to get people moving much sooner after surgery than what occurred in previous generations.

Another way our bodies naturally try to rid ourselves of trauma is by shaking. Often when those who have experienced trauma tell me their stories, I hear the tremor in their voice and ask, "Are you shaking?" Without exception, they say how hard they are trying to stop shaking, usually with

> The release of trauma—held as stress hormones and energy—requires movement. This movement can be internal, such as during a massage, or external, as in dancing. The important point is that the body must move in order to heal.

an apology. They are surprised when I tell them shaking is healthy. Animals, after being chased by a predator, will stand and shake off the trauma in their bodies before moving on.[98] For some reason we have decided this indicates weakness and try to stop our bodies from healing.

The best examples of full-bodied worship have historically been part of the Black church. The first time I watched a Black choir sing, I wanted to sing with them—with my body swaying to the music. I only attended two churches in which moving to the music felt comfortable. One was during a very stressful time in my life, and I looked forward to going to church and moving with the music—which was both loud and artistic (it is possible). As a child, when I heard music, I remember tapping my toes to the beat inside my shoes—moving my body to the music would have been inappropriate. I did not realize until healing that my body constantly longed to release the buildup of stress chemicals. As healing allowed this to happen, I began to feel God's presence and the urge to move with the music.

During the documentary, *The Black Church: This Is Our Song*,[99] I watched in amazement as those in the Black Pentecostal Church were taken in the spirit. The full-body involvement in the documentary looked much like the what the participants experience in the neurogenic tremor classes my friend teaches. In the case of the worshippers, the spiritual experience was very physical.

After experiencing both verbal and physical abuse during slavery, many gravitated to religious experiences that provided full-body involvement in worship. The African rhythms the slaves brought with them to America are embedded in their music and preaching in many of their churches. This included the practice of "serve and return" between the preacher and congregants during sermons—with ample hand waving. For many, the church was a place of healing as they praised God through movement, much like how their indigenous ancestors understood that drum rhythms provided a healing release for both their bodies and communities.

HOW CAN MUSIC CHOICES AFFECT WORSHIP?

Sometimes the words of songs stand in the way of drawing closer to God. A friend who loved attending a particular church had stopped attending. I was curious and asked why he left.

"It changed," he said. "The songs stopped being hopeful and felt condemning. It felt like the old 'worm theology' stuff I left behind, you know, like how wretched I am. It was difficult because I was finally beginning to understand that what happened to me as a kid wasn't my fault. Being told I was sinful every time I walked in the door brought up those old feelings of shame again. So, we left. It was a big church. No one noticed."

I understood this. While healing, it is easy for shame to descend again if we are in a community that emphasizes sin over God's desire for a relationship. It does not take much for unworthiness to rob the survivor's connection with God and others that is so essential to corporate worship. This feeling of being loved by God is inaccessible when one is constantly reminded of unworthiness that feeds the false shame narratives of the traumatized. Do we never talk about sin? Well, maybe not during worship. Loathing our failures is not a healthy form of worship for those impacted by trauma, likely not for anyone.

For every believer, it is essential to find a path to worship. For the traumatized, this is particularly important, especially if the trauma was in the context of the church. I end this section with possibly my favorite of Foster's words: "We are free in Christ to use whatever forms will enhance our worship, and if any form hinders us from experiencing the living Christ—too bad for the form."[100] It is not about form; it is about a relationship.

For those whose history of trauma causes them to feel uncomfortable in traditional church services, this is a key element to encouraging trauma-sensitive worship. So often those things that helped me participate, including tables at the back of the sanctuary, were viewed as unnecessary frills by many others. Probably the most helpful was when I was able to watch my friend paint during the service—I treasure her art along with the memory. Again, it is not about form.

FINAL THOUGHTS

What gave Nathan the sense of expectancy when he attended the concerts? Complete acceptance by God and the unique crowd that attended Calvary Chapel during those years. He could attend as who he was, have a sense of belonging, and feel the hope in the songs.

Nathan contacted me later to follow up with our conversation. "There was another place where I felt the same way. It was the church I attended while I was healing. At this church, people's stories mattered. The pastoral staff was honest about their experiences of having failed. The music reminded me of the concerts. It felt safe there. I could hardly wait to go to the services."

As I wrote, I reflected on how Nathan's story could have been written differently. I felt that his experiences at the concerts held the key. Nathan needed to heal, and God took him to a place where no one would ask him to serve or expect him to be anything other than himself in the presence of God. While Nathan did not seem to remember the concerts as a significant God experience, they were what he needed to find his way through the darkness that gripped his life at the time.

Trauma-sensitive faith communities will always place knowing and being known by God before service. At one church I attended, the pastor said, "If you are in the process of healing, then you need to delay service." What a difference this would have made during the years when Nathan felt so much pressure to serve! The church would have been the place where Nathan was encouraged to heal within an entire community who believed in the power and importance of trauma-sensitive spiritual practices, in all their forms, including worship. (See Appendix 4 for Steps to Worship through a Trauma-Sensitive Lens.)

Chapter 13: Leadership Reflection Questions

- Can you think of examples of service blocking worship (including personal)? What creative policies or plans could be put in place to ensure that this doesn't occur?
- Why is it especially important to include whole-body experiences in worship? To what degree do you feel this is occurring in your ministry? Do you know of, or have you seen examples (beyond moving to the music) when this did take place?
- After comparing the "try harder" approach to worship with that of going to the beach and breathing the air, what were your thoughts on how you and those in your church seem to approach worship (or any other spiritual practice)?
- With a trauma lens, review the music that the worship teams incorporated during the past few weeks. What was the focus? Did you come across any lyrics that would confirm the worthlessness or self-loathing of those who experienced childhood trauma?

Guidance Through a Trauma Lens

T hose like Nathan who have experienced severe trauma often need a village to support them. It is not the fault of the trau- matized when their unmet needs consume their lives and the lives of those around them. Imagine never receiving unconditional love and suddenly discovering a room filled with it. When I began therapy, I was like a starving person as my unmet needs exploded from me. I simply could not get enough! Feeling shame for being "needy" only complicated things. I needed a village.

The spiritual practice of guidance can effectively be used to provide support while people walk through the healing process. Mentoring can be an individual one-on-one relationship, but Foster's corporate Discipline of guidance includes the idea of mentoring by "a village" as he stated in the following: "God does guide the indi- vidual richly and profoundly, but he also guides groups of people and can instruct the individual through the group experience."[101] With boundaries and self-care, this extra layer of support is a gift given to both the professional therapist and client. Everyone needs a village; this is especially true for those who have been affected by trauma and struggle to find communities where they feel accepted.

WHAT DOES IT MEAN TO NEED A VILLAGE?

An example of a village is what Foster described as "meetings for clearness." A young man was seeking guidance about his future. "So, he gathered a group of people who knew him well, had spiritual maturity, and were unafraid to be honest and candid with him."[102] Through a process of discussion, worship, and prayer, "they became a supporting community."[103]

Would Nathan's story have changed if he could have asked a group to gather for a meeting for clearness? Not one of forced reconciliation, but a gathering with those who knew him, knew his story, and recognized the ways the job loss might have triggered his childhood trauma? The clarity might have helped them assist Nathan in seeking professional care. At the very minimum, they could have listened to his side of the story as nonjudgmental listeners. Nathan needed a village.

Like many, Nathan served without a supportive community. During college, while attending classes with much younger students, he became someone they looked up to and sought out for advice. The instructors were focused on the younger students and assumed Nathan had his act together. He was a scrappy survivor who knew how to act normally and do what needed to be done. He quickly became a leader in college, church, and work. Always in leadership roles, Nathan never gathered a group around himself that could have supported him when his world fell apart.

Like Nathan, I have often needed a village to help me when making decisions. While friends can give advice, it often conflicts with the advice of others. A group discussion with those who understood my story would have provided more clarity as they could disagree with each other, and everyone could have reflectively considered the options. During the writing of this book, my publishers and writing mentors have provided these kinds of meetings for clearness. It is a model worth replicating.

What would it be like for those who have experienced trauma to have a group they could call upon for meetings of clearness? How can we gather around those who have been impacted by trauma and help them to effectively access spiritual practices in ways that are trauma-sensitive and feel accessible? How could we support them in their healing process?

WHAT HAPPENS WHEN THE VILLAGE FAILS?

Because I believe so strongly that the church can be the village for those affected by trauma, I never want my writing to dissolve into church bashing. Yet, it became clear that there were issues I did not address when, during the final stages of writing, the Guidepost Solution's report on the mishandling of sexual abuse by the Southern Baptist Convention (SBC) exploded onto the religious landscape. Not that this was the first revelation of this sort, and it is not limited to the SBC, but it was possibly the most damning because it revealed systemic dismissal and often derision of those who suffered sexual abuse within the context of the church. Russel Moore, former President of the Ethics & Religious Liberty Commission of the SBC called it an "apocalypse."[104] It is certainly the most stunning revelation of how badly a village can fail.

Most of the recommendations in the Guidepost Solutions' report focused on prevention and revolved around organizational structures and responsibilities. The following was an exception: "Acknowledge those who have been affected by SBC clergy sexual abuse, through both a sincere apology and a tangible gesture, and prioritize the provision of compassionate care to survivors through providing dedicated survivor advocacy support and a survivor compensation fund."[105]

This recommendation describes how the church becomes a village for those who have experienced trauma within the context of the church. This is certainly a part of the entire picture that cannot be ignored. In my case, the cost of therapy necessary for healing the failure of my village can probably not be imagined by most readers. Yes, the village must prevent abuse, but it also must care for the traumatized who experienced abuse while attending our churches. The village that guides must also be a village that accepts responsibility for the failure.

HOW CAN INTERDEPENDENCE HELP EVERYONE BE VALUED?

Guidance in the early church was something Foster explained as "interdependence": "[Paul] saw that the gifts of the Spirit were given by the Spirit to the body in such a way that interdependence was ensured. No one person possessed everything. Even the most mature needed the help of others. The most insignificant had something to contribute. No one could hear the whole counsel of God in isolation."[106]

> Yes, the village must prevent abuse, but it also must care for the traumatized who experienced abuse while attending our churches. The village that guides must also be a village that accepts responsibility for the failure.

In this scenario, every person has gifts to share, and no one must wear a mask of spirituality to be respected as a member of the community. When these communities are trauma informed and sensitive, everyone's experiences are significant and individuals hold value *because* of their story, not despite it.

I discovered what this kind of community might look like when being interviewed for the Attachment & Trauma Network's board of directors. At the time, there were still many lingering effects of trauma in my life. Thus, I was both excited about the opportunity and anxious about the expectations. When asked if I had any concerns, I responded, "Sometimes I am not okay and may not be able to do what is expected."

The executive director's response changed my life. "We know your story and would not expect you to always be okay. Working with those who have experienced trauma is what we do. When you are overwhelmed, just tell us and we will help you."

In the ensuing weeks, I began to understand what it meant to be valued because of my story, not despite it. My efforts to heal and understand trauma held value in this community. They were a gift that I brought. When I spoke, it was as a voice for the children the organization is dedicated to helping. My perspective was important. This is the type of community that trauma-sensitive churches could also provide—places where no one feels they need to hide their stories. In fact, a place where their stories make them more valuable.

FINAL THOUGHTS

There were many areas of my life in which a trauma-sensitive/informed mentor could have provided life-giving help as I served in leadership roles both at work and in the church. It wasn't just about spiritual guidance, but about learning how to cope in a world for which I was, in many ways, completely ill-prepared. This was true in both general life and spiritually.

Without mentoring relationships and healing, most who have suffered trauma as children will hide their struggles. Those who learned to meet their own needs as children are strongly independent, with carefully hidden unmet needs. Many will put on a mask of spirituality while privately using unhealthy coping strategies or openly using socially acceptable but maladaptive ones. Spirituality becomes a battle to be won instead of a celebration.

The only way to change church culture to become more trauma-sensitive is to recognize the importance of story as well as the strengths and contributions of those who have survived the unspeakable. For me, this person was a therapist, but all of us, with trauma-informed wisdom, can be this person for each other. This recognition of post-traumatic spirituality has the power to revitalize the church. It requires a village involved in mutual guidance.

Chapter 14: Leadership Reflection Questions

- The focus of this chapter was on the corporate aspect of guidance which was identified as being a village for those who are in the process of healing from trauma. Can you identify reasons why this is so important?

- How can the lack of incorporating a village culture around those who deeply need care lead to ministerial burnout? How would a village culture also provide accountability for ministry leaders?

- Mental health needs and/or effects of trauma are often viewed from a deficit viewpoint. How can this be reframed to be seen as a strength and asset to the faith community?

Celebration Through a Trauma Lens

t was my third wedding that weekend. Graduating students often planned their weddings while family and friends were still in town after graduation. I have no idea how many weddings I attended during my twenty years of teaching traditional-aged college students. During the weddings, I looked for something that distinguished the couple's ceremony from the others so I could express how it "felt like them." Over time, most of these weddings became a blur of traditional and semitraditional celebrations, except for one.

As the groom kissed the bride, the distinct sound of Three Dog Night came over the speakers. "Celebrate! Celebrate! Dance to the music!" and the wedding party proceeded to dance down the middle aisle.

The dancing bride and groom may have been the most unexpected event in my life as a Bible college professor. Dancing in the sanctuary was certainly unexpected. Some church experiences did feel dull like Foster described in the following quote: "Celebration is central to all the Spiritual Disciplines. Without a joyful spirit of festivity, the *Disciplines become dull, death-breathing tools in the hands of modern Pharisees.* [emphasis added] Every Discipline should be characterized by carefree gaiety and a sense of thanksgiving."[107]

Being carefree during a celebration requires freedom from the debilitating hold of shame. Curt Thompson explored the deadening effects of shame when he said that "Shame leads the world ultimately to a point of paralysis, vis-à-vis the movement that is required for creative engagement."[108] Shame destroys the possibility of joy.

DOES OBEDIENCE BRING JOY TO THE TRAUMATIZED?

The importance of experiencing joy is echoed by all those who work to help those impacted by trauma heal. It is the one thing the traumatized most long for. Deborah A Dayna, in the book *Anchored*, stated, "When we build a pattern of acting from a survival state, we suffer both physically and psychologically. We may be successful in the world, but we don't feel satisfied or find joy in our experiences." This also sounds true of spiritual experiences based in survival. In a sense, it is spiritual survival and is often very much lacking in joy.[109]

The conundrum of traditional thought about spiritual practices is that practicing them will bring joy. For those who are living with the effects of trauma, joy is almost always elusive. Do they want joy? Yes, but the effects of trauma both impede spiritual practices and block the joy. Well, that sucks, especially if told that the solution is to try harder.

I am always looking for what authors say about Joy. Foster said, "Joy comes through obedience to Christ, and joy results from obedience to Christ. Without obedience, joy is hollow and artificial."[110] That seems like another catch-22. For many, the harder they try to obey, the less joyful they become. I believe the effects of trauma require us to dig deeper for the root cause that robs the traumatized of joy.

Many who struggle to access spiritual practices believe they are living in obedience, yet hollowness and artificiality still describe their spiritual lives. Nonetheless, their desire for God is evident, and they are doing their best to live in obedience—sometimes to the point of legalism.

For most of my life I accepted that my lack of obedience in not diligently participating in spiritual practices prevented joy and kept me from celebration. Only when I began to heal did I understand that it wasn't disobedience, it was my inability to access the abundant life. Trying harder generally made things worse and added layers to my already shame-filled existence. I was not enough. These efforts brought me no closer to experiencing joy in my life.

> Many who struggle to access spiritual practices believe they are living in obedience, yet hollowness and artificiality still describe their spiritual lives. Nonetheless, their desire for God is evident, and they are doing their best to live in obedience—sometimes to the point of legalism.

One friend said, "I was super involved in the church and Bible studies. I always believed everything, but the promises of Jesus just never seemed to apply to me. I didn't know why I was left feeling like I was doing everything right and trying so hard to feel like I was included but just feeling like a fraud because I couldn't ever feel like God included me." In other words, she did not feel invited to the celebration.

I did find ways to feel close to God, but few were at church, and I did not recognize them as spiritual. God completely understood both who I was created to be and the effects of my trauma. This was especially true as my healing journey began. Embracing healing as a part of my spiritual practice eventually opened the door to joy and celebration. For the wounded, to heal is to follow God's leading—which is the true meaning of obey. The paths to joy for those impacted by trauma seldom fit the images of traditional spiritual practices.

WHY IS JOY SO DIFFICULT TO EXPERIENCE?

Only an understanding of the effects of trauma helped me grasp why joy was so elusive. Throughout my life, my heart rate has been elevated. This is common in those who have experienced childhood trauma and is a symptom of PTSD. The resting heart rate is one method Dr. Bruce Perry used to evaluate the effects of trauma in children removed from the Davidian compound.[111] These children all had elevated resting heart rates.

As a teenager, a PE teacher noticed my high heart rate, and my parents took me to a doctor to check my heart. After an X-ray, it was determined that my heart was small and overworked for the size of my body—that was certainly grasping at straws. Since healing, my resting heart rate remains within the normal range, indicating that my inner world is no longer flooded with stress hormones. This change allowed me to begin to experience joy more fully.

In the book *Waking the Tiger: Healing Trauma*, Peter A. Levine and Ann Frederick made the connection between hypervigilance and the loss of joy. "Hypervigilant people are keyed to a state of intense alertness at all times and may actually develop a slightly furtive or fearful, open-eyed appearance due to this constant watchfulness. There is a growing tendency to see danger where there is none, and a diminished capacity to experience curiosity, pleasure, and the joy of life. All of this occurs because, at the core of our beings, we simply do not feel safe."[112]

It is nearly impossible to be hypervigilant and experience joy at the same time. Bessel van der Kolk described the physical manifestations of joy: "When a child is in sync with his caregiver, his sense of joy and connection is reflected in his steady heartbeat and breathing and a low level of stress hormones."[113] This sense of calm, essential for joy, does not exist in those who have experienced severe trauma.

> It is nearly impossible to be hypervigilant and experience joy at the same time.

While healing and longing for joy, I would experience glimmers of it. However, it would vanish almost as quickly as it appeared. These moments gave me hope. What I did not understand was that this experience could only come when my body relaxed from its hypervigilant state. Sometimes this happened while watching a sunset or walking my dog. During most of my life, I depended on laughter to experience moments of joy. "A joyful heart helps healing, but a broken spirit dries up the bones."[114] Yes, laughter helped, but the feeling of joy was as elusive as the sun on a foggy day.

HOW ARE PLAY AND JOY CONNECTED?

Many of those who experience trauma as children miss out on the crucial building blocks learned through play—a primary source of joy. Their play is often aggressive, overly competitive, and repetitive. It lacks the spontaneous creativity of healthy play. Many of those who did not experience healthy play as children do not know how to play in carefree ways. This has many ramifications; one is the loss of joy.

Bessel van der Kolk also made the connection between play and joy when he wrote, "When we play together, we feel physically attuned and experience a sense of connection and joy. . . The moment you see a group of grim-faced people break out in a giggle, you know that the spell of misery has broken."[115] It is clear that play is important in building community.

The Discipline of celebration requires us to recapture our joy. Foster put it this way, "When the power that is in Jesus reaches into our work and play and redeems them, there will be joy where once there was mourning."[116] Our work (service) does not bring the fullness of joy if not accompanied by play. Children who grow up in healthy ways play naturally, and children and adults who are robbed of these experiences require intervention and support to redeem play as an essential part of life.

I was delighted to recognize many attributes of play included in the following paraphrased list of Foster's descriptions of celebration:

- Saves us from taking ourselves too seriously.
- Adds notes of gaiety, festivity, and hilarity to our lives.
- Helps us relax and enjoy the good things of the earth.
- Is an effective antidote for sadness.
- Has the ability to give us perspective.
- Enables everyone to join as equals.[117]

If faith communities play together, it will give everyone an opportunity to be a village that supports healing through play. That would certainly deserve a celebration.

FINAL THOUGHTS

Joy depends on an inner transformation, which for those impacted by trauma means healing. Without this transformation, faith remains joyless. Often the pressure to exhibit joy results in only wearing a mask of spirituality. Those who have suffered trauma often turn to imitations of joy in an attempt to fit in with Christian culture. They go through the motions and wonder why they feel as though they are standing outside of the celebration. As long as the unresolved trauma holds them captive, joy remains out of reach. It is not a spiritual problem; it is a physical problem that requires healing the body, soul, and mind. When this occurs, everyone can join the celebration.

Chapter 15: Leadership Reflection Questions

- How would you define joy? Can you think of several things or experiences in your life that bring you joy?

- How can an understanding of the effects of trauma explain the joyless faith that so many seem to live?

- How might those who experienced trauma struggle to access the attributes of celebration that Foster proposes? What opportunities do church ministries include that would help those who have experienced trauma to build the missing building blocks of play that can then lead to joy?

- How can admonitions to "be joyful" circumvent the healing process of trauma? How can this become a spiritual bypass instead of an authentic spiritual experience?

Section Three

EFFECTIVELY MINISTERING TO THOSE IMPACTED BY TRAUMA

I t is easy to believe that people leave churches because they have spiritual problems that they don't want to address. It is especially easy to believe this when the departure is filled with emotions. The effects of trauma that manifest in a protective fight response, usually fear and anger, distract from the often-valid reasons for leaving. Others like Nathan leave quietly. Many of them have faded into the pandemic-induced loss of normalcy that many felt when churches locked down. Nathan realized that he could feel closer to God and continue healing by not attending. He was one example in a million.

It didn't have to turn out this way. At the same time, nothing Nathan could have done would have changed the situation. While reflecting on this, I wondered how it could have been different. What if, at the very beginning of Nathan's difficulties, the leaders in the church had been able to respond better? What if the leaders and members were trauma informed, sensitive, and responsive? The following is my reimagined story of how a paradigm shift could have made all the difference. Nathan's leaving had been in progress for many, many years.

"Hey, Nathan, I thought I'd give you a call. I hear it's been a rough week for you. I have a project that needs some of your skills at my cabin, and I wondered if you would drive out there with me on Saturday and take a look. We can talk about your week, or not. You don't have to. Some country air might be a good change."

It was the pastor of Nathan's church. Everything in him wanted to say no to this invitation but getting away sounded good. He also knew the pastor was not handy and probably did need help.

Nathan answered, "Yeah, really rough week, don't want to talk, but I'll be glad to help you."

By the time Saturday came, Nathan regretted his choice, but he always kept his word. They headed down a country road and Nathan recognized where he had taken his wilderness wandering. Without really meaning to, he said, "This is where I walked."

The pastor said, "I thought that might have been true. I'm sorry the week was so rough. Anytime you want to talk about it, you can. I want to hear what happened from you. I know the kind of person you are and something doesn't make sense. But you need to be ready to talk. I will not pressure you."

They completed the repair on the cabin, and Nathan understood the repair was just a reason the pastor had made up to spend time with him. This felt uncomfortable, but he accepted his good intentions.

It would be several months and many more interactions before Nathan told this pastor his side of the story. In the meantime, when several other men realized he liked to play racquetball, they reached out to him to join them. He told them he hadn't played in years but agreed to go. During one of the games, they began talking about concerts they attended when they were younger. One mentioned the Calvary Chapel concerts and was surprised to find out Nathan also attended and still enjoyed listening to songs by the concert artists.

Over the next few months, by word-of-mouth recommendations, Nathan's business began to grow and soon there was no time nor need for a second job. With this flexibility, the increased income, and the pastor's encouragement, Nathan began trauma-based therapy.

One day, two men in his racquetball group began to share their own childhood stories and long paths to healing. Their sharing helped Nathan to tell some of his story and how he was healing through therapy.

One of the men asked, "Nathan, how can we support you? This is a courageous thing you're doing."

"I have no idea. It just feels so overwhelming and lonely. I don't know what is normal and some days it's hard to function."

Another friend said, "I get that! It sucks really bad. But it'll be worth it. I'll start texting to check on you during the week. Will that help?"

Nathan nodded his head, and they began another game.

The next Sunday, as he waited for the service to begin, a of song from the Calvary Chapel concert began playing over the speakers, and for the very first time in Nathan's life, he felt as if God, was saying, "Nathan, I love you."

Nathan saw the pastor smiling at him. When the song ended, the pastor walked to the microphone and said, "Let the celebration begin!"

Yes, when we *know* better, we can *do* better—in our personal lives, ministry preparation, and faith communities. Our churches can be the refuge of safety for the most wounded among us. It will take effort, but it is possible.

> ## Section Three: Leadership Reflection Questions
>
> - In what ways does the rewritten story of Nathan's experiences demonstrate the trauma informed, sensitive, and responsive spiritual practices?
> - How does the story demonstrate a village approach to ministering to those who have experienced trauma vs. a programmatic approach to meeting needs?
> - A common theme in the trauma-informed movement is that relational trauma only heals through relationships. How is your church either practicing this principle or poised to do so?

How Can We Be Trauma Responsive in Our Personal Lives?

U p to this point, I have addressed faith communities and ministry leaders to provide the trauma-informed and trauma-sensitive perspectives necessary to compassionately serve those in our churches who have experienced trauma. Before delving into the paradigm shift to trauma-responsive ministry, it is time to apply the change in thinking in our personal lives. In the trauma-informed movement, we know the absolute necessity of doing our own work if we are to even begin to be trauma responsive with others. For this reason, I am going to pause and talk about us.

I would suggest that many who serve in ministry either diminish their own history of trauma or simply do not recognize their experiences as traumatic. This truth was demonstrated when a friend, a licensed therapist, and I presented during a professional development day for teachers at a Christian school. We learned an important lesson regarding the ACE research study.

While I have mentioned this research study several times as it pertains to the effects of trauma, it has not been approached as a personal reflection, which is what we attempted to do that day. To our surprise, we watched as several participants come to the troubling realization that they *had* experienced trauma. Two became so emotionally dysregulated that they were unable to continue the workshop. For this reason, I always approach the information with a warning and do not ask anyone to complete the ACE questionnaire (available online) in public settings, or without support.

UNRAVELING OUR STORIES

The ACE questionnaire asks ten questions. It was never intended to encompass all the various forms of trauma, only those most prevalent before the age of eighteen. Five of the questions are personal—physical, verbal, or sexual abuse, physical or emotional neglect. The other five questions relate to family members—alcoholic parents, domestic abuse of mother, a jailed family member, divorce of parents, and family member diagnosed with a mental illness.

The ACE list is neither a comprehensive nor predictive tool. The number of ACEs does increase one's risk of experiencing trauma-related health issues, but this can be mitigated by positive experiences and compassionate and nurturing adult role models and mentors. The questions also do not address chronic stress or traumas that were ongoing. All the ACE test does is open the window to view how pervasive traumatic experiences are in the childhoods of those we work beside and minister to. It often opens the window to face the reality of our own stories.

For those of us raised in church communities, the silence around trauma is thorough and profound. The admonitions of "honoring your parents" mixed with "not airing your dirty laundry" have silenced entire generations. Vulnerable honesty was rare in church circles unless it was about personal sins. The recent emphasis on gratitude casts anyone's honesty about their difficult or adverse childhood experiences as ungrateful. "Look how blessed you are!" All of this led to that room of Christian schoolteachers who came face-to-face with their traumatic childhood experiences in ways that took my friend and me by surprise. I imagine many readers who have been reading with a desire to help others have occasionally paused to reflect on their own experiences and false internalized messages.

> For those of us raised in church communities, the silence around trauma is thorough and profound. The admonitions of "honoring your parents" mixed with "not airing your dirty laundry" have silenced entire generations.

When I began teaching and parenting young children, my trauma was often triggered, causing me to respond to children and adults in baffling ways that sometimes frightened me, often with over-the-top emotions or reactions to the situation. At no point would I have ever connected these responses to my traumatic childhood experiences. It was much more palatable to believe them to be caused by the sin nature. I would not have recognized my childhood as traumatic, which is the result of both denial and repression. My story of trauma found no place to belong in my home, church, or profession.

Many who work in ministry, as well as other professions, hide the trauma they have experienced because it would hurt them professionally. The pressure of "ministerial perfection" is real. This was especially true for me since my trauma responses were usually attributed to being an emotional female. I hope this destructive aspect of ministry and professionalism is ending; it has not served us well. Watching the younger generation's open and honest vulnerability gives me hope for the future.

WHAT DO WE RISK BY NOT HEALING?

My own painful story is overwhelmingly filled with evidence that those who were leading had not done their own internal work. They likely didn't know that they were unconsciously living out their unresolved trauma in both reactive and protective ways. Beyond the obvious abuse, this shows up in the need to always be right, viewing others as "the enemy," constant hypervigilance and need to control, judgmental attitudes toward others, and rigid black-and-white thinking, to name a few. These are often disguised—even from ourselves. It often feels like we are being spiritually discerning about what is right or wrong.

At the end of the continuum are outright moral failures that grow out of meeting unmet emotional needs or a sense of powerlessness. I do not excuse the leaders who deeply harmed me. Instead, I hold them up as examples of how the avoidance of unresolved pain can cause us to live out our trauma in actions that harm others. Such was the case for Alex.

Alex was invited to a church teen activity by a neighbor. His home life was chaotic, and when his father was home, he was usually drunk. Alex learned to stay out of his father's way on the weekends, and church seemed like a good escape. He had not attended church before and hardly knew what to expect. Alex thought it would be boring, but he soon realized the youth group was fun and energetic. He enjoyed spending time at the church under the leadership of the youth pastor, Evan.

After Alex's first visit, Evan asked him to go to lunch. During lunch, Alex wasn't sure anyone had ever listened so attentively to him. He decided attending church was a good idea, and he became a regular at youth group, slowly beginning to learn what church was all about. He also began reading the Bible Evan gave him.

"I didn't think Evan could do anything wrong," Alex told me. "He taught me what it meant to love God, and I accepted Jesus as my Savior. My life completely changed. I started doing better in school and eventually applied for college. I was disappointed when Evan suddenly moved to another church. It wasn't long before I found out he had gotten one of the teens in the youth group pregnant. It destroyed me. I thought he was different. I struggled for a long time."

> It is imperative that we, as leaders, do our own work to heal childhood wounds before ministering to others.

Those whose childhoods were bereft of stable adults need the kind of spiritual advisors who exemplify the spiritual practice of guidance. It is imperative that we, as leaders, do our own work to heal childhood wounds before ministering to others. Otherwise, it is easy to meet those needs through those who are following us. If followers also have unmet attachment needs, both individuals will find themselves in a vulnerable place. Alex desperately needed Evan to be someone who finally saw the real him. In Alex's eyes, Evan could do no wrong. Falling from this pedestal can have devastating consequences for those who dare to trust.

WHAT HAPPENS WHEN SPIRITUAL GUIDES FAIL?

In truth, Evan had been struggling for years. He experienced neglect as a child and often doubted his ability or worthiness to be a youth pastor. It felt good when Alex told him how much he helped him. Evan thrived on helping others and several teens spent a great deal of time with him. One was a girl who experienced sexual abuse as a young child—another vulnerable teenager.

I asked Alex how he was able to keep his faith after Evan's devastating fall. He said, "It was hard because what Evan taught me about Jesus wasn't wrong. I can see how it is still a part of my faith today. But I had to eventually get some professional help to hold both the 'Evan who failed' and the 'Evan who helped' in my mind at the same time."

I understood what Alex was saying. Some of my abusers taught me foundational elements of my faith. When leaders fail those who are already hurting, it makes sense why so many walk away. It is nearly impossible to climb over the cognitive dissonance of good and evil living in the same person who purports to be a spiritual leader. There are no easy answers. Alex and I both knew that being told to "keep our eyes on Jesus" did little good when the person we believed God brought to help us through our pain morally failed us in such a catastrophic way.

"Evan went on with his life and is now a pastor," Alex said. "The girl didn't fare as well. I think people blamed her for the whole thing. She left the church and gave the baby up for adoption. She eventually got married, but last I heard she was divorced." The story had all the hallmarks of ministry leaders sweeping the moral failures of other leaders under the rug at the expense of the victim.

> When leaders fail those who are already hurting, it makes sense why so many walk away. It is nearly impossible to climb over the cognitive dissonance of good and evil living in the same person who purports to be a spiritual leader. There are no easy answers.

Foster rightly said, "Spiritual directors must be on the inward journey themselves and be willing to share their own struggles and doubts. There needs to be a realization that together they are learning from Jesus, their ever-present Teacher."[118] This requires an attitude of vulnerability *and* our ability as leaders, to do our own work and set boundaries that protect the vulnerable who have deep attachment and abandonment wounds and risk everything to trust a spiritual leader.

Alex's story reminds us of the responsibility we have as leaders, just as this Bible verse admonishes: "So if you think you are standing firm, be careful that you don't fall!"[119] This is especially true if we are trauma survivors who are working with those who have experienced abandonment as part of their childhood trauma. They often enter relationships with us looking for an attachment figure. They may have longed for someone to fill the attachment void since birth. It is the leader's responsibility to set compassionate boundaries—something very difficult for those who have experienced trauma themselves.

HOW DO WE KNOW WE NEED TO "DO THE WORK" OF HEALING?

I conclude with my own story of doing the work of healing. For me, the realization that my childhood was filled with trauma was a disturbing revelation. Being trauma responsive for oneself requires that moment of recognition. I never speak to audiences without someone approaching me with a whispered awareness that they had denied the full truth of their childhood story. It is in that moment of realization that healing begins. This is how that moment came to me.

I was approaching my sixtieth birthday and headed toward my fortieth year as a teacher and teacher educator; life was outwardly bright and inwardly dark. I was the poster child for creating all the appearances of success and happiness while ignoring anything that did not fit into that ideal. No one could have suspected the story of childhood sexual abuse that began to fill the pages of books four years later. My childhood story was carefully edited to be acceptable as a leader in higher education and the church.

Remarkably, while this undercurrent of pain was embedded in my church experiences, my subconsciously repressed memories remained sequestered while living out my faith with a childlike trust in God. It was this childlike faith that enabled me to follow God's prompting to begin therapy. In hindsight, my first appointment seemed to be dedicated to convincing my new therapist that everything in my life was fine. Maybe I just needed a bit of life coaching? On the dark days, this was certainly not the case.

What would soon be apparent was how both my faith and dissociative coping helped me live above the pain but never healed the layers of trauma that included relational betrayals from the time I was three years of age until my early twenties. The effects of trauma were everywhere in my life; they were unconscious drivers fueling my life choices. These effects were also evident in unidentified anxiety, PTSD flashbacks, triggers, and dissociative coping strategies. Though I took antidepressants for over twenty years, neither the cause nor extent of my mental health issues were ever considered.

The possibility of trauma was certainly not considered. Trauma was something that debilitated "those people." It wasn't considered in the life of a Bible college professor. The only sign that a trauma-informed doctor might have recognized was my feeling that I lived at two levels and existed just outside of my own life. I am not sure I could have expressed it. The interesting thing about trauma is that we often do not recognize it in ourselves. We tell our childhood stories carefully and diminish the truth, but our bodies know. Even when I began to acknowledge that my story wasn't as perfect as I wanted it to be, I was completely unaware of the ways that trauma was affecting me. It took me months of therapy to even realize I was dissociating during therapy sessions. It was simply how I lived my life. It felt normal.

What could have helped me understand my need for healing? My inability to access the spiritual practices in any way that brought joy in my life. Being in ministry does not mean that we aren't suffering. For me, it only meant that I could not admit that I needed help.

DISSOCIATIVE DISORDERS[120]

In *Healing the Fragmented Selves of Trauma Survivors*, Dr. Janina Fisher provided a thorough history of the growing research that is helping practitioners better understand and support the healing of dissociative disorders. following paragraph, Dr. Fisher perfectly described the "me" who entered therapy.

"By the time the trauma survivor appears at our doorstep, the neurobiological and psychological effects of a dysregulated autonomic nervous system, disorganized attachment patterns, and structurally dissociated parts will have become a set of well-entrenched, familiar, habitual responses. He or she will be unconsciously driven by post-traumatic implicit procedural learning activated by trauma-related triggers. The symptoms and triggered reactions now will be so familiar and automatic that, subjectively, they feel like 'just who I am.' Although apparently unrelated to the past, these 'just who I am' responses are the conveyors of a narrative that cannot be fully remembered or put into words, a history held by different parts of the personality with different perspectives, triggers, and survival responses."[121]

Dissociative disorders are characterized by an involuntary departure from an individual's current reality. The symptoms of dissociative disorders include significant memory loss of specific times, people, and events; out-of-body experiences, depression, anxiety and/or thoughts of suicide, a sense of detachment from emotions/emotional numbness, and a lack of self-identity.

There are three types of dissociative disorders:

- Dissociative Amnesia – difficulty remembering important information about oneself or life events
- Depersonalization-Derealization Disorder – sense of detachment from thoughts, actions, body sensations, or feelings.
- Dissociative Identity Disorder (DID) – may include elements of all disorders in this category but characterized by alternating between two or more personality states.

FINAL THOUGHTS

Even without therapy, a trauma-responsive culture within the church would have enabled me to heal along the way. The mental-health stigma that permeated the church made it nearly impossible for ministry leaders to seek help. The antagonistic stand that many church leaders took against psychological help, along with their insistence that the Bible held the answer for every human problem, complicated things even further.

Hopefully, our growing understanding of how trauma affects both the mind and body will enable us to move toward trauma-responsive approaches that encourage us to access what we now understand about healing from the effects of trauma. This must begin with us as leaders. Healing is not for *them*; healing is for everyone. Why do I do what I do? Because the difference that healing has made in my life would have transformed the years that I served in faith communities.

> Healing is not for *them*; healing is for everyone.

It is possible to be trauma responsive to our deepest wounds. In hindsight I understand how trauma caused me to fear the very thing that would help me. Shame is the limiter and destroyer of hope and freedom. God will honor anyone willing to do the work of healing. No matter how minimal you believe your difficult childhood experiences were, healing will make a difference. When the Apostle Paul admonishes us to "leave the past behind," we now know the only way that happens is through healing. It will be worth the work!

Chapter 16: Leadership Reflection Questions

- This chapter's focus changes from ministering to others to taking time for self-reflection. In what areas has your previous reading already prompted self-reflection?

- How familiar were you or are you now with the ACE research study? If you have not taken time to complete the survey, this might be an appropriate time to do so (resources available in Appendix 6).

- Many trauma survivors diminish their own experiences by stating, "It wasn't that bad." How has this served as protection?

- Foster stated that spiritual directors must be on the inward journey themselves, do you see this modeled in the ministerial circles in which you fellowship?

- If you have a history of trauma, have you felt professional or ministerial pressure to not reveal this to those you minister to or work with? Has it also caused you to not seek professional help? Who could you choose to safely share your story or help you seek professional help?

How Can We Be Trauma Responsive in Ministry Preparation?

I n a recent conversation with a colleague who is involved in the training of ministry workers, we discussed the lack of emphasis on healing in ministry preparation programs. He said, "I'm fine. I took one class in pastoral counseling!" We laughed together, understanding the ridiculous assumption that offering one class focused on helping others, with a minimal amount of self-reflection, was sufficient to prepare those we send to the front lines of ministry—especially in a world filled with trauma.

During my tenure at a second Bible college, I worked with many students who had come to salvation from rough-and-tumble backgrounds. They surrendered to serving in some form of church-related ministry and arrived on our doorstep—in person or virtually. For many years, I had the privilege of teaching an online intervention in which every student wrote and shared an autobiography. While reading those papers, I unknowingly began to understand the effects of trauma. Only later would I realize what had caused some to fail in their pursuit of full-time Christian ministry.

Many of these students received salvation but seldom accessed professional healing for the effects of their trauma. Knowing what I do now about the ACE research, I imagine many scores were in the 5–10 range. These students were working hard to order their outside world and the church provided structure. They found sincere purpose in submitting to what they believed God desired for them, but surrendering to service without healing can be a path fraught with landmines for those who have experienced trauma. Being placed in leadership too soon beckons them to live an outward life that denies the turmoil within. It was difficult to watch students fail. The failure was sometimes catastrophic.

Utilizing healing as the foundation for ministry preparation seems imperative considering the statistics of depression, suicide, moral failures, and resignations among ministry professionals.[122] Is this trauma related? If one in four adults has a history of sexual abuse, that means twenty-five out of a hundred of those who serve in ministry have this as part of their story, and it's probably higher. This one statistic does not touch the many other forms of trauma.

Previously, we discussed the great cost of not personally doing the work of healing before we lead. Consider how the effects of Evan's childhood experiences caused him to fail so dramatically. Sadly, it is not an unusual tale; I imagine every reader knows a similar story. The time when intervention could have prevented tragedy would have been during his ministry training. There is often a misconception that a call to ministry comes with the necessary spirituality to grow sufficiently during the preparation process. Once again, the problem is not spiritual.

CHILDHOOD DEVELOPMENT IN MINISTRY PREPARATION

One of the courses I taught at Bible colleges was child development. I spent many years begging pastoral majors to take the class as an elective. It was one of my least-successful campaigns. Most would say, "I took psychology." It was impossible to convince them that one psychology class on lifespan development was not enough. Yet when I did, they all thanked me.

One said, "My advisor put this on my schedule. It was the only elective that fit. I was irritated and skeptical, but it may be the most important class I have taken."

Even before understanding the effects of trauma, I knew that the role attachment relationships played in children's development was not given the attention it deserved. In fact, I didn't give it enough emphasis! Now I better understand how our earliest attachment relationships set the foundation for resilience—the ability to recover from adversity.

The natural, healthy progression of development that begins with a secure attachment to a caregiver is a key factor in helping people to arrive in the adult world with the necessary skills to have relationships with others and God. Without these skills, most require help to remain afloat—or they feel the need to pretend they are swimming when they are only treading water. I lived in a grown-up spiritual world that forced me to display outward spirituality. Without healing, my spiritual life depended on imitation (treading water).

> When the honeymoon phase of ministry ends, treading water becomes harder and many who enter ministry never experience the joy of swimming.

When the honeymoon phase of ministry ends, treading water becomes harder and many who enter ministry never experience the joy of swimming. They force themselves to apply spiritual practices and begin serving from a sincere but empty well. Only five years out of college, one very successful young pastor left ministry stating, "It wasn't fun anymore." Leaders scoffed at that as an excuse, but it probably was the most honest explanation anyone has ever given. Treading water was too difficult.

Many leaders, like me, serve with the coping strategies they used to survive during childhood. These strategies served them well as children but not so well as adults. Living as an adult who missed developmental building blocks feels like being thrown into the waters of life without any swimming lessons. I believe many ministry leaders who appear completely competent are secretly struggling, unaware that they missed foundational attachment-related building blocks. It probably feels like a lack of faith, but it isn't. They did not receive the relational care as children that are necessary for being resilient in ministry.

It is the attachment relationship that provides what psychologist Lev Vygotsky calls "scaffolding." Scaffolding involves completing small manageable steps in collaboration with a caregiver, instructor, or mentor. This process involves baby steps that help learners connect what they already understand and what they are working to understand with the help of someone who has walked ahead of them. This needs to be replicated at the adult level for those who have experienced childhood neglect or trauma. They may be completely unaware, as I was, that their survival strategies are not healthy coping strategies. Survival is not resilience.

THE NEED FOR TRAUMA-RESPONSIVE MENTORING

Many who would benefit from healing are competent water-treaders. They are so competent, in fact, that most believe they are swimming. They have figured out how to say, do, and feel all the right things. Survivors are experts at seeming competent. They can also be extremely repentant, self-loathing, for previous moral failures, which is seen as spiritual. Though they might long for mentoring, consciously or unconsciously, they are unlikely to ask. Leadership often assumes they are fine, as in the case of Nathan. Thus, they devote their efforts to mentoring the less competent. None would think the water-treaders need mentoring until it is too late.

> Many who would benefit from healing are competent water-treaders. They are so competent, in fact, that most believe they are swimming. They have figured out how to say, do, and feel all the right things. Survivors are experts at seeming competent.

How could ministry preparation leaders possibly recognize the very competent water-treaders? By asking about their childhood experiences and then listening very carefully. Water-treaders often cannot tell a coherent narrative of their childhood that includes both adverse and positive experiences. If they mention adversity, it is usually with a "but I turned out okay" deflection. Ministry preparation leaders must become skilled at listening to narratives, a skill that therapists have fine-tuned. The intent is not to probe. The intent is to sense the almost-silent cries for help and slowly walk them through the process of accepting the need for professional help.

As mentioned before, in my experience, there is little emphasis on healing in ministry preparation programs. Those who missed these building blocks are at risk for failing those they serve who are most vulnerable. Ministry preparation must involve mentoring relationships that go beyond spiritual guidance. Not addressing childhood trauma, neglect, or adversity leads those being mentored to leave the past behind. In the case of trauma, it is never left behind until resolved.

How often does trauma-responsive mentoring take place before becoming a guide for others? I listen to many spiritual leaders discuss their ministries, and it is rare when they do not mention a mentor. Everyone seems to understand the importance of mentors, but many cannot access the help a mentor could provide. Few are as bold as the student who approached me after class one evening and said, "The professor for my spiritual development course said that we should ask someone to be our mentor. Would you be my mentor?" I admired her courage and agreed. Would she have dared approach me if the assignment hadn't given her permission to do so? Probably not.

THE ONGOING NEED FOR HEALING ACCOUNTABILITY

Despite the precautions, who better to lead the wounded on paths to healing than one who has done the work themselves? As Henri Nouwen stated in *The Wounded Healer: Ministry in Contemporary Society*, "The great illusion of leadership is to think that man can be led out of the desert by someone who has never been there."[123] When we have walked through the desert, we can lead others. This doesn't mean that everyone who leads must have healed from severe trauma; it does mean that everyone who leads must have been willing to heal from any experiences that haunt them. Denial claims we came through childhood unscathed.

The spiritual practice of serving demands healing. Throughout my career, I often suggested that others access therapy. This was true even before I chose to go myself. The irony of this does not escape me. Now I realize that I may have prevented others from a deeper level of healing by continuing to support them as they declined to access therapy. It is easy to become the means of survival when the true path to thriving is beyond what we are qualified to do. I am thankful my therapist helped me to establish boundaries before launching myself back into service.

This then led me to consider how many pastors recommend therapy for others without ever having gone themselves. I hardly ever go to a restaurant that hasn't been recommended by a friend or been reviewed online. A doctor who has never been a patient will lack compassion. Those who have done the work are certainly at an advantage.

Recently a pastor whose wife was in therapy for PTSD asked me, "Do you think I should go to therapy too?" If anyone is living with someone suffering the effects of trauma, the answer is yes! That conversation reminded me of the common concern that therapy breaks up marriages. In a sense, this is often true. Any situation in which one partner experiences growth while the other does not has this potential. It is also true of education. Shared experience is always a plus for relationships.

Leaders who do not take time and effort to heal will end up in situations where they are helping others while still in the desert. Without enough water, they both become too dehydrated to survive. Nouwen addressed this by saying, "Who can listen to a story of loneliness and despair without taking the risk of experiencing similar pains in his own heart and even losing his precious peace of mind? In short: 'Who can take away suffering without entering it?'"[124] Professional counselors and therapists know this danger and are taught to set boundaries and remain accountable to mentors or colleagues.

Leaders who do not take time and effort to heal will end up in situations where they are helping others while still in the desert. Without enough water, they both become too dehydrated to survive.

Even when it feels as if healing is finished, and everyone wants to be done, there are usually new layers. Reaching plateaus is part of the process. Every time I ended therapy, my therapist told me, "You know you can call if you need help." This was easier said than done, but it a was helpful reminder that healing is a continual process. Service depends on being able to set pride aside and ask for help.

Part of my self-care is a monthly accountability appointment with my current therapist. In this safe space, there are often emotional needs that surface. Even when the issue seems to be at the adult level, childhood trauma is always a contributing factor. These needs are easily ignored without some form of accountability. While accountability can take many forms, for those who have experienced childhood trauma, my emphasis is on professional trauma-based therapy. It is a cautionary tale for all who serve without having healed.

HOW CAN LEADERS BE SUPPORTED?

Faith communities sometimes provide too much grace to leaders without requiring accountability. In other situations, no grace is given to leaders who struggle. There seems to be no way to predict this. Grave sins can be swept under the carpet while minor misjudgments, real or perceived, result in modern-day tar and feathering. These reactions are true from both leadership and laypeople. It is much like the lives of children who live with unpredictable parents. It is the perfect storm for chronic stress.

The situation for those who serve in supporting roles as assistant pastors is even more complicated. A young man who had survived several difficult ministry situations said, "The church needs a human resources department. There is no place for young staff members to voice concerns." Most who leave ministry preparation programs accept these types of positions. One of the most frustrating experiences of my career was to work with a student for four years, see tremendous growth and growing excitement to serve, only to be destroyed in their first ministry position. We could not prepare them for what might happen if they made a rookie mistake. For many, there is no coming back from it.

Why does this happen? Why are more and more leaving the ministry? How can we better prepare those who enter ministry? How can leaders thrive in churches that provide heavy doses of chronic stress? And why are our churches dissolving into chaotic conflicts? Trauma. We are sending the wounded out to care for the wounded without ever acknowledging that the underlying problems require more than salvation.

When I was speaking on a panel for teen mental health, one of the other panelists who addresses trauma within policework talked about the necessity of consistently accessing therapy to process her work-related trauma. When mentoring, it is essential to understand the effects of trauma on those we serve and encourage seeking professional help. It is also important to begin this access during ministry preparation. Make going to therapy the norm.

When I suggest seeking therapy, most in ministry will immediately assume that the therapy should involve spiritual mentoring. I think this is an important part of mentoring, not necessarily therapy. Hear me out on this one! Two years ago, I chose to find a new therapist after moving. My work was too important to not do this. Because I was on Medicare, it was impossible to control the process of assigning me to a therapist. The new therapist, while not opposed to my spiritual path, did not affirm my spiritual answers as to why I was choosing to address the church. When I gave spiritual answers, I realized how flat they felt—almost like a betrayal to my own story. This counterbalance provided the space to wrestle. Every ministry leader needs a place to *not* be spiritual.

It is far too common to hear of faith leaders whose lives end by suicide. In any tragedy my immediate thought is, "What happened to them as children?" When the tragedy is a school shooting, the details of the shooter's childhood quickly surface. It is interesting that when it is a faith leader who fails, there is often little to no mention of childhood experiences.

Many unhealed leaders are hiding the inner turmoil of childhood trauma. I know this is true; I was one of them. If healing had been encouraged, it would have helped me walk into therapy much sooner in my life, even though the help might not have been trauma based. Our current and future leaders need permission to say when they are not okay and seek professional trauma-based help.

Every church member and leader would benefit from sitting on a therapist's couch and taking an honest look at their childhood. It does not have to be horrific abuse to unconsciously affect us. Not having childhood needs met is enough. Incorrectly interpreting a childhood event and internalizing the wrong message is enough. Being bullied as a child is enough. Healing is the path to spiritual growth, and there is much at stake when those who have not healed harm those who desperately need someone to care about them. How much better to receive this help as part of their preparation.

FINAL THOUGHTS

According to the Barna Group report *Trauma in America* (completed before the pandemic), when pastors were "specifically asked how well their education or training prepared them to minister to people who have experienced a traumatic event, most chose 'somewhat well' (55%). Only ten percent chose 'very well.' A full one-third thinks their training did not leave them better equipped for trauma care (34% 'not too well' or 'not well at all')."[125] The confidence level for the complicated effects of childhood trauma would be even lower if the depth of necessary knowledge were recognized.

How would the inclusion of trauma-responsive principles, healing in ministry preparation, and professional development opportunities build resilience in those serving in ministry? One difference would be the ability to recognize the effects of trauma in others. When this happens, judgment can be set aside, and it is not necessary to be defensive.

Without healing, it is challenging to be present in the emotions of others without struggling with our own. When the emotions of others make us uncomfortable, we can often feel the need to fix them. We unconsciously seek for them to be better so we can feel better. In reality, no one feels better, neither the fixer nor the fixee. It is an easy trap to fall into even with the purest desire to serve others. This distinction between service and fixing is essential to trauma-responsive ministry preparation. The focus on spiritual leading can blind us to the root cause of the inner turmoil of others. Spirituality becomes the fix for a spiritual problem that doesn't even exist in the individual who is longing for a closer relationship with God.

The inclusion of trauma-responsive principles would also provide the understanding that is necessary to distinguish the difference between the effects of trauma and spiritual conviction. Sermon preparation would expand to encompass more root causes for why humans struggle other than the sin narrative. Teachings on salvation would include an understanding of the importance of healing from traumatic experiences. Healing was always a focus of the ministry of Jesus. In addition, healing would not always be addressed in the language of repentance or forgiveness.

On a personal level, I believe ministry preparation programs addressing childhood experiences as a contributing factor for moral failure could have had the potential to prevent the trauma I experienced when seeking spiritual help for my inner turmoil. These programs might have included courses that studied the neuroscience of trauma and neglect, required at least ten therapy sessions, and taught trauma-sensitive aspects of spiritual practices. I speak for all those who identify with the #ChurchToo movement. With all my being, I believe we can do a better job preparing people for ministry and then supporting them in developing the necessary self-care skills for healthy living and successful ministry.

Chapter 17: Leadership Reflection Questions

- How well did your ministerial training prepare you to reflect on your own trauma history or that of those in your ministry? Was the need to access professional assistance for healing emphasized in your preparation?

- Have you been offered or accessed trauma-informed professional development? If so, in what ways has that enabled you to minister more effectively?

- Have you seen examples of moral failure that you now understand as the result of the individual's trauma history? Does this help you to have increased compassion for yourself and others?

- How might an understanding of the effects of trauma have better prepared you for the challenges of ministry, specifically in interactions or conflicts with congregants? Can you reflect on times when your own story got tangled up in the interaction?

How Can We Recognize Trauma-Responsive Spiritual Practices?

s it possible that those we serve in ministry are involved in spiritual practices that don't fit the traditional definitions we have come to accept? If I were asked if I read my Bible on a daily basis, I would have had to answer no. This feels shameful. Instead, suppose I say that while writing, I continually reflect on the meanings of verses, complete in-depth word studies, and enjoy researching historical backgrounds. Then I feel deeply grateful for how God has enabled me to find unique methods to accomplish the purposes of the spiritual practices.

Late in my teaching career, I became less prescriptive in how adult students met the course objectives. Instead of writing a paper, they could prepare a slideshow, complete a real-life project, take a test, and so on. I discovered many hidden talents when I allowed them to express what they learned in more creative ways. Granted, there was a foundational level of knowledge they had to accomplish before being creative, but they often already knew the modes in which they learned best. My job usually involved helping them believe in their ideas; they were so accustomed to prescriptive teaching. Spiritual practices have often also been prescriptive.

CREATIVELY PARTICIPATING IN SPIRITUAL PRACTICES

As a child, I enjoyed listening to my father lead the responsive congregational readings located in the hymnal. His deep voice and the congregational response provided a sense of belonging as I was learning to read along. As an adult, I continued to write responsive readings and prayers. (See Appendix 1 for a published congregational prayer for the brokenhearted.) If I had understood this was a spiritual practice of equal value for the purpose of drawing closer to God, it would have brought great comfort in my spiritual life.

My writing was the gift I was given to fulfill the purpose of drawing closer to God. What a loss that this was not recognized as an amazing example of what spiritual practices are meant to be. To realize that Richard Foster intended this all along was transformative. The wide range of practices included in *Celebration of Discipline* boggles my mind. How did so many embrace the book and then settle for prescriptive guidelines?

God created us in his creative image and delights in our imaginative responses to him. Using my imagination, I expanded upon several of Foster's suggestions for spiritual practices with a trauma-responsive lens. Two of these, meditation and worship, are included in Appendices 3 and 4, respectively.

Reframing fasting and solitude in trauma-responsive modes were probably the most challenging. After all, fasting is fasting and solitude is solitude. Or are they? And then my tumble into simplicity demonstrated how every aspect of our lives can fulfill the purpose of the spiritual practices. The following twists on traditional practices resulted from following God down completely unexpected paths.

After their completion, it was so much easier to see God coloring outside the lines in leading others down their own unexpected paths.

TRAUMA-RESPONSIVE FASTING

Fasting is one way emotionally healthy people can release control. But for the exhausted adult who experienced childhood trauma, it can become another forced act of "doing." What is needed is a spiritual and emotional fast *from* doing. It would have been easy after the Damascus Road experience for Paul to dive into doing. That is not what God had in mind. Paul needed to heal by not doing. He went from being the man in charge to being in charge of nothing. He went on an involuntary doing fast that helped him release his control over his life.

Going on a doing fast is part of the journey of healing. For many, like me, it is the most difficult part. Being busy is a survival skill.

Jennie had been working hard to heal and reached out to me for help. When I asked her how she was doing, she said, "I guess I'm fine. I just can't do anything."

> Fasting is one way emotionally healthy people can release control. But for the exhausted adult who experienced childhood trauma, it can become another forced act of "doing." What is needed is a spiritual and emotional fast *from* doing.

I groaned empathetically. "How does it feel when you try to get up and do something?"

"Horrible. I'm sure I'll have another panic attack."

Remembering many similar days, I said, "That's a difficult place to be. It won't last forever."

"Are you sure?" Jennie asked.

"Yes, the crucial thing right now is to rest; your body needs rest. Trying to make yourself do things is not a good plan, especially now."

Not long after this conversation with Jennie, another of my friends messaged me. She was progressing with her healing but felt

211

stuck—so stuck that all she wanted to do was lie in bed. I understood this was a serious problem because she was committed in many areas of her life. This phase of healing was extremely inconvenient for her.

"What do I need to do?" she asked.

"Repeat that question for me," I said.

She complied and then I asked, "What was the last word in the question?"

"Um, do?"

"Yes," I answered. "In fact, the word *do* was in the sentence twice. You are healing all the ways you have controlled yourself over the years and now your body has decided that doing is not an option. Your body is telling you to rest." She needed a fast from doing.

For months and months, like my friend, anytime I tried to reassert that crazy trauma-based control, it led to a collapse. It is important to understand that those who have experienced trauma need to avoid trying to heal by controlling themselves. The urge to be "normal" and get back to their life is strong. Some of it must happen out of necessity but with gentleness and self-compassion. The fast from doing is like a tortoise not a hare. They need others to understand this and support them. We have a hard time believing Jesus actually meant to rest our bodies when he said, "Come to me, all you who are weary and burdened, and I will give you rest."[126]

For those who have lived by control, it can be frightening when a doing fast removes the option of forcing ourselves into action. It feels like life is over. *Titration* is the answer—baby steps. Annie Wright, a therapist and blogger, wrote about titrating your experience like a toddler begins to explore the world. She stated, "When we titrate our experience, we take action in small, monitored ways to adjust the amount of stimulation we introduce to our nervous system, proceeding in manageable ways to help keep ourselves in a state of emotional safety and equilibrium."[127]

What was my advice to both of my friends? Think of this process as a spiritual practice. Listen to your body. Figure out how to do essentials and go on a doing fast with the nonessentials. Also, try not to panic. You can slowly return to life through titration. Fasting from doing can ultimately bring us to a place where our choices are no longer driven by the unconscious drives created by trauma. In their place, we can trust God to lead us.

TRAUMA-RESPONSIVE SOLITUDE THROUGH REPETITION

Many spiritual practices require solitude and for those impacted by trauma, solitude requires structure. During the healing process, structured and repetitive practices hold the potential for changing the wiring in our brains. The structured routines we build in our lives are healthy and give us a feeling of control over something, as long as they do not become another form of trying harder. Structured repetitions also build new pathways in the brain. If others said you were worthless again and again when you were a child—and you may have told yourself the same—it will take countless affirmations to build new neural pathways. Repeated affirmations are supported by the following evidence from brain research:

> Scientists aren't yet sure which time intervals supply all the magic. But taken together, the relationship between repetition and memory is clear. Deliberately re-expose yourself to information if you want to retrieve it later. Deliberately re-expose yourself to information more elaborately if you want to remember more of the details. Deliberately re-expose yourself to the information more elaborately and in fixed space intervals if you want the retrieval to be as vivid as possible.[128]

Because false narratives have such power over us in silence and solitude, it is necessary to remind ourselves of the ways God affirms us as created beings. In addition, the unconscious patterns developed because of trauma often feel like conscious thoughts or choices, or even worse, God condemning us. While healing, we need to focus on the truth of God's love. Everything else will eventually get sorted out.

I hesitate to suggest scripture as the source of affirmation since it has been part of the religious trauma many have experienced. There are plenty of verses that feel defeating to those who are healing and working to separate what

> While healing, we need to focus on the truth of God's love. Everything else will eventually get sorted out.

was a deliberate choice from what was the effects of trauma. Some may have erroneously believed the abuse to be their fault and internalized the condemnation from those verses.

I am also aware it might seem like a "be positive" mantra that results in spiritual bypassing. How tragic that our source of encouragement—God's word—has so often been distorted and used to control others. Therefore, to reclaim the goodness God intended, I suggest starting with these affirmations of God's love:

- "'Though the mountains be shaken and the hills be removed, yet my unfailing love for you will not be shaken nor my covenant of peace be removed,' says the Lord, who has compassion on you." Isaiah 54:10 (NIV).
- "And hope does not put us to shame, because God's love has been poured out into our hearts through the Holy Spirit, who has been given to us." Romans 5:5 (NIV).
- "No, in all these things we are more than conquerors through him who loved us. For I am convinced that neither death nor life, neither angels nor demons, neither the present nor the future, nor any powers, neither height nor depth, nor anything else in all creation, will be able to separate us from the love of God that is in Christ Jesus our Lord." Romans 8:37–39 (NIV).

Finally, the only path to becoming comfortable in solitude—a state which is not a form of *dissociative escape*, going off into a space in your mind that disconnects you from reality—is to be comfortable with God and yourself. This requires building new neural pathways—best built through solitude and repetitive affirmations. It is often hard for ministry leaders to understand what baby steps actually look like for those who have been traumatized to develop a trauma-responsive spiritual practice that is not dependent on either control or ignoring the sensations in their bodies. (An example of this type of repetitive practice can be found in Appendix 5.)

TRAUMA-RESPONSIVE SIMPLICITY

While I was writing about the Discipline of simplicity, God helped me to understand that the story I relate next was a deeply spiritual process. It is a reminder to me that God wrings good from our most difficult experiences and coming to terms with the pain is a spiritual practice. There is not an area of our lives that cannot become part of our spiritual practice and healing.

At the end of my first year of healing, simplicity came to me in ways I did not choose. We were renting a five-bedroom condo to care for my elderly father in his final years, and after four years, he decided to move into a nursing home because of his increasing need for medical care. We now had no reason to stay in the condo and our lease was up. In a few weeks, I would be retiring, a decision precipitated by my mental health collapse that I was carefully hiding. Looking around the condo, I was overwhelmed by the massive accumulation of possessions that now needed liquidating.

I invited my daughter and several younger friends to come and tag anything they might want. I enjoyed handing them Post-It note pads and sending them into the condo. Then I made lists and started delivering treasures. I sent essential—or so I thought—items with my daughter who was moving out of state, gave heirloom pieces to relatives, and made endless trips to donation centers. We still filled a storage unit.

After helping my daughter move, it was time to return to Colorado where my husband was still working and living with a friend. When I moved in, we laughed because it felt like an episode of *Friends*. It was temporary; we had no long-term plan. This experience was the closest I ever came to homelessness—with a storage unit. I was a scrappy survivor who generally had a plan of action. This was terrifying! Yet I was learning both the meaning and freedom of simplicity.

The following summarizes Foster's explanation of three attitudes for the Discipline of simplicity:

- "To receive what we have as a gift from God."
- "To know that it is God's business, and not ours, to care for what we have."
- "To have our goods available to others."[129]

These three points are a tall order for someone who since childhood desperately needed to feel in control. Just when things felt completely overwhelming, we learned we only had nine days left in our friend's apartment. He had decided to not renew his lease. Our days continued counting down. We felt no peace about signing a lease since our eventual goal was to relocate near our daughter, but we could not leave my dad in the nursing home and move away. We had no idea why we needed much of what was in storage, so we started posting and selling again.

Marie Kondo's concept of giving gratitude to the objects that have brought us joy before releasing them has helped me to accept simplicity.[130] Two years later, when we moved with only two carloads of possessions, there were many ceremonies as I released more of my possessions. Sometimes I took pictures and discarded the items that would hold no value for others. Sometimes I donated or gifted items. What I kept would probably make little sense to others. My treasures are symbolic of the ways that God has loved me over the years—through friend's gifts and treasures from thrift stores, flea markets, or garage sales.

Self-compassion allows me to honor how collecting possessions helped me to survive. Now when I shop, it is far more intentional—sometimes for joy, sometimes for utility. My brain has built an entirely different freeway for shopping; one that is not based on survival and validation.

A TRAUMA-RESPONSIVE PATH TO SERVICE

Amy and I met through a mutual friend. She had read *Brave*, and during a visit to her area, we were able to meet in person. We sat on my friend's screened-in porch as she shared her story of childhood and young adult trauma.

What impressed me about Amy was both her desire to follow God and her determination to stand strong against the rule book kind of faith that had permeated her childhood. She was beginning to recognize the religious trauma in her past and was working hard to heal.

In the recent Religious Trauma Sociological Study, twenty-five to twenty-eight percent of the surveyed population identified themselves as experiencing some form of adverse religious experience (ARE) or religious trauma (RT).[131]

The results of the survey echoed the effects of Amy's story of trauma within the church and also confirmed that she, like many others, was determined to retain her faith. "Among participants who reported adverse religious experiences, sixty-six percent who tried prayer as a form of coping with ARE said it was helpful. It may seem unexpected that religious trauma victims would find further engagement in faith to be productive. This may suggest that people still find comfort and healing in their faith and spirituality despite negative experiences with religious people and/or institutions." Most of those who have experienced trauma in the church and leave are not giving up on their faith, simply traditional religious practices.

Amy realized that her love for art was the avenue that would bring her both healing and spiritual growth. With the help of art therapy and supportive mentors, she began to transform her life. One day, I received an invitation to her online ordination service. This surprised me since she had not been part of a denomination that ordained women. When I reached out to learn more, I was even more surprised to hear her goal for pursuing ordination. "I am looking toward becoming an art chaplain at the psychiatric unit at our hospital and in other local mental health places." I could not have imagined a better blending of her talents and graduate work in ministry. While this particular goal is still a future dream, she is currently beginning a Healing Art Studio in a local community center. She is also on call with various mental health nonprofit organizations to assist with crisis care.

There was very little in Amy's path of healing that fit the traditional forms of spiritual practices. I watched as some publicly criticized her choices and stepped in to support her. I knew that God's guidance was written throughout her story. God always colors outside the lines when helping those impacted by trauma heal and find their path to service.

FINAL THOUGHTS

For those who have suffered from the effects of trauma, it is essential to encourage all the possible forms of spiritual practices that fulfill the purpose of helping them draw closer to God. Nathan never felt like God communed with him in the ways this happened for me. One day he said, "Well, I know God did that." This was literally the first time I had ever heard words like that come from his mouth in all the long years of our friendship.

"What did you say?" I asked. And he repeated it.

Careful to not overwhelm him with my excitement, I realized two things. The first was how long this had taken, the second was how easily this monumental spiritual moment could have been overlooked. When we as ministry leaders are only looking for the obvious traditional forms of spiritual growth, we miss the miracles of baby steps like Nathan's statement. God not only colors outside of the lines for those who have suffered greatly, but the creator of the universe is also far more patient than we can imagine and never misses the miracle of a small moment of faith.

Chapter 18: Leadership Reflection Questions

- As you read the chapter, did you identify non-traditional forms of spiritual practices that you or others have incorporated without considering them as fulfilling the purpose of drawing you closer to God?

- How can a "doing fast" give those in the process of healing from trauma confidence in their desire to grow closer to God? What have your thoughts been concerning those who suddenly resign from ministries they have previously been devoted to doing? How can understanding the healing process help you to minister more effectively when this happens?

- The effects of trauma cause so many spiritual practices to be almost inaccessible. Are the small baby steps involved in the repetition practice (see Appendix 5) surprising? How can you help those who struggle to accomplish even the smallest baby steps to feel successful?

- Why is self-compassion so essential to the spiritual practice of simplicity (and other practices)?

- In what way is it possible to honor the ways that God colors outside of the lines in the lives of those who have experienced the worst that life can offer?

How Can We Become Trauma Responsive in Our Churches?

To understand the importance of a trauma-responsive approach to "doing church," we need to go to a rat park. In his groundbreaking research study, American psychologist Dr. Bruce Alexander realized that rats placed in isolated cages without any stimulation chose to drink morphine-laced water over plain water to the point of dying from overdose. When the rats were placed in what came to be known as the rat park with other rats, with room to run and explore, they chose to drink plain water. It was a paradigm-shifting study in the treatment of addiction. Addicts treated in centers and sent back out into the world without necessary supports were very likely to return to the coping strategies that soothed them.[132]

Similarly, those who have suffered trauma cannot thrive after "being saved" without being surrounded by a community that is rich with relationships. This includes a church body that accepts their story, does not assume sin as the root cause of their struggle, and provides relational experiences that begin to rebuild decimated foundational building blocks of trust. To do this, the church will need to take the propensity to judge, based on the sin narrative, and bury it in the deepest sea. All behavior is rooted in prior experiences and the body's adaptive stress responses, both healthy and unhealthy.

WHAT DOES THE RAT PARK TEACH US?

How would a trauma-responsive church community be like the rat park? The trauma-responsive goal for churches is to meet others at their point of need and support them as God leads them in healing and spiritual growth. The challenge is to recognize and focus on their strengths. If someone who was traumatized as a child desires faith, this is strength. Establishing the following paradigm-shifting principles of trauma-responsive ministry will go a long way in building communities in which it is safe to explore what it means to heal and draw closer to God.

PRINCIPLE #1: TRAUMA-RESPONSIVE MINISTRY PLACES RELATIONSHIPS FIRST

Jesus always put relationship before repentance when interacting with the wounded and suffering. We should follow this example. While attending more fundamentalist churches, I was taught that if I did not explain the plan of salvation to someone and they died without Jesus, I was responsible for them going to hell. This one teaching, in my mind, caused more damage to what the church was called to be for our hurting world than any other. If I flew on a plane next to someone, I felt compelled to witness. What if the plane crashed? The relationship with that person

> Jesus always put relationship before repentance when interacting with the wounded and suffering.

was my very last concern. I really had no interest in their life, family, hopes, dreams, or pain. This was so far from the example that Jesus set for us.

Now I understand that the only way to help people to engage with Jesus is to show them my own faith and how that faith has made a difference in my life. Talking about how my faith and healing intersected is completely comfortable and natural as I listen to their stories and build relationships. I am eager to return to planes again with expectations for divine meetings.

I can offer trauma-responsive relational care, but where do I tell them to go to find the same relationship in their community? What would I tell them to look for? How would that place feel? Would their story be safe there, or would assumptions be made in a call for repentance? Would the sin narrative overshadow God's desire for healing? Would the effects of trauma on their life be understood as that and not as a spiritual problem? Would the focus be on relationship and not behavior? In other words, can they find a faith community that is trauma informed, sensitive, and responsive? And how will that feel when they arrive?

The answers to these questions could be defined as "spiritual co-regulation." Those who know that peace that originates in nurturing relationships can become the spiritual parents of those who long for it. It comes through unconditional relationships. I do not believe I would have ever experienced this without the co-regulation of a therapist who understood my needs—and helped me to learn to identify them myself.

It is tragic when those who most need to rebuild the essential building block of co-regulation are met with judgment. Just like a child, it will take many relational interactions to repair the wounds and build the missing skills of self-regulation. As we demonstrate how to pause before reacting to their behaviors or protective strategies, they are provided the model that was not present for them. It isn't a strategy. It is a relationship—one that usually requires a support village. And as co-regulation grows, trust in others and God grows organically.

Just as it is not up to a child to learn self-regulation on their own, it is not up to those who have been traumatized or those new to the faith to learn self-regulation on their own. When their misjudgments or mistakes are judged, the inner turmoil is like that of a child with an abusive parent. Generational trauma informs us that the reaction by that parent is likely a result of their unresolved trauma. Everyone must do the work if we are to help one another co-regulate within spiritual communities.

Many of those who helped me through co-regulation and those who I have helped are now part of my village of spiritual co-regulators. Together, we are working through the difficult healing processes that draw us closer to God and each other. It is truly a beautiful image of what the body of Christ should be. Not just "going to church together" but living life together—all of life: the doubts, the pain, the failures, the messiness. So very different from when I sat alone in the pew, hiding my traumatic stories and pain. Spiritual co-regulation is how we bring healing to the trauma within those who sit in the pews.

PRINCIPLE #2: TRAUMA-RESPONSIVE MINISTRY UNCONDITIONALLY RECEIVES STORIES

Can you listen—hold space—for others without judging their actions or sharing spiritual advice? The litmus test for trauma-responsive faith communities is how leaders and laypeople respond to the vulnerable sharing of trauma. While everyone wrestles with listening without offering advice, it adds a layer of spiritual shaming when that advice is spiritual. How could we help those who have been impacted by trauma feel safe sharing their stories? What a difference the following types of responses would make as they build trust and open the door to relation-based, trauma-sensitive spiritual guidance in future conversations:

- Thank you for telling me; that took a lot of courage.
- I am so sorry this happened to you.
- That was not your fault; you did nothing to deserve this.
- You have overcome a lot in your life!
- That is hard; how can I help you?
- What you are feeling is a normal response to trauma.
- I want you to know you are not alone; I am here for you.

Then, what happens after the sharing? When I first shared my story with others, I sometimes felt affirmed by their responses, but when alone, the old messages of shame would surface, telling me it was a mistake to share and that the person was just being nice, and so on. The greatest gift was when I was contacted the next day and thanked again for trusting them with my story. Stories are sacred sharings, and the sharing requires many affirmations.

Once you hold that sacred story, your next step is to support the brave soul who shared it. Sometimes, as mentioned before, this requires a village. What better village than a trauma-responsive church? Support can take many forms, such as encouraging them to seek professional help or providing resources. To be trauma responsive, it is necessary to focus on growth and not behavior. It is a long journey of healing before new neural pathways are built. Off-roading is always a possibility. Modeling compassion allows self-compassion to grow.

PRINCIPLE #3: TRAUMA-RESPONSIVE MINISTRY TEACHES ABOUT TRAUMA

For an entire faith community to become trauma responsive, leaders must be trauma informed and provide opportunities for church members to also explore the effects of trauma. Listening to one webinar on trauma does not accomplish this—neither does reading this book, though the reflections on spiritual practices through a trauma-sensitive lens are a great beginning. Following up with the resources listed in Appendix 6 is an important next step.

I am aware that leaders want strategies. When I'm speaking to teachers, strategies are at the top of their request list. Everyone who sees the effects of trauma wants to know what to do. While I have provided some general directions, these will only be as effective as the degree to which the leader implementing them has shifted

> For an entire faith community to become trauma responsive, leaders must be trauma informed and provide opportunities for church members to also explore the effects of trauma. Listening to one webinar on trauma does not accomplish this—neither does reading this book, though the reflections on spiritual practices through a trauma-sensitive lens are a great beginning.

from judgment to informed compassion. This is not easily accomplished because it requires stepping away from the sin narrative.

During a conversation about trauma, a longtime friend, who at the time was the pastor of a large thriving church, suddenly became silent. Then he asked, "Are you saying that people are not always in control of their behavior?"

"That is really the question, isn't it?" I countered. "As long as you believe they are, the discussion is about sin and not trauma."

He said that he would have to think about that. I understood.

I could have also added, "It is also about controlling behaviors and not healing the source of the pain that causes the behavior."

The following quote attributed to Desmond Tutu says it best: "There comes a point where we need to stop just pulling people out of the river. We need to go upstream and find out why they're falling in." A trauma-responsive church works together to help the traumatized to heal the pain at its source. They also support families and communities in ways that can greatly reduce the traumatic experiences of children.

PRINCIPLE #4: TRAUMA-RESPONSIVE MINISTRY HONORS HEALING

If the purpose of trauma-responsive faith communities is to carry out the mission of Jesus, then we must consider why Jesus came. If Jesus meant what he quoted from Isaiah about healing the broken-hearted, then it is possible that the church is defining its mission too narrowly by not looking more closely at the word "salvation." We have set up salvation in a way that feels incongruous to the healing of trauma. Ben Cremer, pastor of Cathedral of the Rockies-Amity Campus in Boise, Idaho, has provided an explanation of salvation that gives the importance of healing clarity:

> The Greek words we often translate as *salvation* in the Bible are *sózó* and *sótéria*. These are the same words we commonly translate as *healing*. So, when we read that Jesus healed someone and then we read He 'saved' someone, it's the same Greek word. Salvation is healing.
>
> Even the etymology of our English word salvation comes from the Latin word *salve*, as in the ointment we put on burn wounds. So, this idea that Christ's salvation is only spiritual, not physical, only personal, not systematic, is a false compartmentalization. It's not either/or, it's both/and.
>
> When Jesus healed the leper, they were saved. They were restored not only physically, but they were able to re-enter their families, their culture, their religious practices that they were otherwise prevented from doing because of their illness. This physical healing also brought about emotional, spiritual, and relational healing as well.

227

How often we've used our own definitions of salvation as tools for controlling others. As if we are only concerned about eternity for their soul and not for their lives here and now. As if it is only about believing the right things, rather than pursuing healing for their lived reality. Conversely, how much damage we've caused by seeing the absence of desired healing as a lack of salvation or worse, defined an individual as undeserving of salvation.

What if we were as obsessed with finding out what is actually healing for others as we so often are with making sure others believe as we do? What if we pursued healing for our neighbors, really listened to what is hurting them, and work with them towards healing from what minimizes their humanity? Especially if that means we need healing ourselves in how we think about them! People need healing. The church needs healing. Nations need healing. We all need healing. To say that salvation is only for our soul is just too small for what Jesus had in mind. Jesus wants to save, to heal, all that we are. Mind, body, soul, and relationally, communally, economically, and structurally. Or, to quote John 3:16, he actually wants to save/heal the whole world! May we who follow Christ be about that same salvific and healing work."[133]

All throughout the gospels, Jesus stepped into the sometimes messy, often painful lives of the people he came to heal. There was not an aspect of the human experience that didn't apply. He accepted every story as important and understood its effect on the one who stood before him—and made healing a priority.

228

PRINCIPLE #5: TRAUMA-RESPONSIVE MINISTRY IS COMPASSION DRIVEN

Leading others to confessions that have the power to heal requires us to view the sacrifice Jesus made as "entering into" suffering. Foster said, "Jesus knew that by his vicarious suffering he could absorb all the evil of humanity and so heal it, forgive it, redeem it."[134]

Every survivor of relational trauma has a story about the evil of humanity. The story of how Jesus willingly suffered on their behalf, out of love, is the message they need. Foster illustrated a common error when describing the opposite perspective as follows: "People were so bad and so mean and God was so angry with them that he could not forgive them unless somebody big enough took the rap for the whole lot of them."[135]

In a similar vein, Thomas Jay Oord described this God as "Some bully in the sky,"[136] and offered views of God that will assist those who suffer in the process of healing. (See resources for constructing a trauma-sensitive view of God in Appendix 6.)

It is tragic when the abused believe they were so bad that God needed to kill his son to save them from eternal hell. Instead, Jesus came to walk among the wounded and deeply understood their suffering. Foster emphasized how Jesus refused the vinegar (painkiller) so he could "...be completely alert for this greatest work of redemption."[137] Jesus did not have to suffer the pain of the violence inflicted on him. Just as many suffered as innocent children, so did Jesus, without sin, enter into suffering and humiliation. This is the story those who have experienced trauma need to hear. The sin was not their own but instead perpetrated against them. Jesus understands relational betrayal.

When Jesus cries out, "My God, my God, why hast thou forsaken me?" the voices of millions of innocent children can be heard in this cry. It is exactly how each one felt: abandoned. God never abandoned them, but it most often feels that way. The cry of abandonment betrayal is always that of being forsaken, by both God and man.

When the apostle Paul said, "In the same way, the Spirit helps us in our weakness. We do not know what we ought to pray for, but the Spirit himself intercedes for us through wordless groans,"[138] he describes the groans of those who experience trauma and have no words, confession, to describe what happened. At all ages, the Broca, motor speech, area of the brain that controls language shuts down during traumatic events. We are literally scared speechless. The Spirit—the Comforter—fully understands this effect of trauma.

To not approach the death on the cross from this perspective robs the traumatized from knowing that God loved them enough to enter into their suffering. To be willing to feel the pain of relational betrayal and physical abuse that is at the core of the effects of trauma was the ultimate gift of love.

HOW CAN TRAUMA-RESPONSIVE CHURCHES REFRAME THE FUTURE OF THE CHURCH?

What did the church miss on the way to the world-changing events of 2020? The church missed ways that cumulative unhealed trauma would eventually rip at the very fabric of our nation and churches. We were all "doing church" while the ship headed for the proverbial iceberg of trauma that existed just below the surface. When the ship struck the collective trauma of the pandemic, leaders were oblivious to how the pandemic would expose the collective trauma of our nation and church.

A pastor friend was lamenting how attendance in his church—which really did do its best to emphasize relationships—had fallen away during the pandemic. I asked him why he thought that happened. His answer was that the third who left were not committed. I felt his pain and sense of loss and frustration. I had no desire to argue because the pandemic regulations did prevent many of the relational activities that had sustained church growth.

At the same time, I knew of many who felt relief in not forcing themselves into participating in traditional church activities. If possible, what would bring them back? Only relationships can do that. Statistics show that people are leaving the church but not their faith. Leaving is never easy for those who have been impacted by trauma. It is a choice that is not made lightly. For me, my entire life and identity revolved around the church and leaving was a gut-wrenching experience. Why was it necessary? Because the church lacked the five trauma-responsive principles which I proposed above. These would have been necessary to stay while healing.

Some have left because they are troubled by the actions of many ministry leaders during the pandemic—note, not all leaders—and are longing for authentic relationships that view the world through the lens of compassion and not division or judgment. While it seems discouraging, I believe God is rebuilding the church and using an understanding of trauma to help us once again be Jesus to the world.

My hope is that this discussion will help ministry leaders rethink those who leave. Many are looking for a place to celebrate a relationship with God that does not, and maybe never has, fit the rule book. Sometimes this is because they feel the need to leave their stories in the car when they go inside to worship. This is especially true if they have healed childhood trauma and no longer believe the shaming narratives that emphasized their sinfulness. Maybe it felt true when they were filled with self-loathing, but now they understand God delights in them and is proud of the work they did to heal. They often do not feel that their efforts are acknowledged, understood, or celebrated.

The church should be a place where people refuel for service and celebrate the ways that members are living out their faith. In the book *Religious Refugees*, Mark Gregory Karris stated, "People are looking for a holistic, real, and raw religious community-experience. They want to worship with every last bit of their wounded heart, fractured mind, divided soul, and lack of strength."[139] May our churches become places where we vulnerably walk alongside each other in the messy processes of life and healing. This would be the ultimate fulfillment of Jesus bringing heaven to earth.

Who are the future leaders who will move the church toward the next decade? I have been watching them find their voices in a world that is convulsing with trauma. Many of them have not had an easy path within the traditional leadership roles of the church. I am especially interested in those who have healed from the trauma of their childhoods and now exhibit the strengths of post-traumatic growth. When their trauma is religious, I am astounded and thankful that they still believe the church can make a difference.

Thinking back over Nathan's life, I believe there were times when his natural creativity found outlets in church and work. These moments were surprising and brief, extinguished almost immediately in a church and work world that lacked appreciation for how Nathan could have experienced healing and found a path to his own unique spiritual practices.

There is a kindred spirit between those who have once again found the joy lost in childhood. They possess the most stunning examples of childlike faith. They have often walked through hell to find it and can bring a richness to the church that cannot be obtained any other way.

FINAL THOUGHTS

I believe the next generation, with the understanding of the effects of trauma, can create churches where those who have been impacted by trauma can find safety and healing. As I came to the end of my months-long spiritual journey that included my reflections on *Celebration of Discipline*, I had many reasons to celebrate, and finishing the monumental undertaking was among them. At the top of the list was the hope I found that the church could become the compassionate village that would embrace healing alongside salvation.

I cannot imagine a more healing spiritual community than the one described in the concluding pages of *Celebration of Discipline*. It includes the types of experiences that rebuild the building blocks lost during traumatizing childhoods. Foster ends by saying, "Finally, an interesting characteristic of celebration is that it tends toward more celebration. Joy begets joy. Laughter begets laughter. It is one of those few things in life that we multiply by giving."[140] This describes the joy that is so elusive to those impacted by trauma. In trauma-responsive faith communities that value and embrace healing spiritual practices, more and more will come into joyful fellowship—and the joy will be multiplied. This is possible when we are able to respond in trauma-responsive ways to the most vulnerable among us. We can do better when we know better.

Chapter 19: Leadership Reflection Questions

- Why is the story of the rat park significant? How does it relate to the importance of trauma-responsive ministries?
- Reflect on each of the Five Principles of Trauma Responsive Ministries. How does your current ministry fulfill those characteristics? In what ways could it improve?
- How are these characteristics embedded in the Prayer for the Broken Hearted (Appendix 1)? How could this prayer become part of the village culture in your ministry?

ACKNOWLEDGMENTS

M y thanks go out to all those who have supported me, shared their stories, bolstered my faith, and taught me what it means to be trauma informed, sensitive, and responsive. I cannot begin to name all those who walked alongside me as I wrote. I am especially grateful to my husband Scott. Together we are telling the generations that follow us that healing is possible and part of the good that God desires in our lives. We grieve that healing waited so long but are proud of the life we lived and the children—Melinda and Eric—we brought into the world as well as the daughter-in-law Kelly who joined us. Their support for us and their compassion for others is a daily inspiration.

I am deeply grateful for the professional care and support of four therapists. *Trauma in the Pews* is filled with the wisdom gained from my therapist, Susan M. Kwiecien, PhD, LMFT, EMDR II, retired. I continue to pay forward her skillful and compassionate care every day. Thank you Darrick Johns, MA, NA, AAC; and Krista Brown, LICSWA, MHP, CMHS, who helped Scott and me—individually and as a couple—process the difficult life events that we were forced to navigate over the past three years. When the world shut down, you kept us from doing the same. We stand strong because you cared. And finally, thank you Margaret (Peggy) Patterson, LICSW for your invaluable support as I marched toward the finish line for this book.

Thank you to all who continue to love, encourage, laugh with and believe in me. We connected in churches, classrooms, colleges, writing courses, organizations, conferences, book clubs, airplanes, and RV parks. You are friends, relatives, colleagues, fellow trauma warriors, authors, and ministry leaders, and the list goes on. Specifically, I am thankful to Amy for allowing parts of her story of healing to be included. There is no greater emissary for hope than someone who has suffered and come to the other side with purpose and faith.

I am grateful to the staff and friends at Bethel Church of the Nazarene (Spanaway, WA) for the love you demonstrated to our family. Also, to all those who are sincerely following Jesus and graciously love me when you disagree. My vulnerable honesty and hard-earned knowledge are not always comfortable topics. I honor all who have been willing to stretch their understanding of the effects of trauma.

Where would I be without publishers? The *Brave* series, published by Cladach Publishing, Cathy and Larry Lawton, has brought hope for healing to unknown numbers of people across the globe. I will forever be grateful for their willingness to tirelessly work to publish three books in as many years. Their support made me even braver and prepared me to author *Trauma in the Pews*.

Thank you to Berry Powell Press, Carmen Renee Berry, MSW, publisher; Marianne Croonquist, MFT, Author Relations; Valeri Mills Barnes, Senior Editor; Abigail Dengler, Director of Editorial Services, and Carolyn Rafferty, Director of Publishing; and PageMill Press, co-owners Roy M. Carlisle and Robert D. Frager, PhD for recognizing the significance of my message. I could not have done this without this team! Your mentoring, affirmations, and laughter have helped bring the message of *Trauma in the Pews* to life in ways I could not have imagined. Our journey together not only brought a book into the world; it transformed me.

A special thanks to Pat Tremaine, who read every draft. Her feedback, engagement, and encouragement helped me more than words can say. Also, a special thanks to Julie Beem, MBA, Attachment & Trauma Network, executive director, for our friendship and faith conversations that were essential in making the connections between the effects of trauma and the spiritual struggles of so many. To my students in the Tabor College MEd program, watching the understanding of trauma move you to even greater compassion was the inspiration I needed to finish *Trauma in the Pews*.

And a shout-out to all the ATN staff, fellow board members, conference speakers, attendees, and volunteers who give me hope for a future in which trauma-informed, sensitive, and responsive care is the norm in our schools and communities. They have inspired me to take this message to ministry leaders and the church. To the trauma movement in general, I give my thanks. I have done my due diligence to give credit when possible but am sure that the firehose of information I have been privileged to absorb over the past seven years may have resulted in some thoughts unintentionally showing up as my own. If so, please accept my apology and consider it as a compliment to the collective hive!

Finally, I am thankful for every person who has healed and is now demonstrating the powerful influence post-traumatic growth can have on a hurting world. Together with God, we are a force of love and justice that can change the world. May faith communities embrace the wisdom of those whose faith has been strengthened through healing.

APPENDIX 1

Prayer for The Brokenhearted[141]
(Based on Psalm 34:18)

God, wherever we go, we walk among those
who hide unspeakable pain.
In our desire to give hope, help us to create
safe spaces for the hurting.
May this space also be a place where they
can seek help and share their pain.
Empower us to be Jesus to the broken.

**The LORD is close to the brokenhearted and
saves those who are crushed in spirit.**

We all have stories. Every story is important.
Our stories mold and form us.
Our stories break and transform us. God, help
us to value the stories each other hold.
Help us to create sacred spaces to hold those stories in safety.

**The LORD is close to the brokenhearted and
saves those who are crushed in spirit.**

Help us to be your tangible love through
the conscious choices we make.
Help us to courageously enter into the other's pain.
Allow us to share your love in creative ways.
Help us wisely tell the victims that their
wounds were never part of your plan.

**The LORD is close to the brokenhearted and
saves those who are crushed in spirit.**

Let us pray this prayer of dedication,
Asking God's guidance for seeing others' brokenness
As our opportunity to show God's love.

Congregation:
God help me to see others for who they are
and not what has happened to them.
Help me to see their pain without judging their behavior.
Help me to act in ways that will be a bridge
of trust between you and the hurting.
Help me to hear your prompting, demonstrating your active love.
And step into broken lives in ways that make a difference.
Help me to not control behavior in others
but instead, love them to wholeness.
Allow me to speak hope into their lives.

All in unison:
We are the eyes that see the pain.
We are the feet who walk beside.
We are the ears that listen.
We are the arms that hold them as they heal.
**The LORD is close to the brokenhearted and saves
those who are crushed in spirit. Amen.**

APPENDIX 2

What Is Our Perception of Discipline?

The definition of "discipline" in the Oxford Dictionary states: "The practice of training people to obey rules or a code of behavior, using punishment to correct disobedience."[142] The Merriam-Webster Dictionary states: "Control gained by enforcing obedience or order." The second definition is a bit more palatable yet does not convey Foster's intent of the Spiritual Disciplines acting as a means of drawing us closer to God—in a relationship.

I wondered what others might feel about the word discipline. Would it be like the first definition? Have we culturally changed the meaning of discipline? My curiosity led me to Facebook Messenger, where I randomly asked forty friends who did not know about this book the following question: "I need your help! Answer this question for me, the first thing that comes to mind: What picture does the word 'discipline' create in your mind?"

Thirty-eight people responded and two-thirds of the responses aligned with the first punitive definition. The demographics involved an age range from the thirties to seventies, most were parents, there were many educators, and several pastors or chaplains, male and female. They all had some level of connection with the church. While this was not a research-quality survey, it was informative and confirmed the need to explore the idea of discipline.

There are other definitions of discipline, as was pointed out by one friend who explained the following three types and said, "I think what these all have in common is discipline as a type of structure or frame."

1. The type of discipline that makes me put my butt in my chair and write or grade papers or else get myself to the kitchen to make dinner.
2. Another borders on punishment: time-outs, spankings, even natural consequences.
3. And, of course, academic disciplines.

The general idea of a framework comes closest to the intended purpose of the Spiritual Disciplines as proposed by Foster. It is a framework that provides the means to developing a closer relationship with God. Yet he was adamant that it is not the human effort of "trying harder" that brings results. God's grace meets us even in our most limited efforts.

Other replies also followed this bent. One with a military background likened discipline to "a runner training for a race . . . training daily . . . or a soldier in basic training completing mission tasks." Another said her gut response was "dedication." Another's secondary response was, "Discipline is what you're good at. There is order, it's consistent, it makes sense, and the outcome is extraordinary."

There was also an interesting undercurrent of discipline through control of self. This is part of my own story, so I recognized it when one person stated, "Beating up self? Staying the course?" Another described this as, "When I started working at home, I had to discipline myself to hold to a routine. Get up, make my bed, eat breakfast, go to my downstairs home office by 9:00 a.m. to start my work." I believe both align with the necessary part of creating habits within the context of spiritual practices. When one said, "Self-control to focus on an unpleasant task," I wondered how many are disciplined in their spiritual practices but found it unpleasant.

The purpose of using discipline to bring about order was evident in other responses. One teacher explained it as, "Library books neatly put in their place on the bookshelves." Another person gave a similar word picture: "A room full of children sitting at attention listening to the teacher." Another person explained the opposite of this sense of order as "chaos."

Several comments did feel like a celebration of discipline. One from a young mother was particularly touching: "I think of leading and guiding. Helping others to know better so they can do better. I guess I would think of it in the way that we are parenting our son. As he's two, there is a lot he can't do and needs help with. And there are things we help him with to keep him safe because he doesn't know yet. As we lead and guide him in his growing and learning, there is a process."

She went on to explain how she and her husband are lovingly teaching their son to respect boundaries in their yard and ended with, "We would tell him how much we love him, give him hugs. and make sure we keep the relationship intact. When he would stay in the yard the whole time we played outside, we would praise him for following our directions and give him hugs and love."

The following responses also portrayed discipline as loving guidance:

- "A loving parent."
- "A loving father gently guiding a child to learn a new way of being in the world."
- "Teacher or parent with their arm around the shoulders of a child as they listen to the child's reasoning and if needed, explain a better choice to make."
- "First thing was a loving parent hugging a child. I suspect that's going to be a weird (probably unique) answer."

The final responder on this list was right—hers was a unique answer, though several who described discipline as punitive followed

243

up with a different, "more acceptable" answer. Several apologized for their first answer, even knowing my desire for them to be honest. One said that cognitively they would have given a different answer, but the punitive one was their first response. One was surprised by her gut reaction. She stated, "A parent with a switch raised over their head. That's kind of funny for this to be the first image that comes to mind because I was never spanked with anything but an open hand on my bottom."

Two responses reflected the shift from punitive thoughts about discipline to those of a loving guide. One mentioned something punitive but went on to say, "The first picture that comes to my mind is an adult kneeling on one knee holding a child's arms to seek eye contact and connection, slowed action, and dialogue."

The other comment provided a glimpse at deep reflection about the initial answer. She said: "Unfortunately, I think the first thing that comes to mind is an angry parent exercising power over a child. However, my mind then went to the noun meaning. I was thinking about a musical or athletic discipline where someone trains to become better at their particular skill. This definition then impacted my first thought on discipline. It made me wonder what parental discipline would look like if it was lived out more closely to this definition."

Yes, I also wondered this because the following answers that rapidly appeared on my computer screen were usually focused on initial thoughts of discipline as punitive. (This list includes those who made additional comments to display how uncomfortable their gut-level responses felt to them.)

- "A mother scolding her child. Isn't that pathetic?"
- "Being corrected for doing wrong. 'Stop that!' Ideally, I know discipline is training and guiding, but that is my knee-jerk reaction."
- "Belt or Rod. I know there's more to it, but that's where my mind went first. I see a petrified child waiting to be punished. I hate it that this was my background."

- "Being spanked by my mom. If I thought more about it, I would have said God for the verse says, those He loves He disciplines."
- "Being harshly brought into line with what an authority wants. I almost wanted to say something lovely about Jesus and being a disciple but realized that wasn't honest."
- "Spanking, but I know that's not God's way, just my past."
- "Not so much a picture as it is a word combined w/ feeling: shame . . . little scared girl who has done something wrong."
- "Superiority, shame, condescension. Yes. I know discipline is not those things in my head. My heart says otherwise."
- "Honestly . . . the very first picture is stern correction. That's not what I want to say, but it's the first thing that came into my mind."

The following list expresses fear without an added caveat. These were the most difficult to read since I knew the backstory of horrific abuse that some of these individuals experienced as children.

- "Hand or paddle."
- "A belt often for things I did not do."
- "Punishment with a stick."
- "I immediately get the picture of someone who is angry at me and therefore wants to hurt me. They scare me."
- "Picture of me holding my breath waiting for the worst—fear. I'm trying to remember examples of where discipline was good. This seems like an oxymoron."

By the time all the answers had arrived, the lists of implements for discipline included the following: switch, rod, stick, belt, hand, paddle, and voice. The opposite discipline methods were loving arms, hugs, and expressions of affection. For many, these were never part of their childhood. For some who had done the arduous work of healing, using these words demonstrated a profound and intentional shift—a shift that feels essential to the purpose of this book.

HOW ARE DISCIPLINE AND
PUNISHMENT DIFFERENT?

While including the responses, I realized this discussion could appear to be a cleverly disguised case against corporal punishment. So be it. Though it wasn't my intent, it does make the case for how our interactions with children develop mindsets that continue to plague them as adults. Their own words tell the story.

Much pain has resulted from an incorrect interpretation of "the rod." No shepherd ever beats the sheep. The rod was used as a guide for the protection of the sheep. The idea that we must harm the sheep to protect them makes no sense. Does it work? Yes, through shame and fear that result in lifelong ramifications. Strong relationships based in unconditional love do counteract this, but there are better methods for discipline.

What about those who have experienced childhood trauma connected to spiritual teachings such as not sparing the rod? One response I received described a long series of childhood "spiritual corrections" that left her bloodied and unable to sit in chairs. There are many similar stories among those I did not ask. Many who experienced abuse within religious settings will diminish their pain as an attempt to retain their faith and remain in the church. The pain of physical abuse lives on at a neurobiological level and unconsciously affects spiritual growth. The continuing desire of these individuals to have a relationship with God astounds me!

APPENDIX 3

Meditation Types Through a Trauma-Sensitive Lens

Four types of meditation are included in *Celebration of Discipline*. Some strike at the core of what makes them challenging. The first is to meditate on scripture, which is a challenge that I will discuss as an alternative to reading and listening, often hearing the voices of those who taught me *and* did great harm. I joined a Bible journaling class at a nearby church. We would arrive to find all the supplies we needed to creatively express the personal meaning of a verse on the pages of our Bibles. My efforts were childlike in comparison to some of the true artists in the group, yet over the weeks, my Bible became a testament to healing as the chosen verses took on new meaning. "The written Word [became] a living word addressed to [me]."[143]

The second type of meditation is what I would call *grounding*, a central part of healing. It is the realization that we cannot change the past or control the future. We are loved and safe in this current moment. This is very difficult to embrace when we have never felt safe.

The Quaker practice of *centering down* is described by Foster as "a time to become still, to enter into the recreating silence, to allow the fragmentation of our minds to become centered."[144] One of the vital skills for self-regulation is inherent in this practice. It is a sense of calm and quiet that is not dependent on circumstances. The problem arises with the number of times centering needs practicing before one can feel it. The challenge of centering is exponentially greater for the traumatized. There will probably never be a day when this essential practice will be easy for me, but healing has made it possible.

One centering practice I employ when helping my friends who have experienced trauma ground themselves is to ask them to name five things in the room. It can be taken a step further, which requires them to move to a higher cognitive level, by asking them to name one thing they can see, one they can touch, something they can hear, another they can smell, and finally something they can taste. Actual touching, tasting, and so on takes this to an even greater level. Why do we eat when stressed? It grounds us. Many of our traditions involve all these sensations. At the Last Supper, the Disciples saw, heard, tasted, felt, and smelled. Meditation can be active and sensory.

It is helpful when meditation utilizes concrete objects. Sand Play therapy, not just for children, involves choosing miniature symbolic objects of people, animals, buildings, motor vehicles, and so on to create a picture in the sand. We unconsciously gravitate to objects that symbolize what needs processing. I "borrowed" my therapist friend's sand tray several times for what I now understand was meditation. One day I created a picture of my sense of self—the center was empty. Once I realized this, I began to select objects that felt true to who I knew myself to be instead of what others wanted me to be. This process, which fulfills the purpose of meditation, helped release some of the unconscious false messages that drove my life and prevented intimate communion with God.

The third type is a meditation upon God's creation. One characteristic of healing is a growing appreciation for nature. Many turn to photography during a time of healing. It is as if we have never seen the world before. Every minute detail becomes vivid and we long to capture the beauty. My cell phone holds many pictures of sunsets and clouds! My Facebook feed is also filled with photos of mountains, creeks, and animals.

One summer day, my friend Jenn and I met at a lake for lunch and a walk. We laughed at how often we stopped to stare at roots, or ferns, or ducks. Not everyone who walks with me understands my need to absorb and photograph every detail. If anyone desires to experience this form of meditation, grab someone who is healing from trauma and go walking. You will find someone who understands Foster's words: "So give your attention to the created order. Look at the trees, really look at them. Take a flower and allow its beauty and symmetry to sink deep into your mind and heart. Listen to the birds—they are the messengers of God. Watch the little creatures that creep upon the earth. These are humble acts, to be sure, but sometimes God reaches us profoundly in these simple ways if we will quiet ourselves to listen."[145]

The fourth type of meditation is that of holding current events before God for insight and discernment. This meditation is both challenging and necessary for those who have experienced great evil in our world. Those who live with the fear caused by trauma can be easily swayed by those who would use that fear to control for their own purposes. When trust never grew as a child, it is easy to believe that no one can be trusted and follow those who tell them to be afraid. Most political or marketing campaigns are built around the fear of something.

The answer for many Christians is to say that God is in control. To fully embrace this belief, one must believe that God uses evil to bring about good. This belief permeated most of my life as a survivor. If God was in control, then my abuse was part of the plan. Nothing stood in the way of opening my heart to the voice of God any more than believing God had created me to suffer and then live my life helping others. Everything bad that happened in my life and the world was part of that plan.

Now, realizing that God never desired, planned, or allowed my abuse helps me view the world differently. Yes, there is evil. Most who inflict pain on others suffer from their own unresolved (unhealed) trauma. Understanding the effects of trauma on the world helps me to view current events differently. I can hold the events and those who create those events up to the lens of how the healing has the power to change people, churches, communities, and the world. This perspective allows the following verse to come to life through meditation—not denying the evil but focusing on the good: "Finally, brothers and sisters, whatever is true, whatever is noble, whatever is right, whatever is pure, whatever is lovely, whatever is admirable—if anything is excellent or praiseworthy—think about such things."[146]

APPENDIX 4

Steps to Worship Through a Trauma-Sensitive Lens

Worship is not confined to church services. *Celebration of Discipline* includes seven steps to worship that I have used as a foundation to specifically address those who struggle from the effects of trauma. Often their hypervigilance makes worship challenging to achieve. Each of these steps begins with Foster's statement and is followed by a trauma-sensitive application. These are intended as suggestions to draw everyone into a mutual corporate experience of worship.

"First, learn to practice the presence of God daily."[147] Look for ways that God chooses to surprise and delight you during the week. While healing, ladybugs held special meaning for me and appeared in unlikely places. On difficult days, the sunsets were often the most beautiful. God is always working to show up in the ordinary moments of our life. If you know someone who is struggling, reach out and ask them to text and share one these experiences. They may not realize this is how God is stepping into their life.

"Second, have many different experiences of worship."[148] While some may like to hide in large worship venues, they often still don't feel comfortable expressing themselves. Others feel the same way about small groups, especially when there is an expectation to participate in some way, such as everyone raising their hands—please stop requesting this. The key is *felt safety*, which is based on safe relationships. It is a huge ask to expect anyone to feel comfortable in either large or small groups without relational care. With creativity it can happen. For instance, during the pandemic shutdown, our church worship leader held Zoom worship gatherings one night a week. In the safety of my home, I muted myself and sang along!

"Third, find ways to really prepare for the gathered experience of worship."[149] Our early discussion of anxiety demonstrated why this is problematic. The church bulletin is part of my positive childhood memories, so this example may be specific to me. It may also provide ideas for relieving anxiety while preparing for worship. For those who experienced chaos in their childhood, the buzz in the sanctuary can be unsettling. Bulletins that include an order of the service provide predictability and can feel calming. Announcements can be grounding when they provide a way to order our lives. The inclusion of reflective questions can help ease the anxiety of a rapidly filling room. Without this, I depend on my cell phone!

The fourth and fifth will be covered together. "Fourth, have a willingness to be gathered in the power of the Lord."[150] Foster explained this as being of one mind in believing God will speak not just individually but to the entire group. "Fifth, cultivate holy dependency. Holy dependency means that you are utterly and completely dependent upon God for anything significant to happen."[151] There is something powerful that happens during worship when both steps are taken corporately. Most often I watched this as an outsider, not fully entering into the experience. Yes, it was significant, and I witnessed it but felt nothing. It was very uncomfortable.

During a worship experience, a friend looked across the room and saw me staring vacantly. She left her place and came to stand beside me and held me tightly as I began to cry. I felt God's presence in her embrace. This compassionate gesture then enabled me to become part of the corporate worship experience.

"Sixth, absorb distractions with gratitude."[152] None are any more distracted than those whose trauma causes them to constantly survey their surroundings. Since I was a child, my inability to sit still and focus has been a source of shame. Foster's suggestion to "become willing to relax with distractions—they may be a message from the Lord"[153] is a breath of loving care from God! How brilliant to reframe the effects of trauma into an ongoing conversation with God during church.

"Seventh, learn to offer a sacrifice of worship."[154] When I choose to walk into church to worship, it is very intentional because it is not a comfortable place for me. This is not my church's fault—I deeply love my church—nor is it my own. It simply is. I have felt this way my entire life. My spiritual mask and denial of my story helped make it possible, but never easy.

It is honoring for survivors when our attendance—on the days it is possible—is acknowledged as an intentional choice. It is life giving when attending or not attending receives equal acknowledgment as a legitimate form of self-care. Providing online options that feel like community is helpful to many survivors who are doing the best they can.

APPENDIX 5

An Embodied Spiritual Practice of Solitude and Affirmations

The traditional views of most spiritual practices involve control, specifically of the mind and body. M. Elizabeth Lewis Hall stated, "It is important to note that self-control or self-discipline involving the body is not the problem in and of itself. These practices can be problematic, however, when they arise out of rejection of or disdain for the body and a sense of superiority of the mind, and when they are practiced in order to minimize bodily experiences."[155]

An emphasis on controlling the body requires those who have experienced trauma to distance themselves from the sensations in their bodies—their emotions. The suppression of emotions is a major cause of trauma-related dysregulation and impedes the healing process. Hall continues, "An embodied spirituality is one that would take seriously the emotions—not to suppress them, but to help us discover what is going on in our souls. . . . being aware enough of our bodies to know what we are feeling is essential to living out our embodied spirituality."[156] What Hall has described is a faith that lives in harmony with the body, not at war with it.

The following Embodied Spiritual Practice of Solitude and Affirmations is designed to bring the trauma survivor back in touch with his or her body. It also is based on three important parts of the healing process.

First, one of the most difficult challenges for those who experienced trauma as children is to speak positive affirmations to themselves. A second challenge is sitting in silence. The third is to gaze at oneself in the mirror without judgmental thoughts. The following practice of titrated silence and repeated affirmations is intended to assist in accomplishing all three together as a way to build new neural pathways and increase resilience. It is also intended to help those healing from trauma to listen to the needs that the body is communicating. Learning to listen to the body requires sitting with uncomfortable feelings while learning *not* to use control to accomplish the practice. Thus, it assumes no standard amount of time that the individual "should be able to" participate.

Day One: Find a comfortable place to sit and choose a selection of instrumental music to play in the background. This can be outdoors, a place with a window view, or simply a corner with favorite objects. Sit quietly and begin the music. Sit for as long as you can. When you begin to feel anxious or experience uncomfortable inner sensations, stop. This is your body communicating with you—it is enough. This may only last a few minutes. It is more important to listen to your body than try to stay longer.

Day Two: As you did the first day, settle into the same spot or choose another. Begin playing your chosen music and as it plays read the following portion of the verse aloud. Note: If your story involves religious abuse that is triggered by scripture, then simply repeat, "God Loves Me" in place of the verse. Repeat as long as feels comfortable, then remain silent and continue listening until your body communicates that you should stop.

"'... my unfailing love for you will not be shaken nor
my covenant of peace be removed,' says the Lord,
who has compassion on you." Isaiah 54:10 (NIV).

Day Three: As you did on previous days, settle into the same spot
or choose another. Begin playing your chosen music and listen until
your body communicates to stop. This time, use your phone to re-
cord a selfie video as you read the verse to yourself (or repeat "God
loves me"). Watch the video you recorded and then sit quietly until
you feel uncomfortable. At this point, you can either listen to the
video, repeat the verse, or return to the music. When your body communicates to stop, congratulate yourself for how you are increasing
the length of time spent in the practice.

Day Four: This time begin by identifying five objects in your view
that either comfort you or bring delight. Then watch the recorded
video and then sit in complete silence until your body indicates that
you should stop. Watch the video for several repetitions and then
either end the practice or listen to instrumental music until your
body indicates that it needs to stop.

Day Five: As you did on previous days, settle into the same spot or
choose another. The goal for this day is silence, but you may choose
any of the additional parts of the practice to soothe yourself when
the silence feels uncomfortable. You can also simply go back to another day's practice where you felt most comfortable. Again, silence
should be a goal.

Ending Reflection: Take some time to answer any of the following
questions—you choose:

1. What did you learn about how your body communicates
   with you?

2. What parts of the practice felt most comfortable? Most uncomfortable?

3. What did you notice as you moved through the days? (length of silence, need for variety, choice of setting, etc.)

4. What might you want to add to the practice as you begin the second round of five days? Only your imagination limits these ideas.

APPENDIX 6

Trauma-Informed Resources

This is not the typical resource list for those in ministry. The resources selected for this list are books and other resources that helped me understand the effects of trauma and restore my faith while healing. These are also not the more technical books written for clinicians, though I did a deep dive into those also. I recommend any book by the authors on this list. The ministry resources are those leaders whose work I found helpful and those who have walked alongside or spoken with me at conferences or engaged in conversations/collaborations. Again, it is not an exhaustive list. Other resources are available at my website (https://www.janyne.org/) and the Attachment & Trauma Network Bookshop (https://bookshop.org/shop/attachmenttraumanetwork).

Trauma-Informed Resource

Deborah A. Dana, *Anchored: How to Befriend Your Nervous System Using Polyvagal Theory* (Boulder, CO: Sounds True, 2021).

Nadine Burke-Harris, *The Deepest Well: Healing the Long-Term Effects of Childhood Adversity* (NY: Houghton Mifflin Harcourt, 2018).

Peter A. Levine and Ann Fredrick, *Waking the Tiger: Healing Trauma* (Berkley, CA: North Atlantic Books, 1997).

Gabor Mate, *In the Realm of Hungry Ghosts* (London: Vermillion, 2018).

Donna J. Nakazawa, *Childhood Disrupted: How Your Biography Becomes Your Biology, and How You Can Heal* (New York, NY: Atria Books, 2015).

Bruce D. Perry and Maia Szalavitz, *The Boy Who Was Raised as a Dog: And Other Stories from a Child Psychiatrist's Notebook: What Traumatized Children Can Teach Us About Loss, Love, and Healing* (New York: Basic Books, 2008).

Stephen W. Porges, *The Pocket Guide to the Polyvagal Theory: The Transformative Power of Feeling Safe* (New York: W.W. Norton, 2017).

Bessel van der Kolk, *The Body Keeps the Score: Brain Mind and Body in the Healing of Trauma* (New York: Penguin Books, 2015).

Barry K. Weinhold and Jane B. Weinhold, *Developmental Trauma: The Game Changer in the Mental Health Profession.* (Colorado Springs, CO: CICRCL Press, 2018).

Oprah Winfrey and Bruce D. Perry, *What Happened to You?: Conversations On Trauma, Resilience, and Healing* (New York: Flatiron Books, 2021).

Shame & Vulnerability Resources

Brené Brown, *Braving the Wilderness: The Quest for True Belonging and the Courage to Stand Alone.* (New York: Random House, 2017).

Janice Morgan Strength, *Healing Shame and Guilt: A Guide for Ministers, Therapists and Spiritual Directors* (Los Altos, CA: PageMill Press, 2022).

Curt Thompson, *Anatomy of the Soul: Surprising Connections Between Neuroscience and Spiritual Practices That Can Transform your Life and Relationships* (Carol Stream, IL: SaltRiver, 2010).

Curt Thompson, *The Soul of Shame: Retelling the Stories We Believe About Ourselves* (Downers Grove, IL: InterVarsity Press, 2015).

Faith Resources

Center for Action and Contemplation, Ed. Vanessa Guerin. *Oneing: Trauma* (Albuquerque, NM: CAC Publishing, 2021).

Mark G. Karris, *Religious Refugees: (De)Constructing Toward Spiritual and Emotional Healing.* (Orange, CA: Quoir, 2020).

McLaren, Brian. *Faith After Doubt: Why Your Beliefs Stopped Working and What to Do About It.* (New York: St. Martin's Essentials, 2022).

Thomas J. Oord, *God Can't!: How to Believe in God and Love after Tragedy, Abuse, or Other Evils.* (Grasmere, ID: SacraSage, 2019).

Trauma-Informed Websites

ACEs Too High: https://acestoohigh.com/

Arizona Trauma Institute: https://aztrauma.org/

Attachment & Trauma Network (ATN): https://www.attachment-traumanetwork.org/

Center for Disease Control (CDC) Adverse Childhood Experiences: https://www.cdc.gov/violenceprevention/aces/index.html

Harvard Center on the Developing Child (In Brief: The Science of Resilience): https://developingchild.harvard.edu/resources/inbrief-the-science-of-resilience/

PACEs Connection: https://www.pacesconnection.com/

Polyvagal Institute: https://www.polyvagalinstitute.org/

Trauma Research Foundation: https://traumaresearchfoundation.org/

Trauma-Informed Ministry Resources

Becky Haas, author, speaker, trainer: https://beckyhaas.com/index.php/practice-areas/#faithbased

Embodied Faith Podcast on Relational Neuroscience, Spiritual Formation, and Faith, Geoff Holsclaw: http://geoffreyholsclaw.net/embodiedfaithpodcast/

Hope Made Strong (Canada) Laura Howe, Founder: https://hope-madestrong.org/

Pathway to Hope (Kansas City) Kiersten Adkins, Executive Director: https://pathwaytohope.org/

Paul Ward Ministries, spiritual life coordinator, speaker, author: https://prward.com/

The Faithful City, Arizona Trauma-Informed Faith Community (AZTIFC), Sanghoon Yoo, MSW, MDiv, Founder: https://www.the-faithfulcity.org/

Trauma and the Church Course, The Movement for Moral Care, Michel Hannagan: https://michaelhanegan.com/trauma-and-church

ABOUT THE AUTHOR

J anyne McConnaughey, PhD, became a trauma-informed advocate the moment she heard the phrase, "There isn't anything wrong *with* you; something bad happened *to* you." Today she is a nationally known trauma-informed author, speaker, and activist. At the age of sixty-one, Janyne entered therapy where she came to an understanding of the effect that childhood sexual abuse and trauma had on her, beginning from the time she was three years old. Realizing healing is possible for survivors, she has authored three books describing the effects of childhood trauma and the paths to healing that changed her life. Janyne's passion is encouraging other survivors of trauma to seek healing.

Janyne draws from her life-long involvement in church ministry and a thirty-three-year career training teachers and ministry workers at colleges and universities. She holds a PhD in Educational Leadership and Innovation from Colorado State University–Denver and is currently a Distinguished Visiting Professor at Tabor College (Master of Education: Neuroscience and Trauma).

Janyne also serves as President of the Board of Directors for the Attachment & Trauma Network (ATN), a non-profit with the mission to promote healing of children impacted by trauma through supporting their families, schools, and communities. For more information, visit ATN's website at www.attachmenttraumsnetwork.org.

Janyne and her husband, Scott, have lived in California, Missouri, Colorado, and now reside south of Seattle with their rescue dog

Weber. They enjoy exploring the Pacific Northwest and spending time with their children and grandchildren.

To contact Janyne to schedule speaking engagements, consultation and podcasts, you are invited to contact her through website at www.janyne.org.

ENDNOTES

Section One

1   E-3 Module Five Participant Manual: *Trauma and Stressor-Related Disorders* (Olathe, KS: Pathway to Hope, Inc., 2021) 1. (Portions of this information were originally written and published in this manual and have been included and/or adapted with permission.)
2   American Psychiatric Association, *Diagnostic and Statistical Manual of Mental Disorders: DSM V, 5th ed.* (Washington, DC: American Psychiatric Association, 2013).
3   SAGE, *Can over-the-counter pain meds influence thoughts and emotions?* ScienceDaily. www.sciencedaily.com/releases/2018/02/180206090700. htm (accessed March 4, 2022).

Chapter One

4   E-3 Module Five Participant Manual: *Trauma and Stressor-Related Disorders* (Olathe, KS: Pathway to Hope, Inc., 2021) 7. (Information was originally written and published in this manual and has been included and/or adapted with permission.)

Chapter Two

5   David Michael Henderson, *John Wesley's Class Meeting: A Model of Making Disciples* (Nappanee, IN: Evangel Pub, 1997).
6   Bessel van der Kolk, *The Body Keeps the Score* (New York: Penguin Books, 2014), Kindle loc. 247-251 of 9327, (italics mine).
7   E-3 Module Five Participant Manual: *Trauma and Stressor-Related Disorders* (Olathe, KS: Pathway to Hope, Inc., 2021) 8-9. (Information was

originally written and published in this manual and has been included and/or adapted with permission.)

8   For further information see Stephen W. Porges, *The Pocket Guide to the Polyvagal Theory: The Transformative Power of Feeling Safe* (New York: W.W. Norton, 2017).

9   E-3 Module Five Participant Manual: *Trauma and Stressor-Related Disorders* (Olathe, KS: Pathway to Hope, Inc., 2021) 9-10. (Information was originally written and published in this manual and has been included and/or adapted with permission.)

Chapter Three

10   Centers for Disease Control, *About the CDC–Kaiser ACE Study* [web page], n.d., accessed October 28, 2021, https://www.cdc.gov/violenceprevention/aces/about.html.

11   E-3 Module Five Participant Manual: *Trauma and Stressor-Related Disorders* (Olathe, KS: Pathway to Hope, Inc., 2021) 1-2. (Information was originally written and published in this manual and has been included and/or adapted with permission.)

12   Carol Tucker, *The 1950s—Powerful Years for Religion*, (USC News, June 16, 1997), accessed October 29, 2021, https://news.usc.edu/25835/The-1950s-Powerful-Years-for-Religion/#:~:text=On%20a%20typical%20Sunday%20morning%20in%20the%20period%20from%201955,to%2063.3%20percent%20in%201960.

13   History, *PTSD and Shell Shock History* [Blog]: (A&E Television Network, August 21, 2021), accessed May 15, 2022, https://www.history.com/topics/inventions/history-of-ptsd-and-shell-shock.

14   The State of Religion & Young People 2020: *Relational Authority* (Bloomington, MN: Springtide Research Institute, 2020).

15   Kristen Caldwell, *Boise Church Deconsecrates and Removes Stained Glass Window Depicting Confederate General Robert E. Lee as it Repents of Racism*: (Oregon-Idaho Conference of the Methodist Church [web page], August 8, 2020), accessed May 14, 2022, https://www.umoi.org/newsdetail/boise-idaho-church-deconsecrates-and-removes-stained-glass-window-depicting-confederate-general-robert-e-lee-as-it-repents-of-racism-14145799.

16   Centers for Disease Control and Prevention. *What is Epigenetics*, (Atlanta: U.S. Department of Health and Human Services) [web page], accessed May 15, 2022, https://www.cdc.gov/genomics/disease/epigenetics.htm.

Section Two: Part One

17 Bessel van der Kolk, *Body Keeps Score*, 206.
18 Bessel van der Kolk, *Body Keeps Score*, 279.

Chapter 4

19 Richard J. Foster, *Celebration of Discipline*, Special Anniversary Edition (New York: HarperCollins, 2018), 22.
20 EMDR International Association, *About EMDR Therapy* [Webpage], n.d., accessed October 28, 2021, https://www.emdria.org/about-emdr-therapy/. ("Eye Movement Desensitization and Reprocessing (EMDR) therapy is an extensively researched, effective psychotherapy method proven to help people recover from trauma and other distressing life experiences, including PTSD, anxiety, depression, and panic disorders.").
21 Excerpts from: EMDR Institute, Inc, *What is EMDR: For Clinicians,* [web page], retrieved April 16, 2022, https://www.emdr.com/what-is-emdr/.
22 Curt Thompson, *The Soul of Shame* (Downers Grove, IL: Intervarsity Press, 2015), Kindle loc. 146 of 3225.
23 Thompson, *Soul of Shame*, Kindle loc. 915 of 3225.
24 Thompson, *Soul of Shame*, Kindle loc. 915 of 3225.
25 van der Kolk, *Body Keeps Score*, 13–14.
26 Richard Rohr, "Introduction," "Trauma," in *Oneing*, vol. 9, no. 1 (Albuquerque, NM: CAC Publishing, 2021), 18.

Chapter 5

27 Foster, *Celebration*, 40.
28 Raylene M. Phillips, *The Sacred Hour: Uninterrupted Skin-to-Skin Contact Immediately after Birth*, Newborn & Infant Nursing Reviews 13, no. 2 (June 2013): 67–72, http://dx.doi.org/10.1053/j.nainr.2013.04.001.
29 Information about therapeutic parenting can be found the Attachment & Trauma Network website: https://www.attachmenttraumanetwork.org/parenting/
30 Thompson, *Soul of Shame*, Kindle loc. 729 of 3225.
31 James 4:3 (NIV).
32 Foster, *Celebration*, 35.

33 Mark Gregory Karris, *Divine Echoes: Reconciling Prayer with the Uncontrolling Love of God* (Orange, CA: Quoir, 2018) 152.

34 John 15:7 (NIV).

35 Janice Morgan Strength, *Healing Shame and Guilt: A Guide for Ministers, Therapists, and Spiritual Directors* (Alameda, CA: PageMill Press, forthcoming 2022), 25.

36 Foster, *Celebration*, 41.

Chapter 6

37 Centers for Disease Control, *About the CDC–Kaiser ACE Study* [Webpage], n.d., accessed October 28, 2021, https://www.cdc.gov/violenceprevention/aces/about.html.

38 David A. Wiss and Timothy D. Brewerton, *Adverse Childhood Experiences and Adult Obesity: A Systematic Review of Plausible Mechanisms and Meta-Analysis of Cross-Sectional Studies*, Physiology & Behavior 223 (September 2020), https://doi.org/10.1016/j.physbeh.2020.112964.

39 Vasiliki Michopoulos, Aimee Vester, and Gretchen Neigh, *Posttraumatic Stress Disorder: A Metabolic Disorder in Disguise?* Experimental Neurology 284, pt. B (October 2016): 220–229, https://doi.org/10.1016/j.expneurol.2016.05.038.

40 ScienceDaily, *High Blood Sugar Causes Brain Changes that Raise Depression Risk*, (June 23, 2014), accessed October 28, 2021, https://www.sciencedaily.com/releases/2014/06/140623092011.htm.

41 Foster, *Celebration*, 55.

42 I Corinthians 9:27 (NIV).

43 Foster, *Celebration*, 54.

44 Oprah Winfrey and Bruce D. Perry, *What Happened to You? Conversations on Trauma, Resilience, and Healing* (New York: Flatiron Books, 2021), 183.

45 Tim Clinton and Gary Sibcy, *Why You Do the Things You Do: The Secret to Healthy Relationships* (Nashville, TN: Thomas Nelson, 2006), 228.

Chapter 7

46 Richard L. Gaskill and Bruce D. Perry, *Child Sexual Abuse, Traumatic Experiences and Their Effect on the Developing Brain*, in Paris Goodyear-Brown, ed., Handbook of Child Sexual Abuse: Identification, Assessment and Treatment (New York: Wiley, 2012), 29–49.

47 Global Center for Religious Research, *What is Religious Trauma?* [web page] (Denver, CO: https://www.gcrr.org/religioustrauma#:~:-text=This%20is%20why%20GCRR%20had,definition%20of%20%E2%80%9Creligious%20trauma.%E2%80%9D), Accessed April 22, 2022.

48 Neurodiversity Awareness: Inclusion for All, *Learning Independence for Tomorrow* [website],April 4, 2022, accessed May 31, 2022, https://liftfrc.org/neurodiversity-awareness-inclusion-for-all/

49 Psalm 56:8 (AMP).

50 Foster, *Celebration*, 64.

51 Brené Brown, *The Power of Vulnerability*, TEDTalk, June 2010. http://www.ted.com/talks/brene_brown_on_vulnerability?language=en.

52 *What is Religious Trauma?* [web page] (Denver, CO: Global Center for Religious Research) https://www.gcrr.org/religioustrauma#:~:-text=This%20is%20why%20GCRR%20had,definition%20of%20%E2%80%9Creligious%20trauma.%E2%80%9D), Accessed April 22, 2022.

53 Journey Free, *RTS: An Historical Overview (CORT talk)* [web page] accessed May 15, 2022, https://journeyfree.org/rts-an-historical-overview-cort-talk/.

54 Janja Lalich, *Characteristics Associated with Cults*, [web page] accessed April 23, 2022, https://janjalalich.com/help/characteristics-associated-with-cults/.

55 van der Kolk, *The Body Keeps the Score* (New York: Penguin Books, 2014), Kindle loc. 1552-1558 of 9327.

56 Foster, *Celebration*, 63.

Part Two

57 van der Kolk, *Body Keeps Score*, 2–3.

Chapter 8

58 Foster, *Celebration*, 79.

59 Foster, *Celebration*, 87.

60 Thompson, *Soul of Shame*, loc. 263–266 of X, Kindle loc. 263 of 2335

61 Brené Brown, Oprah Winfrey, and Bruce D. Perry, *Trauma, Resilience, and Healing*, May 5, 2021, in *Unlocking Us*, podcast, https://brenebrown.com/podcast/brene-with-oprah-winfrey-and-dr-bruce-d-perry-on-trauma-resilience-and-healing/.

Chapter 9

62 Jonathan Baylin and D. A. Hughes, *The Neurobiology of Attachment-Focused Therapy* (New York: W. W. Norton & Co., 2016), 101.

63 Foster, *Celebration*, 99.

64 Janyne McConnaughey, "Brave: What I Chose to Tell," Attachment & Trauma Network Blog, August 14, 2018, accessed October 28, 2021, https://www.attachmenttraumanetwork.org/brave-what-i-chose-to-tell/.

65 Peter A. Levine, *An Unspoken Voice: How the Body Releases Trauma and Restores Goodness* (Berkley: North Atlantic Books, 2010). Kindle

66 Foster, *Celebration*, 100.

67 Foster, *Celebration*, 101.

68 Foster, *Celebration*, 101.

69 Foster, *Celebration*, 101.

70 Nancy Stella, *Fear Traps: Escape the Triggers that Keep You Stuck* (Glendora, CA: Berry Powell Press, 2021) 32.

71 Foster, *Celebration*, 96.

72 Thompson, *Soul of Shame*, loc. 711–713 of X, Kindle loc. 710 of 3225

73 Foster, *Celebration*, 103.

74 Foster, *Celebration*, 96.

Chapter 10

75 McLaren, Brian. *Faith After Doubt: Why Your Beliefs Stopped Working and What to Do About It.* (New York: St. Martin's Essentials, 2022). Kindle loc. 3047 of 4730.

76 Foster, *Celebration*, 111.

77 Foster, *Celebration*, 111.

78 Online Personality Test, *16 Personalities* [Website], n.d., accessed October 28, 2021, https://www.16personalities.com/. (Examples of questions that identify trauma/shame-based traits: "Even a small mistake can cause you to doubt your overall abilities and knowledge"; "When someone thinks highly of you, you wonder how long it will take them to feel disappointed in you"; "You are still bothered by mistakes that you made a long time ago.")

79 Foster, *Celebration*, 114.

80 Foster, *Celebration*, 112.

81 Thompson, *Soul of Shame*, Kindle loc. 120 out of 3225

82 Matthew 10:39.

Chapter 11

83 Foster, *Celebration*, 128.

84 Janyne McConnaughey, *A Brave Life: Survival, Resilience, Faith, and Hope after Childhood Trauma* (Greeley, CO: Cladach Publishing, 2020).

85 Foster, *Celebration*, 128.

86 Winfrey and Perry, *What Happened?*, 263.

87 Foster, *Celebration*, 128.

Part Three

88 Jeffrey M. Jones, *U.S. Church Membership Falls Below Majority for First Time*, (Gallup, March 29, 2021), accessed October 28, 2021, https://news.gallup. com/poll/341963/church-membership-falls-below-majority-first-time. aspx. (The Gallup Poll statistical analysis found that "Among religious groups, the decline in membership is steeper among Catholics (down 18 points, from 76% to 58%) than Protestants (down nine points, from 73% to 64%).")

89 Renovaré, *Celebration of Discipline*, n.d., accessed October 28, 2021, https://renovare.org/books/celebration-of-discipline.

90 Gabor Maté, *In the Realm of Hungry Ghosts: Close Encounters with Addiction* (Toronto: Knopf Canada, 2008), 33.

91 Maté, *Realm of Ghosts*, 137.

Chapter 12

92 van der Kolk, *The Body Keeps the Score* (New York: Penguin Books, 2014), 32, Kindle loc. 764 of 9327.

93 Foster, *Celebration*, 146.

94 Foster, *Celebration*, 157.

Chapter 13

95 Foster, *Celebration*, 158.

96 Foster, *Celebration*, 170.

97 Foster, *Celebration*, 169.

98 Peter Levine and Ann Frederick. *Waking the Tiger: Healing Trauma* (Berkeley, CA: North Atlantic Books, 1997)16.

99 *Black Church: This Is Our Story, This Is Our Song*, PBS, written, hosted, and produced by Henry Louis Gates, Jr., a production of McGee Media, Inkwell Media, and WETA Washington, DC, in association with Get Lifted, n.d., accessed October 28, 2021, https://www.pbs.org/weta/black-church/.

100 Foster, *Celebration*, 159.

Chapter 14

101 Foster, *Celebration*, 176.

102 Foster, *Celebration*, 181.

103 Foster, *Celebration*, 181.

104 Russel Moore, *This is the Southern Baptist Apocalypse*, Christianity Today Blog, accessed May 27, 2022, https://www.christianitytoday.com/ct/2022/may-web-only/southern-baptist-abuse-apocalypse-russell-moore.html.

105 Guidepost Solutions, LLC, *The Southern Baptist Convention Executive Committee's Response to Sexual Abuse Allegations and an Audit of the Procedures and Actions of the Credentials Committee*, (Washington, DC: Guidepost, 2022) accessed May 27, 2022, https://static1.squarespace.com/static/6108172d83d55d3c9db4dd67/t/628bf-ccb599a375bece1f66c/1653341391218/Guidepost+Solutions+Independent+Investigation+Report_.pdf, 14.

106 Foster, *Celebration*, 179.

Chapter 15

107 Foster, *Celebration*, 191 (emphasis mine).

108 Thompson, *Soul of Shame*, Kindle loc. 966 of 3225.

109 Deborah A. Dana, *Anchored: How to Befriend Your Nervous System Using Polyvagal Theory* (Boulder, CO: Sounds True, 2021), Kindle loc. 67 of 231.

110 Foster, *Celebration*, 192.

111 Bruce D. Perry, *The Boy Who Was Raised as A Dog, and Other Stories from a Child Psychologist's Notebook* (New York: Basic Books, 2008).

112 Peter A. Levine and Ann Frederick, *Waking the Tiger: Healing Trauma* (Berkley: North Atlantic Books, 1997), 157.

113 van der Kolk, *Body Keeps Score*, 112.

114 Proverbs 17:22 (CEB).

115 van der Kolk, *Body Keeps Score*, 215.

116 Foster, *Celebration*, 193.

117 Foster, *Celebration*, 195–196.

Chapter 16

118 Foster, *Celebration*, 186.

119 I Corinthians 10:12.

120 E-3 Module Five Participant Manual: *Trauma and Stressor-Related Disorders* (Olathe, KS: Pathway to Hope, Inc., 2021) 5-6. (Information was originally written and published in this manual and has been included and/or adapted with permission.)

121 Janina Fisher, *Healing the Fragmented Selves of Trauma Survivors: Overcoming Internal Self Alienation* (New York: Taylor and Francis, 2017) 29-30, Kindle loc. 802-807 of 6839.

Chapter 17

122 SoulShepharding, *Pastor's Statistics*, [Webpage], n.d., accessed October 28, 2021, https://www.soulshepherding.org/pastors-under-stress/.

123 Henri Nouwen, *The Wounded Healer: Ministry in Contemporary Society* (New York: Image Books, 1979) 72.

124 Nouwen, *Wounded Healer*, 72.

125 Leaders & Pastors, *Do Pastors Feel Well-Equipped to Help Congregants Heal from Trauma?* (August 4, 2020), https://www.barna.com/research/pastors-trauma-care/.

Chapter 18

126 Matthew 11:28 (NIV).

127 Annie Wright, *Titrating Your Experience: What Would a Toddler Do?* [Blog], (March 7, 2021), accessed October 28, 2021, https://www.anniewright.com/titrating-your-experience-what-would-a-toddler-do/.

128 John Medina, *Brain Rules: 12 Principles for Surviving and Thriving at Work, Home, and School* (Seattle: Pear Press, 2008), 150–151.

129 Foster, *Celebration*, 88–89.

130 Mari Kondo, *KonMari Method Fundamentals of Tidying*, [Video], accessed October 28, 2021, https://learn.konmari.com/?campaign=WPBanner/.

131 Darren M. Slade et al., *Religious Trauma Sociological Study*, Socio-Historical Examination of Religion and Ministry 4, no. 2 (Winter 2022): forthcoming.

Chapter 19

132 B. K. Alexander, B. L. Beyerstein, B. F. Hadaway, and R. B. Coombs, *Effect of Early and Later Colony Housing on Oral Ingestion of Morphine in Rats*, Pharmacol Biochem Behav. 15, no. 4 (October 1981): 571–576, https://doi.org/10.1016/0091-3057(81)90211-2.

133 Ben Cremer, Facebook Post, October 29, 2021, accessed October 29, 2021, https://www.facebook.com/ben.cremer (emphasis mine).

134 Foster, *Celebration*, 143.

135 Foster, *Celebration*, 143.

136 Thomas Jay Oord, *God Can't: How to Believe in God and Love after Tragedy, Abuse, and Other Evils* (Grasmere, ID: Sacrasage Press, 2019), 14.

137 Foster, *Celebration*, 143.

138 Romans 8:26 (NIV).

139 Mark Gregory Karris, *Religious Refugees: (De)Constructing toward Spiritual and Emotional Healing* (Orange, CA: Quoir, 2020) 35.

140 Foster, *Celebration*, 198–199.

Appendix 1

141 Adapted and included with permission from Mark Gregory Karris, *Divine Echoes: Reconciling Prayer with the Uncontrolling Love of God* (Orange, CA: Quoir, 2018) 202-203.

Appendix 2

142 Oxford Dictionary, s.v. "discipline (n.)," accessed March 6, 2022, https://www.lexico.com/en/definition/discipline.

Appendix 3

143 Foster, *Celebration*, 29.

144 Foster, *Celebration*, 30.

145 Foster, *Celebration*, 31.

146 Philippians 4:8 (NIV).

Appendix 4

147 Foster, *Celebration*, 170.
148 Foster, *Celebration*, 171.
149 Foster, *Celebration*, 171.
150 Foster, *Celebration*, 171.
151 Foster, *Celebration*, 171–172.
152 Foster, *Celebration*, 172.
153 Foster, *Celebration*, 172.
154 Foster, *Celebration*, 172.

Appendix 5

155 M. Elizabeth Lewis Hall, *What are Bodies for? An Integrative Examination of Embodiment*, Christian Scholar's Review, 39, no. 2 (January 15, 2010): 159-175, https://christianscholars.com/what-are-bodies-for-an-integrative-examination-of-embodiment/
156 Hall, *What are Bodies for?*

Berry Powell Press

Berry Powell Press is a hybrid publishing house that publishes authors with transformational perspectives on timely personal and societal challenges. Our authors are provided in-depth mentorship & collaborative assistance to create life-changing books and to build book-based businesses that can impact the largest audience possible. We publish fiction and non-fiction for adults and children.

PageMill Press

A California based publishing house launched to showcase the insights of transpersonal, humanistic, and positive psychology while highlighting stories of spiritual renewal. PageMill Press's multi-disciplinary pursuit of research incorporates the use of various psychological and spiritual perspectives. And the Press aims to tackle the most challenging contemporary issues of modern living and global concerns by encouraging qualified scholars and writers to produce thoughtful and inspiring books.

Made in United States
Orlando, FL
26 August 2022

21618346R00181